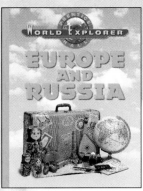
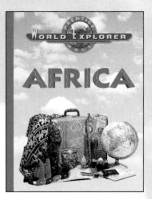
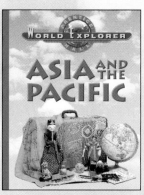

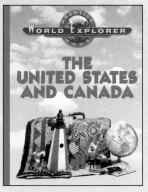

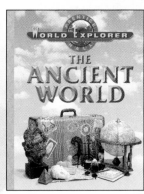

The world studies program that lets you choose.

 PRENTICE HALL
Simon & Schuster Education Group
A VIACOM COMPANY

Upper Saddle River, New Jersey
Needham, Massachusetts

ISBN 0-13-424938-0

1 2 3 4 5 6 7 8 9 10   01 00 99 98 97

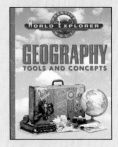  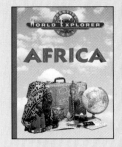

studies program curriculum.

for your course of study.

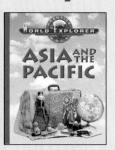 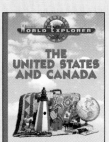  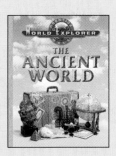 

ASIA AND THE PACIFIC	THE UNITED STATES AND CANADA	LATIN AMERICA	THE ANCIENT WORLD	MEDIEVAL TIMES TO TODAY
ASIA AND THE PACIFIC				
	THE UNITED STATES AND CANADA	LATIN AMERICA		
			THE ANCIENT WORLD	MEDIEVAL TIMES TO TODAY
	THE UNITED STATES AND CANADA		THE ANCIENT WORLD	
ASIA AND THE PACIFIC	THE UNITED STATES AND CANADA	LATIN AMERICA		
ASIA AND THE PACIFIC	THE UNITED STATES AND CANADA	LATIN AMERICA		

Available in single, hard-bound volume

Only World Explorer provides this many management resources— built right into the program.

Designed from the start to have more time-saving resources for middle grades teachers, the World Explorer program has brand-new ways to help you coordinate your program, scheduling, assessment, team teaching, interdisciplinary connections, and other valuable resources.

- **Managing Time and Instruction**
- **Block Scheduling**
- **Assessment Opportunities**
- **Activities and Projects**
- **Resource Pro ™ CD-ROM**
- **Technology Options**
- **Flexible Planning Guide**

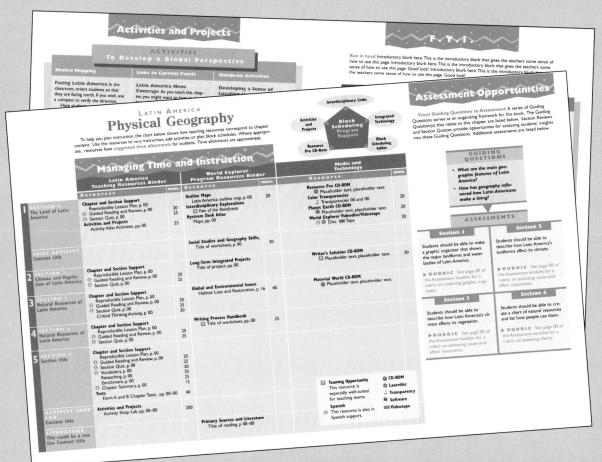

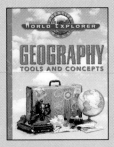

TECHNOLOGY OPTIONS

- Teacher's Edition wraparound with barcodes
- Point-of-use technology references
- Integrated video presentations

Guided Reading Audiotapes *
Computer Test Bank
 (MAC/Windows)
 World Video Explorer
     Videodiscs *
     Videotapes
Resource Pro™ CD-ROM
Material World CD-ROM
Planet Earth CD-ROM
Writer's Solution CD-ROM
*available in Spanish

FLEXIBLE PLANNING GUIDE

This key supplement makes it easy to plan, schedule, and coordinate World Explorer's multi-book program.

- Course configurations
- Pacing charts
- Scope and sequence of skills
- Correlations to national standards

RESOURCE PRO™ CD-ROM

- Teaching Resources
- Planning Express™
- Computer Test Bank

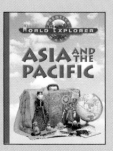

Coverage of all World Explorer program skills is provided in the Student Edition and Teacher's Edition.

Skills Activity
Students learn, practice, and apply core social studies skills through the use of hands-on activities.

Skills Mini-lessons
These lessons supplement and reinforce core social studies skills that are not formally presented in the student book.

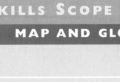

GEOGRAPHY: TOOLS AND CONCEPTS SKILLS SCOPE AND SEQUENCE

MAP AND GLOBE SKILLS

SKILL	BOOK	PAGE
Using Regional Maps	STUDENT	113
Using Isolines to show Elevation	TEACHER	57
Using Distribution Maps	STUDENT	70–71
Using Route Maps	TEACHER	41

CRITICAL THINKING SKILLS

SKILL	BOOK	PAGE
Expressing Problems Clearly	STUDENT	20–21
Identifying Central Issues	TEACHER	83
Distinguishing Facts From Opinons	TEACHER	115
Recognizing Bias	TEACHER	89
Recognizing Cause and Effect	TEACHER	81
Drawing Conclusions	TEACHER	67

CHART, GRAPH, AND ILLUSTRATION SKILLS

SKILL	BOOK	PAGE
Interpreting Graphs	TEACHER	109
Interpreting Diagrams and Illustrations	TEACHER	37
Understanding Special Geography Graphs	STUDENT	48–49

READING AND WRITING SKILLS

SKILL	BOOK	PAGE
Previewing	TEACHER	31
Reading Actively	TEACHER	16
Assessing Your Understanding	TEACHER	17
Using the Writing Process	TEACHER	59
Writing for a Purpose	STUDENT	122–123

STUDY AND RESEARCH SKILLS

SKILL	BOOK	PAGE
Locating Information	STUDENT	98–99
Organizing Information	TEACHER	85
Organizing Your Time	TEACHER	13

Use this daily pacing chart to help plan a nine-week course or a twelve-week course for Geography: Tools and Concepts.

	9-WEEK COURSE	12-WEEK COURSE
ACTIVITY ATLAS	2 DAYS	3 DAYS

CHAPTER 1
THE WORLD OF GEOGRAPHY

	9-WEEK COURSE	12-WEEK COURSE
Section 1 The Five Themes of Geography	1.5	2
Section 2 The Geographer's Tools	1.5	2
SKILLS ACTIVITY Expressing Problems Clearly	1.5	2
CHAPTER 1 REVIEW, ACTIVITIES, AND ASSESSMENT	1.5	2
ACTIVITY SHOP Interdisciplinary	1.5	2

CHAPTER 2
EARTH'S PHYSICAL GEOGRAPHY

	9-WEEK	12-WEEK
Section 1 Our Planet, the Earth	1.5	2
Section 2 Land, Air, and Water	1.5	2
Section 3 Climate and What Influences It	1.5	2
Section 4 How Climate Affects Vegetation	1.5	2
SKILLS ACTIVITY Using Special Geography Graphs	1.5	2
CHAPTER 2 REVIEW, ACTIVITIES, AND ASSESSMENT	1.5	2
ACTIVITY SHOP Lab	1.5	2

CHAPTER 3
EARTH'S HUMAN GEOGRAPHY

	9-WEEK	12-WEEK
Section 1 Where Do People Live?	1	1.5
Section 2 A Growing Population	1.5	2
Section 3 Why People Migrate	1.5	2
SKILLS ACTIVITY Using Distribution Maps	1.5	2
CHAPTER 3 REVIEW, ACTIVITIES, AND ASSESSMENT	1.5	2
LITERATURE	1	1

CHAPTER 4
CULTURES OF THE WORLD

	9-WEEK COURSE	12-WEEK COURSE
Section 1 What Is Culture?	1.5	2
Section 2 Social Groups, Language, and Religion	1.5	2
Section 3 Economic and Political Systems	1.5	2
Section 4 Cultural Change	1.5	2
SKILLS ACTIVITY Locating Information	1.5	2
CHAPTER 4 REVIEW, ACTIVITIES, AND ASSESSMENT	1.5	2
LITERATURE	1	

CHAPTER 5
EARTH'S NATURAL RESOURCES

	9-WEEK	12-WEEK
Section 1 What Are Natural Resources?	1.5	2
Section 2 How People Use the Land	1.5	2
Section 3 People's Effect on the Environment	1	1.5
SKILLS ACTIVITY Writing for a Purpose	1.5	2
CHAPTER 5 REVIEW, ACTIVITIES, AND ASSESSMENT	1.5	2

	9-WEEK	12-WEEK
TOTAL NUMBER OF DAYS	**45**	**60**

WORLD EXPLORER
PRENTICE HALL

Choose from this wide variety of resources for management, extensions, and assessment.

Components

- Student Editions
- Teacher's Editions
- Teaching Resources Binders
  - Chapter and Section Support
  - Spanish Support
  - Activities and Projects
  - Tests
  - Social Studies and Geography Skills
- Program Teaching Resources Binder
  - Primary Sources and Literature Readings
  - Long-term Integrated Projects
  - Outline Maps
  - Environmental and Global Issues
  - Writing Process Handbook
  - Assessment Handbook

- Technology in the Classroom
  - Social Studies Educator's Handbooks
  - Nystrom Desk Atlas
  - Posters

- Teacher's Flexible Planning Guide
- Color Transparencies with Overlays

- Guided Reading Audiotapes *
- Computer Test Bank (MAC/Windows)
- World Video Explorer
  - Videodiscs *
  - Videotapes
- Resource Pro™ CD-ROM
- Material World CD-ROM
- Planet Earth CD-ROM
- Writer's Solution CD-ROM
- Interdisciplinary Explorations

* Available in Spanish

 **See us on the Internet**  **http://www.phschool.com**

Contact your local representative or call **1-800-848-9500.**

PH PRENTICE HALL MultiMedia

PRENTICE HALL
Simon & Schuster Education Group
A VIACOM COMPANY

GEOGRAPHY
TOOLS AND CONCEPTS

PRENTICE HALL
Needham, Massachusetts
Upper Saddle River, New Jersey

Program Authors

Heidi Hayes Jacobs

Heidi Hayes Jacobs has served as an educational consultant to more than 500 schools across the nation. Dr. Jacobs is an adjunct professor in the Department of Curriculum on Teaching at Teachers College, Columbia. She completed her undergraduate studies at the University of Utah in her hometown of Salt Lake City. She received an M.A. from the University of Massachusetts, Amherst, and completed her doctoral work at Columbia University's Teachers College in 1981.

The backbone of Dr. Jacobs's experience comes from her years as a teacher of high school, middle school, and elementary school students. As an educational consultant, she works with K–12 schools and districts on curriculum reform and strategic planning.

Brenda Randolph

Brenda Randolph is the former Director of the Outreach Resource Center at the African Studies Program at Howard University, Washington, D.C. She is the Founder and Director of Africa Access, a bibliographic service on Africa for schools. She received her B.A. in history with high honors from North Carolina Central University, Durham, and her M.A. in African studies with honors from Howard University. She completed further graduate studies at the University of Maryland, College Park, where she was awarded a Graduate Fellowship.

Brenda Randolph has published numerous articles in professional journals and bulletins. She currently serves as library media specialist in Montgomery County Public Schools, Maryland.

Michal L. LeVasseur

Michal LeVasseur is an educational consultant in the field of geography. She is an adjunct professor of geography at the University of Alabama, Birmingham, and serves with the Alabama Geographic Alliance. Her undergraduate and graduate work are in the fields of anthropology (B.A.), geography (M.A.), and science education (Ph.D.).

Dr. LeVasseur's specialization has moved increasingly into the area of geography education. In 1996, she served as Director of the National Geographic Society's Summer Geography Workshop. As an educational consultant, she has worked with the National Geographic Society as well as with schools to develop programs and curriculum for geography.

Special Program Consultant

Yvonne S. Gentzler, Ph.D.
School of Education
University of Idaho
Moscow, Idaho

PRENTICE HALL
Simon & Schuster Education Group
A VIACOM COMPANY

Upper Saddle River, New Jersey
Needham, Massachusetts

ISBN 0-13-433702-6

1 2 3 4 5 6 7 8 9 10   01 00 99 98 97

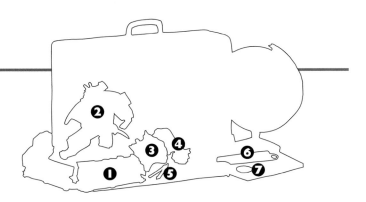

On the Cover

❶ Model of locomotive and freight cars
❷ Antique sextant
❸ Conch shell
❹ Mineral samples
❺ Calipers
❻ Thermometer
❼ Compass

Content Consultants for the World Explorer Program

Africa
Barbara Brown
Africa Studies Center
Boston University
Boston, Massachusetts

Ancient World
Maud Gleason
Department of Classics
Stanford University
Stanford, California

East Asia
Leslie Swartz
Harvard University
East Asian Outreach
Program at the
Children's Museum
of Boston
Boston, Massachusetts

Latin America
Daniel Mugan
Center for Latin American
Studies
University of Florida
Gainesville, Florida

Middle East
Elizabeth Barlow
Center for Middle
Eastern and North
African Studies
University of Michigan
Ann Arbor, Michigan

North Africa
Laurence Michalak
Center for Middle East
Studies
University of California
Berkeley, California

Religion
Michael Sells
Department of Religion
Haverford College
Haverford, Pennsylvania

**Russia, Eastern Europe,
Central Asia**
Janet Valliant
Center for Russian,
Eastern European, and
Central Asian Studies
Harvard University
Cambridge,
Massachusetts

South Asia
Robert Young
South Asia Regional
Studies
University of
Pennsylvania
Philadelphia,
Pennsylvania

Western Europe
Ruth Mitchell-Pitts
Center for West European
Studies
University of North
Carolina
Chapel Hill, North
Carolina

Teacher Advisory Board

Jerome Balin
Lincoln Junior High
School
Naperville, Illinois

Linda Boaen
Baird School
Fresno, California

Nikki L. Born
Harllee Middle School
Bradenton, Florida

Carla Bridges
Concord Middle School
Concord, North Carolina

Bruce L. Campbell
Walled Lake Middle
School
Walled Lake, Michigan

**Barbara Coats
Grabowski**
Russell Middle School
Omaha, Nebraska

David Herman
North Carroll Middle
School
Hampstead, Maryland

Fred Hitz
Wilson Middle School
Muncie, Indiana

William B. Johnson
La Mesa Junior High
School
Canyon Country,
California

Kristi Karis
West Ottawa Middle
School
Holland, Michigan

Kristen Koch
Discovery Middle School
Orlando, Florida

Peggy McCarthy
Beulah School
Beulah, Colorado

Deborah J. Miller
Whitney Young Middle
School
Detroit, Michigan

Lawrence Peglow
Greenway Middle School
Pittsburgh, Pennsylvania

Lyn Shiver
Northwestern Middle
School
Alpharetta, Georgia

The World Explorer Team

*The editors, designers, marketer, market researcher, manager, and manufacturing buyer who made up
the World Explorer team are listed below.*

Jackie Bedoya, Bruce Bond, Ellen Brown, David Lippman, Catherine Martin-Hetmansky,
Nancy Rogier, Olena Serbyn, Carol Signorino, John Springer, Susan Swan

TABLE OF CONTENTS

GEOGRAPHY TOOLS AND CONCEPTS 1

OF SPECIAL INTEREST

A hands-on, active approach to practicing and applying key social studies skills

Engaging, step-by-step activities for exploring important topics in geography

High-interest selections by authors that help geographic concepts come to life

MAPS

CHARTS, GRAPHS, AND TABLES

Activating Prior Knowledge

Three sets of reading strategies are introduced on pages viii and ix. Before students read the strategies, use questions like these to prompt a discussion about reading:

- Before you read, what do you do to help you read better?

- How do you figure out the meaning of what you read?

- Do you take a different approach to different kinds of reading, such as a paperback novel or your math textbook?

Discussion of their answers will help students become aware of their own reading processes.

Introducing the Strategies

Point out to students that reading is a process. If students are conscious of their process, they can improve their reading. Point out that there are three sets of reading strategies: **Before You Read, While You Read,** and **After You Read.** Explain that these are the behaviors that good readers exhibit. As students practice these strategies, they too will increase their reading fluency and comprehension.

Be sure to reinforce the idea that students might use several of these strategies at the same time, or they might go back and forth among them. There is no set order for applying them.

READ ACTIVELY

How can I get the most out of my social studies book? How does my reading relate to my world? Answering questions like these means that you are an active reader, an involved reader. As an active reader, you are in charge of the reading situation!

The following strategies tell how to think and read as an active reader. You don't need to use all of these strategies all the time. Feel free to choose the ones that work best in each reading situation. You might use several at a time, or you might go back and forth among them. They can be used in any order.

BEFORE YOU READ

Give yourself a purpose

The sections in this book begin with a list called "Questions to Explore." These questions focus on key ideas presented in the section. They give you a purpose for reading. You can create your own purpose by asking questions like these: How does the topic relate to your life? How might you use what you learn at school or at home?

Preview

To preview a reading selection, first read its title. Then look at the pictures and read the captions. Also read any headings in the selection. Then ask yourself: What is the reading selection about? What do the pictures and headings tell about the selection?

Reach into your background

What do you already know about the topic of the selection? How can you use what you know to help you understand what you are going to read?

Ask questions

Suppose you are reading about the continent of South America. Some questions you might ask are: Where is South America? What countries are found there? Why are some of the countries large and others small? Asking questions like these can help you gather evidence and gain knowledge.

Predict

As you read, make a prediction about what will happen and why. Or predict how one fact might affect another fact. Suppose you are reading about South America's climate. You might make a prediction about how the climate affects where people live. You can change your mind as you gain new information.

Connect

Connect your reading to your own life. Are the people discussed in the selection like you or someone you know? What would you do in similar situations? Connect your reading to something you have already read. Suppose you have already read about the ancient Greeks. Now you are reading about the ancient Romans. How are they alike? How are they different?

Visualize

What would places, people, and events look like in a movie or a picture? As you read about India, you could visualize the country's heavy rains. What do they look like? How do they sound? As you read about geography, you could visualize a volcanic eruption.

Respond

Talk about what you have read. What did you think? Share your ideas with your classmates.

Assess yourself

What did you find out? Were your predictions on target? Did you find answers to your questions?

Follow up

Show what you know. Use what you have learned to do a project. When you do projects, you continue to learn.

Developing Student Reading

Point out to students that the sections in this book have a Before You Read feature. Each one is enclosed in a yellow box (see page 9 for an example). It includes Reach Into Your Background, which helps students think about what they already know so that they can apply their prior knowledge to what they're reading. Before You Read also includes Questions to Explore, which focus on the main ideas in the section. Each Question to Explore relates to one of the Guiding Questions for the book. See the list of Guiding Questions on the following page.

Students will also find Read Actively margin notes in every section. Encourage them to respond to these prompts to reinforce their active reading process.

Supporting English Language Learners

Preview and predict Suggest that students look at the title, headings, maps, charts, and photos to guess what the section is about.

Ask questions Tell students that every fact an author writes has a purpose. Have them question the purpose of details as they read them. As they find answers and discover meaning, they can formulate new, deeper questions.

Visualize Have students think how the places they read about would affect their senses. What would it smell like there? What would they see and hear and feel?

Assess Have students review their predictions and see how well they did. What helped them make good predictions?

This book was developed around four Guiding Questions about geography. They appear on the reduced Student Edition page to the right. The Guiding Questions are intended as an organizational focus for the book. All of the chapter content, activities, questions, and assessments relate to the Guiding Questions, which act as a kind of umbrella under which all of the material falls. You may wish to add your own Guiding Questions to the list in order to tailor them to your particular course. Or, as a group activity, you may want to ask your class to develop its own Guiding Questions.

Ask a volunteer to read the Guiding Questions out loud to the class. These questions will guide students as they learn about geography.

Introducing the Project Preview

The projects for this book are designed to provide students with hands-on involvement in the content area. On the reduced Student Edition page to the right, students are introduced to the projects. Complete information about them appears on pages 126–127. You may assign projects as cooperative activities, whole class projects, or individual projects. Each project relates to at least one of the Guiding Questions.

GEOGRAPHY
TOOLS AND CONCEPTS

Are you curious about our Earth? Do you want to know why some places in the world are cold and some are hot? Have you wondered why more people live in cities and fewer people live in other places? Would you like to find mountaintops or valleys to explore? If you answered *yes* to any of these questions, you want to know more about geography. Farmers grow corn, traders cross the ocean, and you walk or take a bus to school. Geography explains all of these activities—and many more.

Guiding Questions

The readings and activities in this book will help you discover answers to these Guiding Questions.

- What is the Earth's geography like?
- Where do the world's people live?
- What is a culture?
- How do people use the world's resources?

Project Preview

You can also discover answers to the Guiding Questions by working on projects. Preview the following projects and choose one that you might like to do. For more details, see page 126.

The Geography Game Create a team game the whole class can play. Write clues about the unique physical features, climate, population, culture, and natural resources of a country.

World News Today Prepare a short speech about a country's economy and natural resources. Use a collection of newspaper articles.

Focus on Part of the Whole Set up a classroom map and picture display based on your research of the geography, climate, and population of a country.

Desktop Countries Make a desktop display. Include food samples, a flag, souvenirs, and other items typical of a country from which your ancestors came.

Teaching Resources

Book Projects, in the Activities and Projects booklet, provide students with directions on how to complete one of the projects described on these two pages. You may wish to assign or have students choose a project at the beginning of the course.

Program Resources

Long-Term Integrated Projects booklet, in the Program Resources Binder, provides opportunities for students to make comparisons across regions through a variety of long-term projects. You may wish to assign or have students choose a project at the beginning of the course.

Houses near San Francisco cling to the hills in the picture at the left. At the top, a cargo ship carries goods from one country to another. In the picture above right, Japanese women work in rice fields.

EXPLORER'S JOURNAL

A journal can be your personal book of discovery. As you explore geography, you can use your journal to keep track of the things you learn and do. You can also record thoughts about your explorations. For your first entry, write about how you can use maps to find your way around.

Invite students to discuss the three photographs. Use them as a prompt for discussion of what students know about geography. You may want to begin a K-W-L chart on the chalk board with the headings What We **K**now About Geography, What We **W**ant to Know About Geography, and What We **L**earned About Geography. Have students fill in the first column with several things they agree they already know. Then ask them to brainstorm what they would like to know about geography to add to the second column. Students can fill in the third column as they work through the text.

Using the Explorer's Journal

Have students begin their Explorer's Journal as the paragraph on the student book page suggests. If at all possible, encourage students to use a separate small notebook for their Explorer's Journal entries. They can add to this Journal as they learn more about Geography.

Teacher's Flexible Planning Guide includes a guide to the Prentice Hall World Explorer Program, a skills correlation, and a variety of pacing charts for different course configurations. You may wish to refer to the guide as you plan your instruction.

Resource Pro™ CD-ROM allows you to create customized lesson plans and print all Teaching Resources and Program Resources, plus the Computer Test Bank, directly from the CD-ROM.

Lesson Objectives

❶ Define the term *geography* and explain what geographers do.

❷ Describe the features of physical, population density, climate, and vegetation maps.

❸ Explain how physical, population, climate, and vegetation maps are used.

Lesson Plan

1 Engage

Warm-Up Activity

Tell students to imagine that they are creating a twin community to your own. To begin, have them describe your community's geography. Encourage students to include human geography as well. If necessary, prompt students with questions such as *What is the land like? What is the weather like? How many people live in a neighborhood?*

Activating Prior Knowledge

Ask students to name as many map types as they know. Post the common suggestions on the chalkboard and define them as a class. Talk about how the maps differ and what their possible uses might be.

DISCOVERY ACTIVITIES ABOUT

Geography

Learning about geography tools and concepts means being an explorer, and no explorer would start out without first checking some facts. Use the activities on the following pages to begin exploring the world of geography. They will help you learn what geography is and how it can help you.

▲ Why do people in this place wear this type of clothing?

▼ Why do relatively few people live in this area?

World: Physical

2　GEOGRAPHY: TOOLS AND CONCEPTS

Resource Directory

Teaching Resources

Activity Atlas in the Activities and Projects booklet, pp. 3–5, provides a structure that helps students complete the activities in the Geography Activity Atlas and encourages discovery learning.

PLACE

I. Explore the Meaning of Geography Think about the word *geography*. The word part *geo* comes from a Greek word meaning "earth." *Graphy* means "science of," from an earlier word that meant "to write." How would you define *geography*?

People who are interested in geography are very curious about our world. They often ask questions such as "Where are things?" and "Why are they where they are?"

Look at the pictures on these two pages. The question that accompanies each picture is the type of question that geographers ask. For each picture, write another question a geographer might ask.

▲ Why did ancient people in this area become expert sailors?

▶ Why do visitors to this area become short of breath easily?

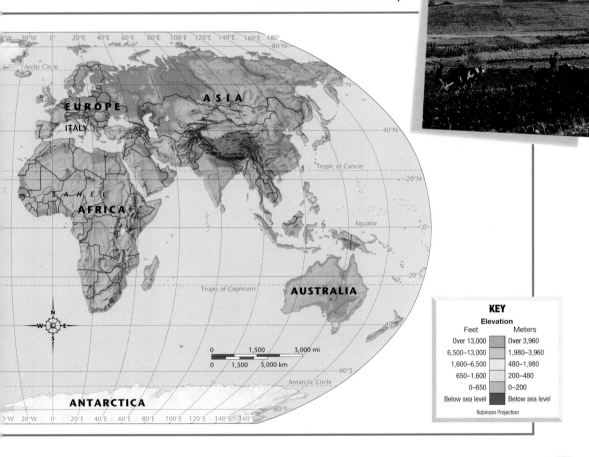

KEY

Elevation

Feet		Meters
Over 13,000		Over 3,960
6,500–13,000		1,980–3,960
1,600–6,500		480–1,980
650–1,600		200–480
0–650		0–200
Below sea level		Below sea level

Robinson Projection

2 Explore

Generate, discuss, and record questions that must be answered in order to describe clearly your community's geographic twin. Then have students carefully read the Activity Atlas materials. Ask them to list new questions that arise as they read. Discuss how maps might help answer each question.

3 Teach

Begin a concept web about geography by writing the word *geography* on the chalkboard. Have a volunteer write a sentence in the center of the web defining the term. Students can then complete the web by adding a second row of elements describing the maps geographers use and a third row explaining the information each map provides.

4 Assess

Concept webs should define geography as the science of the Earth and should list physical, population density, climate region, and vegetation region maps as well as the information each map provides.

Answers to ...

PLACE

I. Geography is the science of the Earth.

Possible questions: How do people adapt to their environment? What makes a place an attractive location to live? What challenges face people living at great elevations? What major body of water influences life in a town?

Practice in the Themes of Geography

Place Have students use the material in the Activity Atlas to write one or two sentences describing a chosen place. Explain that each place can be described in terms of its physical or human geography. (Possible answer: Alaska is a sparsely populated, harsh land in the far north of North America.)

Location Ask students to name the continent on which Italy is located (Europe). Then ask them what two continents are nearest (Asia and Africa).

Movement Tell students to imagine that their family wants to relocate from one continent to another. Ask students which continent their family would be on if they had to cross a large body of water to reach any other continent (Australia).

Regions Ask students what nation occupies most of the region of South Asia (India).

Human-Environment Interaction Ask students to explain why a great port city arose in the city of Karachi. (It is on the coast and is connected to inland communities by a river. The location enables people to move goods in and out of the region.)

LOCATION

2. What Kinds of Maps Does Geo Leo Need?

Geographers do more than ask questions about the Earth. They also gather, organize, and analyze geographic information. Geographers use many different types of maps to do this work.

Examine the map below and the maps on the next page. Be sure to read the title of each map so you know what the map is about. Then help Geo Leo plan a trip to South Asia, an area that includes the countries of Afghanistan, India, Pakistan, and Bangladesh.

A. *"If I wanted to find out how many people live in the city of Mumbai, India, which map would I use?"*

B. *"On my trip to South Asia, I want to search for gigantic insects that live in tropical rain forests. Which map do I use to find the tropical rain forests?"*

C. *"South Asia is a region that has many different types of climate. Which map will help me bring the right gear for Pakistan's arid climate?"*

GEO LEO

BONUS

Which type of vegetation grows in only one South Asian country?

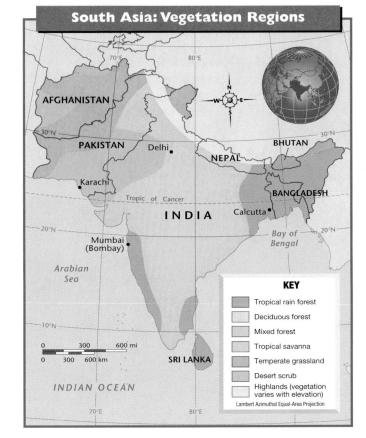

South Asia: Vegetation Regions

KEY
- Tropical rain forest
- Deciduous forest
- Mixed forest
- Tropical savanna
- Temperate grassland
- Desert scrub
- Highlands (vegetation varies with elevation)

Lambert Azimuthal Equal-Area Projection

Answers to ...

LOCATION

2. A. population density
   B. vegetation region
   C. climate region
   Bonus deciduous forest

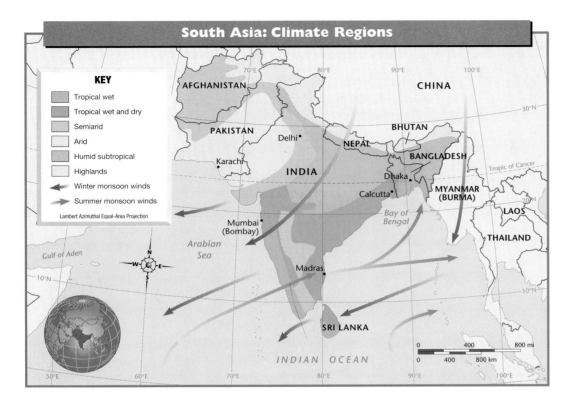

South Asia: Climate Regions

KEY
- Tropical wet
- Tropical wet and dry
- Semiarid
- Arid
- Humid subtropical
- Highlands
- ← Winter monsoon winds
- → Summer monsoon winds

Lambert Azimuthal Equal-Area Projection

AFGHANISTAN
PAKISTAN
Delhi
Karachi
INDIA
NEPAL
BHUTAN
CHINA
BANGLADESH
Dhaka
Calcutta
MYANMAR (BURMA)
LAOS
THAILAND
Mumbai (Bombay)
Madras
Bay of Bengal
SRI LANKA
Arabian Sea
Gulf of Aden
INDIAN OCEAN

| 0 | 400 | 800 mi |
| 0 | 400 | 800 km |

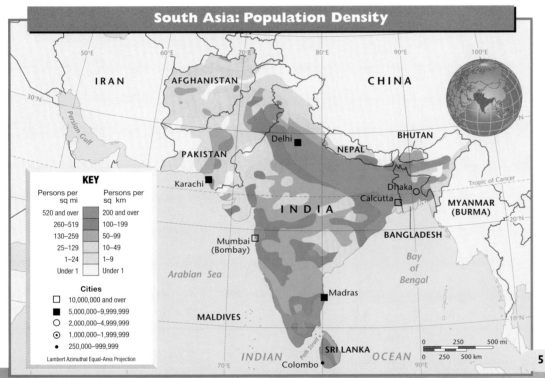

South Asia: Population Density

IRAN
AFGHANISTAN
CHINA
PAKISTAN
Karachi
Delhi
NEPAL
BHUTAN
INDIA
Dhaka
Calcutta
MYANMAR (BURMA)
BANGLADESH
Mumbai (Bombay)
Persian Gulf
Tropic of Cancer
Bay of Bengal
Arabian Sea
Madras
MALDIVES
Polk Strait
SRI LANKA
Colombo
INDIAN OCEAN

KEY

Persons per sq mi	Persons per sq km
520 and over	200 and over
260–519	100–199
130–259	50–99
25–129	10–49
1–24	1–9
Under 1	Under 1

Cities
- ☐ 10,000,000 and over
- ■ 5,000,000–9,999,999
- ○ 2,000,000–4,999,999
- ◉ 1,000,000–1,999,999
- • 250,000–999,999

Lambert Azimuthal Equal-Area Projection

| 0 | 250 | 500 mi |
| 0 | 250 | 500 km |

Background

Links Across Time

Geography has played an important role in the history of South Asia. The towering Himalaya Mountains are the world's highest mountains, with peaks as high as Mount Everest's 29,028 feet (8,848 m). For centuries, these mountains kept the ancient cultures of South Asia largely isolated from the rest of the world. Protected from invasion, complex cultures arose in the region. For example, in the Indus River Valley (in modern Pakistan), ancient Indians built the city of Mohenjo-Daro. This carefully planned city was laid out on a grid of streets. Important public buildings were grouped on a raised citadel area. A system of pipes provided drainage for household waste, public and private baths, and rainfall. The culture of Mohenjo-Daro also produced advanced science and fine art. The city flourished, apparently unthreatened, until about 1500 B.C. Weakened by constant battles with the devastating yearly floods of the Indus River, Mohenjo-Daro was conquered.

Interdisciplinary Connections

Math Have students use an almanac and locate population per square mile data for the five most densely populated cities in the world (Hong Kong: 247,501; Lagos, Nigeria: 142,821; Dhaka, Bangladesh: 138,108; Jakarta, Indonesia: 130,026; and Bombay, India: 127,461). Stress that population density is different than the total number of people. Then, for each city, have students use the projected population figure for the year 2000 and area in square miles to calculate population per square mile for the year 2000 (Hong Kong: 258,956; Lagos: 223,714; Dhaka: 202,875; Jakarta: 168,473; and Bombay: 161,652). Ask them to describe the population trend. (While students' data may differ, the trends should be similar—all the cities are getting more crowded.)
Kinesthetic

Answers to...

REGIONS

3. South Asia, the Far East, Eastern Europe, and the northeastern United States; Antarctica and other polar areas; the land, climate, and resources make these places most livable; possible answer: Cities are often located near bodies of water.

REGIONS

3. Analyze Density As you explore geography, you can find out where things are and why they are there. Geography can also help you figure out where people are and why. Study this population density map. Which places have many people? Which areas have the fewest? Why do you think people live where they do? Look back at the first map in this Activity Atlas for some clues. Try to draw conclusions about how physical features influence where cities are located.

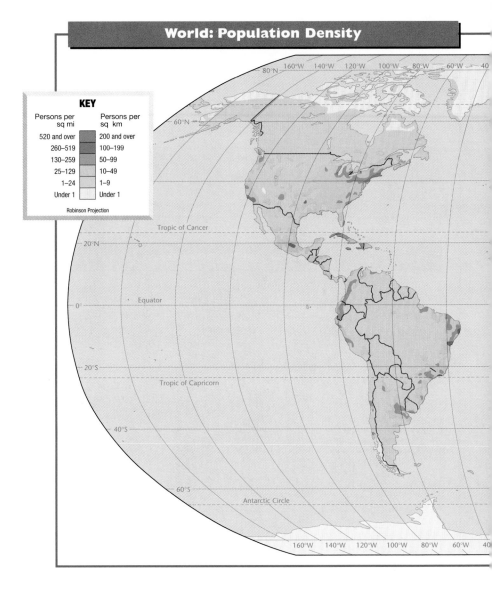

World: Population Density

KEY

Persons per sq mi	Persons per sq km
520 and over	200 and over
260–519	100–199
130–259	50–99
25–129	10–49
1–24	1–9
Under 1	Under 1

Robinson Projection

MOVEMENT

4. Create a "Mental Map" Mental maps exist in people's minds, not on paper. Each of us has a file of mental maps, which show the routes to and around places such as school, home, or the mall. To put a mental map on paper, simply choose somewhere you like to go, and draw a map of how you get there. Include as many details as you can—landmarks, streets, buildings, and other details. Then, test the map by giving it to another person to follow. Is it clear? If not, make corrections. Finally, compare it with the maps on the previous pages. What is different? What is the same?

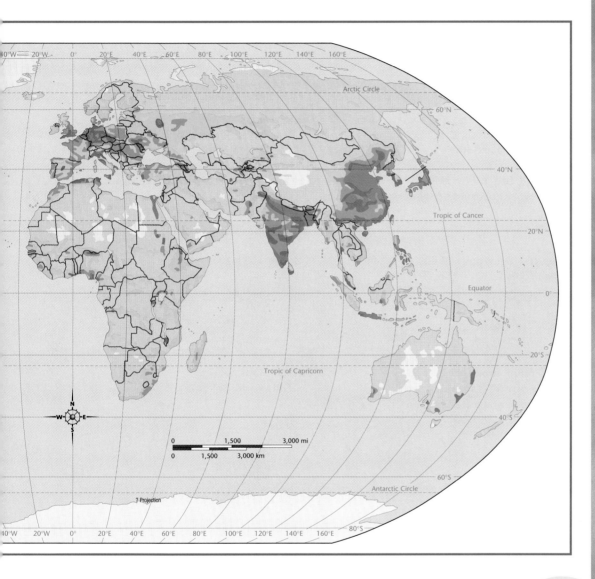

Discovery Learning

Global Geography Game
To play the game, you will need a globe or a world map and a game piece that can be attached to either. Start the game by prompting students with a location clue. Clues may include data from the Atlas maps, photos, or text. Continue giving clues until the students identify the correct place and tell what kind of map would include the clue information. Place the game piece on the location.

The student who identifies the location then gives clues for a second location to another student. Once that location is identified, move the game piece to the next location. Continue the game until all students have correctly identified one place. *Kinesthetic*

Activity

Journal Writing

Tell students to imagine that they are visiting their community's geographic twin. Ask them to write a descriptive letter to a friend back home. Letters should include descriptive language.

Answers to...

MOVEMENT

4. Students should note that their maps show a smaller area in greater detail. They also show routes between places, a feature not on any of the Atlas maps. Students' maps also show relationships between places and locate important details, features that are included in Atlas maps.

The World of Geography

To help you plan instruction, the chart below shows how teaching resources correspond to chapter content. Use the resources to vary instruction, add activities, or plan block schedules. Where appropriate, resources have **suggested time allotments** for students. Time allotments are approximate.

Managing Time and Instruction

	Geography: Tools and Concepts Teaching Resources Binder		World Explorer Program Resources Binder	
	Resource	**mins.**	**Resource**	**mins.**
1 SECTION 1 The Five Themes of Geography	**Chapter and Section Support** Reproducible Lesson Plan, p. 3		**Outline Maps** The World: Physical, p. 2	20
	ⓢ Guided Reading and Review, p. 4	20	The United States: Physical, p. 14	20
	ⓢ Section Quiz, p. 5	25	**Nystrom Desk Atlas**	
	Social Studies and Geography Skills,		ⓣ **Primary Sources and Literature**	
	Understanding Latitude and Longitude,		Readings	40
	p. 10	30	**Writing Process Handbook**	
	Understanding Hemispheres, p. 7	30	Locating Information, pp. 17–18	25
SKILLS ACTIVITY Expressing Problems Clearly	**Social Studies and Geography Skills,** Expressing Problems Clearly, p. 40	30		
2 SECTION 2 The Geographer's Tools	**Chapter and Section Support** Reproducible Lesson Plan, p. 6		**Outline Maps** The World: Political, p. 5	20
	ⓢ Guided Reading and Review, p. 7	20		
	Critical Thinking Activity, p. 19	30		
	ⓢ Section Quiz, p. 8	25		
	ⓢ Vocabulary, p. 10	20		
	Reteaching, p. 11	25		
	Enrichment, p. 12	25		
	ⓢ Chapter Summary, p. 9	15		
	Tests Forms A and B Chapter Tests, pp. 2–7	40		
	Social Studies and Geography Skills, Using the Map Key, p. 3	30		
ACTIVITY SHOP: INTERDISCIPLINARY A Five-Theme Tour	ⓣ Activity Shop: Interdisciplinary, p. 7	30		

Block Scheduling
PROGRAM SUPPORT

- Block Scheduling Folder — PROGRAM TEACHING RESOURCES
- Activities and Projects
- Interdisciplinary Links
- Resource Pro™ CD-ROM
- Media and Technology

Media and Technology

Resource	mins.
📀 📀 Ⓢ World Video Explorer	20
📀 Planet Earth CD-ROM	20
▭ Color Transparencies 1, 3, 98, 99, 155	20
▭ Color Transparency 100	20
🎧 Ⓢ Guided Reading Audiotapes	20
▭ Color Transparency 171 (Graphic organizer web template)	20
📀 The Writer's Solution CD-ROM	30
💾 Computer Test Bank	30

T **Teaming Opportunity** This resource is especially well-suited for teaching teams.

Ⓢ **Spanish** This resource is also in Spanish support.

📀 **CD-ROM**

📀 **Laserdisc**

▭ **Transparency**

💾 **Software**

📀 **Videotape**

🎧 **Audiotape**

Assessment Opportunities

From Guiding Questions to Assessment A series of Guiding Questions serves as an organizing framework for this book. The Guiding Question that relates to this chapter is below. Section Reviews and Section Quizzes provide opportunities for assessing students' insights into these Guiding Questions. Additional assessments are listed below.

GUIDING QUESTION

- *What is the Earth's geography like?*

ASSESSMENTS

Section 1	Section 2
Students should be able to create a chart that names and defines the five themes of geography.	Students should be able to write a report that describes the advantages and disadvantages of different kinds of maps and globes.
▶ **RUBRIC** See the Assessment booklet for a rubric on assessing charts.	▶ **RUBRIC** See the Assessment booklet for a rubric on assessing a report.

Activities and Projects

Mental Mapping

Plenty of Latitude Draw a horizontal line on the chalkboard and label it EQUATOR. Draw two parallel lines equidistant from the Equator line and label them TROPICS. Draw a compass rose near the lines to indicate north, south, east, and west. Then write UNITED STATES just above the northern tropics line.

Invite students to suggest other countries to be placed north of the northern tropics line. Then ask them to name countries they think are between the northern tropics line and the Equator, countries on the Equator, countries that are located between the Equator and the southern tropics line, and countries south of the southern tropics line.

Give students a chance to look at a world map that shows lines of latitude to check their guesses.

Links to Current Events

Geography on the Newsstand Today, more people than ever are interested in geography. Have students look at copies of *National Geographic, National Geographic World, Geo, Faces, Kids Discover,* and other magazines that are devoted wholly or partially to geography.

As students look through an issue of a geography magazine, ask them to list the main topics they see covered in the magazine. Then have students get together in small groups to compare their lists. Ask them to share the variety of topics they find with the class as a whole.

Hands-On Activities

Many Maps Ask students what they think of when they think of a map. Explain that there are many kinds of maps for many kinds of purposes. Ask students to brainstorm maps they know about. They might mention road maps, political maps, weather maps, zip code maps, and physical maps. Suggest that there are also maps of train and airplane routes, climate maps, elevation maps, navigational charts, street maps, tourist maps, maps of buildings and shopping malls, and historical maps.

Ask students to work in pairs to make maps. Have each pair choose a different type of map to make. They may choose to make maps of the local area, the world, or a purely fictional locale. Remind them to include map elements such as a title, key, and compass rose.

Five Themes Ask students to make a graphic organizer with one column for each of the five themes of geography. In each column, have them list ways that each theme could be used to look at their town or city, their state, and their country. *Challenging*

Map Exhibit Have students find as many different types of maps as they can. They may use library reference materials as well as magazines, brochures, and flyers. They can photocopy maps from books or magazines that cannot be cut up. Then ask them to create a display of the maps they find. Under each map, they should write a brief description of how someone could use it. *English Language Learners*

Geography Collage Ask each student to choose three of the five themes. Have them draw or cut out a picture that they think represents that theme. Then have all the students work together to make a big Geography Collage to display in the school or classroom. *Basic*

Latitude and Longitude Let students play a location game. Put a large world map marked with lines of latitude and longitude on a bulletin board. Provide, or let students provide, locations using the grid of latitude and longitude. For example, 42°N and 71°W would be Boston, Massachusetts. Give pairs of students a chance to race one another to find the place described by the location information. You might give them map pins to pinpoint their location. You could also structure this as an elimination competition that would allow the best of each pair of students to compete against each other. *Average*

This page can help you extend your own and students' understanding of the concepts in this chapter. You may want to browse through some of the suggestions in the **Bibliography. Interdisciplinary Links** can connect social studies understandings to areas elsewhere in the curriculum through the use of other Prentice Hall products. **National Geography Standards** reflected specifically in this chapter are listed for your convenience. Some hints about appropriate **Internet Access** are also provided. **School to Careers** provides insights into the practical uses of some of the concepts in this chapter as they might pertain to various careers.

BIBLIOGRAPHY

FOR THE TEACHER

The Dorling Kindersley Geography of the World. Dorling Kindersley, 1996.

Eyewitness History of the World. Dorling Kindersley, 1995. CD-ROM.

Geography: Five Themes for Planet Earth. National Geographic, 1992. Videocassette.

FOR THE STUDENT

Easy
VanCleave, Janice. *Janice VanCleave's Geography for Every Kid: Easy Activities That Make Learning Geography Fun.* Wiley, 1993.

Average
Meltzer, Milton. *The Amazing Potato: A Story in Which the Incas, Conquistadors, Marie Antoinette, Thomas Jefferson,*

Wars, Famines, Immigrants, and French Fries All Play a Part. HarperCollins, 1992.

Where in the World is Carmen Sandiego? Broderbund, 1995. CD-ROM.

Challenging
Lasky, Kathryn. *The Librarian Who Measured the Earth.* Little Brown, 1994.

LITERATURE CONNECTION

Fisher Staples, Suzanne. *Shabanu: Daughter of the Wind.* Knopf, 1989.

Houston, James. *Drifting Snow: An Arctic Search.* McElderry, 1992.

INTERDISCIPLINARY LINKS

Subject	Theme: Discovery
MATH	Middle Grades Math: Tools for Success Course 1, Lesson 5-2, **Napier's Rods** Course 2, Lesson 1-4, **Mean, Median, and Mode**
SCIENCE	Prentice Hall Science *Exploring Planet Earth,* Lesson 4-4, **Topographic Maps**
LANGUAGE ARTS	Prentice Hall Literature *Copper,* **The Strange Geometry of Stonehenge** *Bronze,* **Circle of the Seasons**

NATIONAL GEOGRAPHY STANDARDS

Students explore the 18 National Geography Standards throughout *Geography: Tools and Concepts.* Chapter 1, however, concentrates on investigating the following standards: 1, 2, 3, 4, 5, 7, 8, 9, 11, 12, 14, 15, 16. For a complete list of the standards, see the *Teacher's Flexible Planning Guide.*

SCHOOL TO CAREERS

In Chapter 1, The World of Geography, students learn about the themes and tools of geography. Additionally, they address the skill of expressing problems clearly. Understanding geography can help students prepare for careers in many fields such as history, geography, geology, archaeology, urban planning, and so on. Expressing problems clearly is a skill particularly useful for teachers, administrators, office managers, politicians, and others. The curriculum presented in this book, as in all eight titles of Prentice Hall's *World Explorer* program, is designed to prepare students not only for careers but also for good citizenship—of the world as well as of this country.

INTERNET ACCESS

Many social studies teachers and students use Internet browsers, or search engines, to investigate particular topics. For the best results, use narrow rather than broad topics. Try these for Chapter 1: geography, mapmaking, Equator. Finding age-appropriate sites is an important consideration when using the Internet. For links to age-appropriate sites in world studies and geography, visit the Prentice Hall Home Page at: **http://www.phschool.com**

Connecting to the Guiding Questions

As students complete this chapter, they will focus on the five themes of geography and the advantages and disadvantages of various types of maps. Content in this chapter thus corresponds to this Guiding Question:

● What is the Earth's geography like?

Using the Picture Activities

Discuss with students several features they can identify in the picture. Ask students to tell whether the features are natural or human-made.

• Students should mention such natural features as land and water forms and such cultural features as bridges, dams, and other human-made structures.

• Students' maps should contain information from the photo in the form of symbols. The missing information that they need to make a map is the distances between places.

Heterogeneous Groups

CHAPTER **1**

The World of Geography

SECTION 1
The Five Themes of Geography

SECTION 2
The Geographer's Tools

PICTURE ACTIVITIES

This photograph of San Francisco, California, was taken from the air. Pictures like this tell something about the world of geography. The following activities will help you understand how.

Study the picture
Find several natural features such as forests, hills, or oceans. Notice things that people have made such as roads, towns, and industries. If someone in a plane took a photograph of your region, what do you think the picture would show?

Make a prediction
In this picture, dense fog all but covers San Francisco's Golden Gate Bridge. How do you think the fog might affect traffic across the bridge and ships in the water?

Resource Directory

Media and Technology

Journey Over the World, from the World Video Explorer, introduces students to major landforms throughout the world.

Five Themes of Geography, from the World Video Explorer, enhances students' understanding of the five themes of geography through an examination of the Pacific Islands.

Chapter 2

Chapter 3

The Five Themes of Geography

Reach Into Your Background

If you were going to tell someone how to get to your school from where you live, what would you say? You might say something like "Go six blocks north and one block east." Or you might say your school is next to a local park or shopping center. These directions are examples of geography at work in your everyday life.

Questions to Explore

1. What is geography?

2. How can the five themes of geography help you understand the world?

Key Terms

geography
latitude
parallel
degree
Equator
longitude
meridian
Prime Meridian
plain

What would it be like to look at the Earth from a spaceship? Michael Collins, an astronaut who went to the moon, did just that. In his book *Carrying the Fire,* Collins described what he saw in July 1969 from his space capsule, 200 miles above the Earth. Even that far away, Collins could see natural features of the planet and evidence of the Earth's people.

"The Indian Ocean flashes incredible colors of emerald jade and opal in the shallow water surrounding the Maldive Islands; then on to the Burma [Myanmar] coast and nondescript green jungle, followed by mountains, coastline, and Hanoi. We can see fires burning off to the southeast, and we scramble for our one remaining still camera to record them. Now the sun glints in unusual fashion off the ocean near Formosa [Taiwan]. There are intersecting surface ripples just south of the island, patterns which are clearly visible and which, I think, must be useful to fishermen who need to know about these currents. The island itself is verdant—glistening green the color and shape of a shiny, well-fertilized gardenia leaf."

▼ From hundreds of miles in space, huge clouds drifting over the Indian Ocean look like haze. What features can you see on the land?

Teaching Resources

📁 **Reproducible Lesson Plan** in the Chapter and Section Resources booklet, p. 3, provides a summary of the section lesson.

📁 **Guided Reading and Review** in the Chapter and Section Resources booklet, p. 4, provides a structure for mastering key concepts and reviewing key terms in the section. Available in Spanish in the Spanish Chapter and Section Resources booklet, p. 3.

Program Resources

📁 Material in the **Primary Sources and Literature Readings** booklet extends content with a selection related to the concepts in this chapter.

📁 **Outline Maps** The World: Physical, p. 2 The United States: Physical, p. 14

Section 1

Lesson Objectives

❶ Define the scope of geography.

❷ Identify the five themes of geography and relate each theme to real-world examples.

❸ Use the five themes as a way to organize information about places.

Lesson Plan

1 Engage

Warm-Up Activity

Have students do a quick-write about what they think the subject of geography covers. Let them share their thoughts in a discussion. Ask students to create a preliminary definition of *geography*. Suggest that they record their definitions and check them once or twice as they read the chapter. Encourage them to revise or rewrite their definitions as they learn more about geography.

Activating Prior Knowledge

Have students read Reach Into Your Background in the Before You Read box. Ask volunteers to describe how to get from their home to school. Use the directions as a springboard for listing other occasions in which students use geography.

Answers to . . .

CAPTION

mountains

2 Explore

After students read the section, discuss the following aspects of geography: Why is the study of people and their activities part of geography? What is the difference between a natural and a cultural feature of a place? What are the two main questions that geographers ask? What are some reasons for which people move from one place to another?

3 Teach

Ask students to list the five themes of geography and then use them to create a chart with the following headings: *Theme, Definition, Example*. Tell students that they can use examples from the text, but that original examples are preferred. With the class, create a definition of *geography* that includes the five themes.

4 Assess

See answers to the Section Review. You may also use students' charts as an assessment.

Acceptable charts include accurate definitions and examples from the text.

Commendable charts include some original examples.

Outstanding charts have all original examples.

Answers to ...

MAP STUDY

Australia

The Study of the Earth

From his high perch, Michael Collins described the colors of the ocean and the plant life on the land. He wrote about how land and water looked. He saw fires set by human beings. Collins was looking at the world as a geographer does.

Geography is the study of the Earth, our home. Geographers analyze the Earth from many points of view. They may discuss how far one place is from another. You do this when you tell someone directions. But they also study such things as oceans, plant life, landforms, and people. Geographers study how the Earth and its people affect each other.

The Themes of Geography: Five Ways to Look at the Earth

In their work, geographers are guided by two basic questions: (1) Where are things located? and (2) Why are they there? To find the answers, geographers use five themes to organize information. These themes are location, place, human-environment interaction, movement, and regions.

Location   Geographers begin to study a place by finding where it is. Location is like the address of a place. There are two ways to talk about location—its absolute location and its relative location. Absolute location is an exact spot on the Earth. You might call absolute location a geographic "address." Geographers identify the absolute location by

READ ACTIVELY

Predict What do you think each of the five geographic themes means?

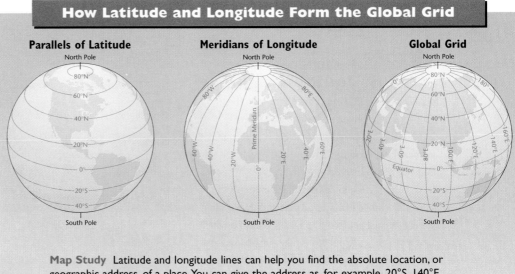

How Latitude and Longitude Form the Global Grid

Parallels of Latitude   **Meridians of Longitude**   **Global Grid**

Map Study Latitude and longitude lines can help you find the absolute location, or geographic address, of a place. You can give the address as, for example, 20°S, 140°E.
Location Find 20°S, 140°E on the Global Grid. What continent surrounds this address?

Resource Directory

Teaching Resources

Understanding Latitude and Longitude in the Social Studies and Geography Skills booklet, p. 10, provides additional skill practice.

Program Resources

Nystrom Desk Atlas

The Hemispheres

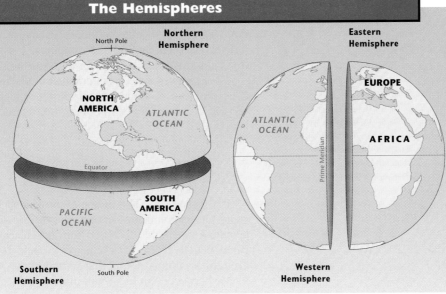

Map Study The Equator and the Prime Meridian both divide the Earth in two. Each half is called a hemisphere. The Equator divides the Earth into Northern and Southern hemispheres. The Prime Meridian divides the Earth into Eastern and Western hemispheres. **Location** The United States is in North America. In which of the hemispheres is the United States located?

North Pole · Northern Hemisphere · Eastern Hemisphere · NORTH AMERICA · ATLANTIC OCEAN · Equator · PACIFIC OCEAN · SOUTH AMERICA · Southern Hemisphere · South Pole · EUROPE · ATLANTIC OCEAN · Prime Meridian · AFRICA · Western Hemisphere

Activity

Drawing Conclusions

Suitable as a whole class activity. Point out to students that there are seven continents. (North and South America, Europe, Asia, Africa, Australia, and Antarctica) Ask students to refer to the illustration and list the names of the continents that lie mostly or completely in the Southern Hemisphere. Which lie in the Western Hemisphere? Have students evaluate their responses and then draw a conclusion identifying any additional information they may need to complete their lists.

using two kinds of imaginary lines around the Earth: latitude and longitude. With these lines, they can pinpoint any spot on the Earth.

Lines of **latitude** are east-west circles around the globe. They are also called **parallels,** because they are parallel to one another. They never meet. These circles divide the globe into units called **degrees.** In the middle of the globe is the parallel called the **Equator,** which is 0 degrees latitude. Geographers measure locations either north or south of the Equator. The farthest latitude north of the Equator is 90° north, the location of the North Pole. The farthest latitude south of the Equator is 90° south, the location of the South Pole.

Geographers also must pinpoint a place from east to west. For this they use lines of **longitude.** These lines, also called **meridians,** circle the globe from north to south. All meridians run through the North and South poles. The **Prime Meridian,** which runs through Greenwich, England, is numbered 0 degrees. Geographers measure locations as east or west of the Prime Meridian. The maximum longitude is 180°, which is halfway around the world.

Geographers also discuss relative location. This explains where a place is by describing places near it. Suppose you live in Newburg, Indiana. You might give Newburg's relative location by saying: "I live in Newburg, Indiana. It's about 180 miles southwest of Indianapolis."

Place Geographers also study place. This includes a location's physical and human features. To describe physical features, you might say the climate is hot or cold. Or you might say that the land is hilly. To emphasize human features, you might talk about how many people live in a place and the kinds of work they do.

LINKS TO MATH

Dividing Longitude
Consider these facts.
(1) Your house makes a complete circle every 24 hours. That is because your house sits on the Earth, which makes one turn on its axis every day. (2) A circle has 360 degrees. Therefore, time is connected to longitude—the location of your house. As a result, geographers divide each degree of longitude into 60 minutes and each minute into 60 seconds.

Media and Technology

 Planet Earth CD-ROM includes satellite maps of the whole Earth.
Color Transparencies 1, 3, 98, 99, 155

Teaching Resources

Understanding Hemispheres in the Social Studies and Geography Skills booklet, p. 7, provides additional skill practice.

Answers to . . .

MAP STUDY

Northern and Western

Human-Environment Interaction The theme of interaction stresses how people affect their environment, the physical characteristics of their natural surroundings. Perhaps they deliberately cut trails into the mountainside. Or perhaps they cleared large forest areas.

Geographers also use interaction to discuss how people react to the consequences of their actions. For instance, most farms in Turkey receive little rain. So people have built dams and canals to irrigate the land. On the good side, everyone in the region has more food. On the bad side, irrigation makes salt build up in the soil. Then farmers must treat the soil to get rid of the salt. As a result, food could become more expensive.

Movement The theme of movement helps geographers understand the relationship among places. Movement helps explain how people, goods, and ideas get from one place to another. For example, when people from other countries came to the United States, they brought traditional foods that enriched the American way of life. The theme of movement helps you understand such cultural changes.

Regions Geographers use the theme of regions to make comparisons. A region has a unifying characteristic such as climate, land, population, or history. For instance, the Nile Valley region is a snake-shaped region on either side of the Nile River. The region runs through several countries. Life in the valley is much different from life in the regions alongside the valley. There the landscape is mostly desert.

The Rift Valley—Lake Naivasha

Edwin Rioba
Age 16
Kenya
The Great Rift Valley of East Africa was formed over millions of years by earthquakes and volcanic eruptions. Running from Syria in Asia to Mozambique in Africa, it stretches some 4,500 miles (7,200 km). **Place** Based on this picture, what landforms do you think are commonly found in the Great Rift Valley?

Physical Regions

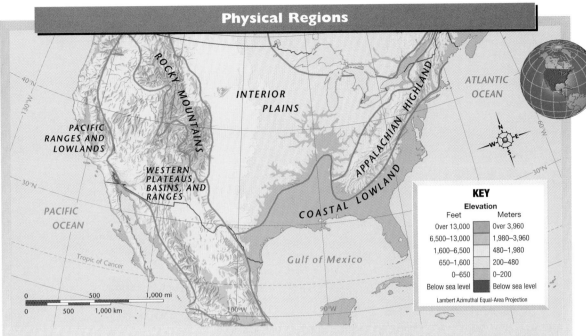

Map Study Suppose that you wanted to drive from the west coast to the east coast of North America. A map like this one gives you an idea of the landforms you might find. **Regions** What obstacle would you have to cross to go from the west coast to the Interior Plains?

KEY
Elevation

Feet	Meters
Over 13,000	Over 3,960
6,500–13,000	1,980–3,960
1,600–6,500	480–1,980
650–1,600	200–480
0–650	0–200
Below sea level	Below sea level

Lambert Azimuthal Equal-Area Projection

On maps, geographers use color and shape or special symbols to show regions. One map may show a **plain,** a region of flat land. The map above shows different regions of elevation, to show the height of land above sea level. A place can be part of several regions at the same time. For example, Houston, Texas, is in both a plains region and an oil-producing region.

SECTION 1 REVIEW

1. **Define** (a) geography, (b) latitude, (c) parallel, (d) degree, (e) Equator, (f) longitude, (g) meridian, (h) Prime Meridian, (i) plain.

2. What are two questions geographers ask when they study the Earth?

3. List the five themes of geography.

4. Give an example of how each theme can be used.

Critical Thinking

5. **Identifying Central Issues** You decide to start a geography club. When you invite a friend to join, she tells you she thinks geography is boring. She would rather learn about people, not just places. What could you say to change her mind?

Activity

6. **Writing to Learn** Make a chart listing the five geography themes. Find the location of your town or city on a map. Write down a relative location that tells where your city or town is. Then, take a walk around your neighborhood and think about the other four themes. Complete the chart by adding descriptions of your neighborhood that relate to each theme.

Lesson Objectives

1. Analyze the problem of accurately representing a globe on a flat map.

2. Evaluate the advantages and disadvantages of various kinds of map projections.

3. Interpret the information provided on maps.

Lesson Plan

1 Engage

Warm-Up Activity

Prepare the following demonstration for the class. Draw two same-size circles on an orange, one near the "equator" of the orange, another near one of the "poles." Ask students what they think will happen to the circles when the orange is peeled and the peel is laid flat. Peel the orange and flatten the peel. Point out that the circles no longer appear to be the same size.

Activating Prior Knowledge

Have students read Reach Into Your Background in the Before You Read box. Lead a discussion in which students list the kinds of maps they are familiar with. Prompt the discussion by asking how they find a particular store in a mall or how they find the fiction books in a library.

The Geographer's Tools

SECTION 2

BEFORE YOU READ

Reach Into Your Background

Skulls-and-crossbones. Ships with black sails. Cannons. Swords. Treasure maps. That's right, MAPS. These things are all tools in great pirate tales. Maps are also one of the most important tools geographers use. Geographers and movie pirates aren't the only ones who use them. You do too!

Questions to Explore

1. What are some of the different ways of showing the Earth's surface and why do geographers use them?

2. What are the advantages and disadvantages of different kinds of maps and globes?

Key Terms
globe
scale
distortion
projection
compass rose
cardinal direction
key

Key People
Gerhardus Mercator
Arthur Robinson

You might expect a map to be printed on a piece of paper. But hundreds of years ago, people made maps out of whatever was available. The Inuit (IN oo it) people carved detailed, accurate maps on pieces of wood. The Inuits were once called Eskimos. These Native Americans have lived in northern regions of the world for centuries. They needed maps that were portable, durable, and waterproof. Carved maps remind us that making maps is not just an exercise in school. People rely on maps, sometimes for their very survival.

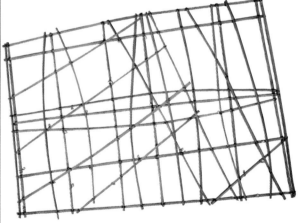

▼ The Marshall Islanders made wood maps of the southwest Pacific Ocean. Curved palm sticks show ocean currents and shells show islands.

Globes and Maps

Hundreds of years ago, people knew very little about the land and water beyond their own homes. Their maps showed only the areas they traveled. Other places either were left out or were only an empty space on their maps. Sometimes they filled the empty spaces with drawings of lands, creatures, and people from myths and stories.

As people explored the Earth, they collected information about the shapes and sizes of islands,

Resource Directory

Teaching Resources

📁 **Reproducible Lesson Plan** in the Chapter and Section Resources booklet, p. 6, provides a summary of the section lesson.

📁 **Guided Reading and Review** in the Chapter and Section Resources booklet, p. 7, provides a structure for mastering key concepts and reviewing key terms in the section. Available in Spanish in the Spanish Chapter and Section Resources booklet, p. 5.

Media and Technology

 Color Transparency 100

continents, and bodies of water. Mapmakers wanted to present this information accurately. The best way was to put it on a **globe,** a round ball like the Earth itself. By using the same shape, mapmakers could show the continents and oceans of the Earth much as they really are. The only difference would be the **scale,** or size.

But there is a problem with globes. Try putting a globe in your backpack every morning. Try making a globe large enough to show the details of your state or community. A globe just cannot be complete enough for people to use and at the same time be small enough to be convenient. People, therefore, invented flat maps.

Flat maps, however, present another problem. The Earth is round. A map is flat. Could you flatten an orange peel without tearing it? There will be wrinkled and folded sections. The same thing happens when mapmakers create flat maps. It is impossible to show the Earth on a flat surface without some **distortion,** or change in the accuracy of its shapes and distances. Something is going to look larger or smaller than it is.

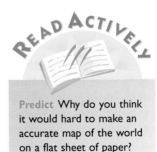

READ ACTIVELY

Predict Why do you think it would hard to make an accurate map of the world on a flat sheet of paper?

An Orange Peel Map

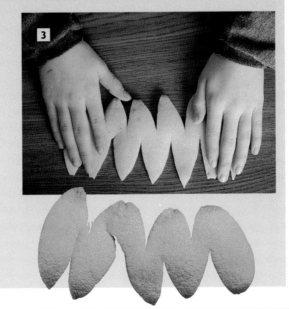

Chart Study It is almost impossible to flatten an orange peel. The peel tears, wrinkles, and stretches. Mapmakers can make a flat map of an orange—or of the Earth—by using mathematics. But even a map laid out to look like this flattened orange peel is not accurate. **Critical Thinking** Look carefully at the photographs. As the orange peel is flattened, what distortions do you think might occur?

Program Resources

📁 **Outline Maps** The World: Political, p. 5

2 Explore

Have students read the section. Then review with them the illustrations showing the variety of map projections. Help students use clues in the illustrations to answer the questions in each caption. Record their answers on the chalkboard.

3 Teach

Ask students to work in small groups to develop a chart listing the advantages and disadvantages of each type of projection. Challenge students to find at least three disadvantages—involving distance, shape, or size—in each map. Discuss why the Robinson map is the least distorted.

4 Assess

See the answers to the Section Review. You may choose to use students' charts of advantages and disadvantages as an assessment.

Acceptable charts include three disadvantages per map.

Commendable charts include additional disadvantages per map and present an example in each category: distance, shape, and size.

Outstanding charts explain why there is distortion in each map.

Answers to . . .

AN ORANGE PEEL MAP

Accept any reasonable answer. The distances will be distorted.

Map Perspectives The way a culture draws its maps can tell us how people in that culture see their world. For example, the Aborigines of Australia believed that the world was created by the dreams of ancestral beings. Aboriginal maps have abstract designs of circles and wavy lines and represent how the world looked to the ancestral beings. In the 1600s in China, maps showed China at the center and the direction south was at the top of the map. This allowed the Chinese emperor to look out over the world he claimed to rule. Today, we in the United States place our country at the center of world maps—other countries often place themselves at the center.

Getting It All on the Map

In 1569, a geographer named Gerhardus Mercator (juh RAHR duhs muhr KAYT uhr) created a flat map to help sailors navigate long journeys around the globe. To make his map flat, Mercator expanded the area between the longitudes near the poles. Mercator's map was very useful to sailors. They made careful notes about the distortions they found on their journeys. More than 400 years after he made it, those notes and the Mercator **projection,** or method of putting a map of the Earth onto a flat piece of paper, is used by nearly all deep-sea navigators.

When Mercator made his map, he had to make some decisions. He made sure that the shape of the landmasses and ocean areas was similar to the shapes on a globe. But he had to stretch the spaces between the longitudes. This distorted the sizes of some of the land on his map. Land near the Equator was about right, but land near the poles became much larger than it should be. For example, on Mercator's map Greenland looks bigger than South America. Greenland is actually only one eighth as large as South America.

Geographers call a Mercator projection a conformal map. It shows correct shapes but not true distances or sizes. Other mapmakers used other techniques to try to draw an accurate map. For instance, an equal area map shows the correct size of landmasses but their shapes are altered. The Peters projection on the next page is an equal area map.

Mapmakers have tried other techniques. The interrupted projection (see next page) is like the ripped peel of an orange. By creating gaps in the picture of the world, mapmakers showed the size and shape of land accurately. The gaps make it impossible to figure distances correctly. You could not use this projection to chart a course across an ocean.

Today, many geographers believe Arthur Robinson's projection is the best world map available. This projection shows the size and shape of most of the land quite accurately. Sizes of the oceans and distances are also fairly accurate. However, even a Robinson projection has distortions, especially in areas around the edges of the map.

There are many other types of projections. Each has advantages and draw-backs. It all depends on how you want to use each one. The illustrations on this page and the next page show several projections.

Ask Questions What would you like to ask Gerhardus Mercator about the map he made in 1569?

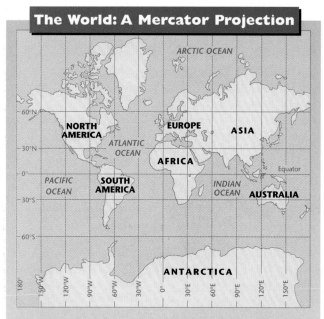

The World: A Mercator Projection

Map Study Mercator maps make areas near the poles look bigger than they are. This is because on a globe, the lines of longitude meet at the poles, but on a flat Mercator map, they are parallel. However, Mercator maps are useful to navigators because the longitude and latitude lines appear straight. Navigators can use these lines and a compass to plot a ship's route. **Place** Here Greenland looks bigger than it really is. It actually is about the size of Mexico. What other areas do you think might look larger than they should? Why?

Answers to . . .

MAP STUDY

Antarctica, and possibly northern North America and Asia. Areas near the poles look bigger than they are.

SKILLS MINI LESSON

Reading Actively
You can **introduce** the skill by indicating to students that they can improve their understanding if they try to picture the action described in the text. Help students **practice** the skill by directing their attention to the description of how Mercator developed his projection by stretching the spaces between the longitudes on a globe. Encourage students to try to visualize or see this action in their minds as if they were watching a movie. Encourage students to **apply** this skill as they read about how other forms of map projections were developed.

The World: Interrupted, Equal Area, and Peters Projections

Interrupted Projection

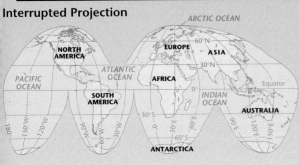

Map Study There are many ways to show a globe on a flat map. The interrupted projection map, on the left, shows the real sizes and shapes of continents. The equal area map, below left, shows size accurately. The Peters projection, below, shows land and ocean areas and correct directions accurately. **Location** Compare each projection with the more accurate Robinson projection below. What do each of these three projections distort?

Equal-Area Projection

Peters Projection

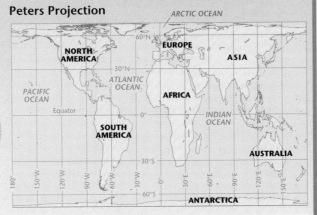

The World: A Robinson Projection

Map Study In 1988, the National Geographic Society adopted the Robinson projection as its official projection for world maps. While the Robinson projection does distort the globe a little, it shows the sizes and shapes of countries most accurately. **Movement** Do you think the Robinson projection would be as useful to a navigator as the Mercator projection? Why or why not?

SKILLS MINI LESSON

Assessing Your Understanding
To **introduce** the skill, point out to students that only they can judge whether or not they understand what they have read. Suggest that they **practice** the skill by asking themselves the following questions after they have read the section. Point out that if they are unsure of any answer, this is the best time to reread the text and reexamine the illustrations.

- Which map shows the correct shapes of landforms but not the true distances or sizes?

- Which map shows the real sizes and shapes of landforms but not the correct distances between places?

- Which map shows the correct sizes, but alters the shapes of landforms?

Background

Biography

Gerhardus Mercator, (1512–94), was born and educated in Flanders, a country whose land is now part of Belgium, France, and the Netherlands. His map of Flanders was deemed to be so accurate that he was chosen as the official geographer to Emperor Charles V. Mercator went on to create an accurate map of Europe and to achieve fame with his world map, the Mercator projection, in 1569.

Background

Links Across Time

Atlas's Task An ancient legend tells the story of a battle between the Titans and the Greek gods. The Titans were defeated and one of them, Atlas, was made to hold the whole world on his shoulders. Maps made hundreds of years ago showed a drawing of Atlas holding the world on his shoulders. That is why Mercator coined the term *atlas* to describe a collection of maps.

Answers to ...

MAP STUDY

The interrupted projection distorts distance, and the equal area and Peters projections distort shapes.

MAP STUDY

The Robinson projection would not be as useful as the Mercator projection for navigation, because the lines are not straight.

Math Have students draw a map of a room in their home or at school to scale. The scale might be 1 inch equals 1 foot, or 1 inch equals 2 feet, depending on the size of the room. Provide a compass so that students can correctly place a compass rose on their map. Encourage students to create a legend or key with symbols for various objects in the room. This activity can be extended by having students draw a map of the school building to scale as a class project. *English Language Learners, Kinesthetic*

Background

Links Across Time

River Maps The Mississippi River has changed course many times over thousands of years. Archaeologists use a map of these past courses to find evidence of ancient settlements. Hydrologists use this same map to predict where the Mississippi will flow in the future, using the information to decide where to build dams and to predict floods.

Answers to ...

MAP STUDY

West End International Airport

The Parts of a Map

Look at the two maps below. One is an imaginary pirate map. The other is a map of the Grand Bahama Island, in the Caribbean Sea. Believe it or not, the pirate map has some features that you will find on any map. Of course, regular maps don't have the X that tells where the treasure is, but you will find a mark of some sort that shows your destination.

A Pirate Map and a Road Map

Map Study Almost all maps have some things in common. A compass rose shows direction. A key explains special symbols. A grid often shows longitude and latitude. The road map below has a grid of numbers and letters to help locate places.

Location What airport is located at B-1?

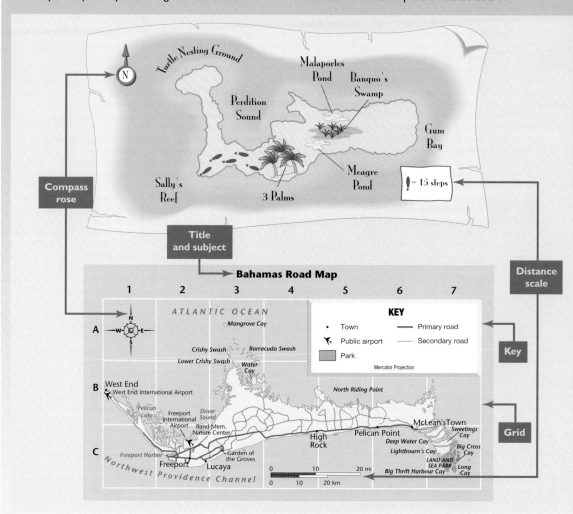

Resource Directory

Teaching Resources

Critical Thinking Activity in the Chapter and Section Resources booklet, p. 13, helps students apply the skill of drawing conclusions.

Section Quiz in the Chapter and Section Resources booklet, p. 8, covers the main ideas and key terms in the section. Available in Spanish in the Spanish Chapter and Section Resources booklet, p. 6.

Vocabulary in the Chapter and Section Resources booklet, p. 10, provides a review of key terms in the chapter. Available in Spanish in the Spanish Chapter and Section Resources booklet, p. 8.

Reteaching in the Chapter and Section Resources booklet, p. 11, provides a structure for students who may need additional help in mastering chapter content.

The pirate map has an arrow pointing north. On the regular map, you will find what geographers call a **compass rose,** which is a model of a compass. It tells the **cardinal directions,** which are north, south, east, and west.

On a pirate map, marks will tell you how many paces to walk to find the treasure. On a conventional map, an indicator for scale tells you how far to go to get to your destination. The scale tells you that one inch on the map represents a particular distance on the land. Scales vary, depending on the map. On one map, an inch may equal one mile. On another map, an inch may equal 100 miles.

On the pirate map, special symbols indicate landmarks such as trails, an oddly shaped rock, a tree with a broken branch, a small stream, or a cave. Regular maps also have symbols. They are explained in the section of the map called the **key,** or legend. It may include symbols for features such as national and state parks, various types of roads, sizes of towns and cities, or important landmarks.

A regular map includes some things that the pirate map doesn't. For instance, the pirate map doesn't have a map title. On a regular map, a title tells you the subject of the map.

A treasure map does not have a grid, either. Some maps use a grid of parallels and meridians. Remember that parallels show latitude, or distance north and south of the Equator. Meridians show longitude, or distance east and west of the Prime Meridian. On some maps, the area is too small for longitude and latitude to be helpful. These maps usually have a grid of letters and numbers to help people find things.

Every part of a map has a very simple purpose. That is to make sure that people who use maps have accurate information they need. The more you know about maps, the easier it will be for you to use them well—even if you're hunting for buried treasure!

READ ACTIVELY

Connect What parts of a map do you think are most helpful to you?

SECTION 2 REVIEW

1. **Define** (a) globe, (b) scale, (c) distortion, (d) projection, (e) compass rose, (f) cardinal direction, (g) key.

2. **Identify** (a) Gerhardus Mercator, (b) Arthur Robinson.

3. What are some advantages and disadvantages of using a globe to show the Earth's surface?

4. Why are there so many different types of map projections?

5. How can knowing the parts of a map help you?

Critical Thinking

6. **Making Comparisons** You are planning a hiking trip with your family to a nearby state park. Your family uses two maps: a road map and a map of the park. What advantages does each map have?

Activity

7. **Writing to Learn** Think of a place that you like to visit. How would you tell a friend to get there? Make some notes about directions and landmarks you could include in a map. Then make a map that shows your friend how to get there.

Lesson Objectives

1 Explain how to identify and express problems clearly.

2 Practice expressing problems in context.

Lesson Plan

1 Engage

Warm-Up Activity

Write the skill title on the chalkboard. Have a volunteer **introduce** the lesson by reading the opening paragraphs. Talk with students about times in their studies when they have not understood a topic or concept. What strategies have they used to solve this problem?

Activating Prior Knowledge

Let students take turns telling what they think *Expressing Problems Clearly* means. They might suggest some possible steps used in the skill.

SKILLS ACTIVITY

Expressing Problems Clearly

Geographers know that geography is not just about maps and where places are. Geography is about change. After all, the Earth is always being changed by natural forces. You and the nearly six billion other people on the planet also change it. Geographers use geography to view and understand these changes.

"Geography," as one of the world's leading geographers put it, "turns out to be much more, and much more significant, than many of us realized."

Are you still having a problem understanding what geography is? You can help yourself by expressing that problem clearly.

▲ What can a geography walk teach you about your surroundings?

Get Ready

One way geographers help organize their study of the Earth is to use the five themes of geography. Look for them in Chapter 1. Understanding the five themes will help you express the meaning of geography.

Try It Out

A. Identify the problem. You may think that geography is only about maps and the names of countries. You need to know what geography really is.

B. Think about exactly what the problem is. You know that the five geography themes should help you figure out what geography is. But maybe you have trouble understanding the five themes.

Resource Directory

Teaching Resources

📁 **Expressing Problems Clearly** in the Social Studies and Geography Skills booklet, p. 40, provides additional skill practice.

C. Put the problem into words. Write a sentence that tells the problem. There are many sentences that will work. Perhaps you will think of one something like this.

> What are the five geography themes, and how are they connected to what I know about the world?

Apply the Skill

Practice understanding the five themes of geography by going for a geography walk. Find out how the themes are reflected in the world around you. You don't have to walk near mountains or rivers. You can walk near your home or school.

① Take a notebook and a pencil. You will need to take notes on your walk. Put into the notebook a list of the five geography themes and their definitions.

② Take someone with you. Walk with a family member or a friend. Be sure to walk in a safe place.

③ Look for geography. As you walk, look for examples of the five themes. Does a delivery truck drive by? That is an example of movement. Is it carrying bread? Wheat for the bread was grown on a farm. That's human-environment interaction.

④ Record the geography around you. Find as many examples of each theme as you can. Record each one in your notebook.

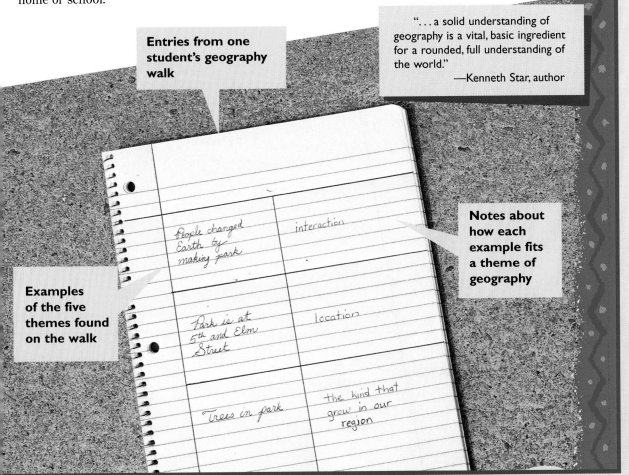

Entries from one student's geography walk

"...a solid understanding of geography is a vital, basic ingredient for a rounded, full understanding of the world."
—Kenneth Star, author

Notes about how each example fits a theme of geography

Examples of the five themes found on the walk

(notebook notes:)
People changed Earth by making park — interaction
Park is at 5th and Elm Street — location
Trees in park — the kind that grow in our region

2 Explore

After students read the text under Get Ready, have a student list on the chalkboard the five themes of geography from Chapter 1. Explain that one way to express problems clearly is to develop questions about a topic. Then direct students to read the rest of the skills activity.

3 Teach

Give students the opportunity to **practice** the steps described in Try It Out. Then work through the steps a second time as a class. Write on the chalkboard some of the sentences or questions students wrote to define the problem.

For additional reinforcement, have students tell a partner about a topic they know well. Partners should then write a sentence or question expressing a problem they have with the information.

4 Assess

The final activity section gives students the chance to **apply** their new skill in a real context. You may want to read through the directions with students, stressing the safety precautions. Point out that in this case, they will be listing examples rather than questions. You can **assess** students' ability to place each thematic example under one of the theme headings on the chalkboard. Encourage class discussion about each example and how it fits under a particular heading.

Together, develop definitions for the themes and statements linking them to the study of world geography.

Reviewing Main Ideas

1. (a) Geographers ask where it is located and why it is located there. (b) Geographers use maps for latitude and longitude to tell the absolute location of a place and what it is near or relative to. Geographers may look at natural features of a place to find out why people have moved there. They may look at human-made features for the same reason.

2. absolutely by giving the latitude and longitude and relatively by naming a nearby place

3. Answers will vary. Students may mention *place*—the natural and cultural features of a location. *Human-Environment Interaction*—how a highway might affect environment and people living along the route of the highway. *Movement*—where most of the people and goods of the region will be moving to or from. *Regions*—whether the rainfall or landforms in the region will affect the highway users.

4. Students should indicate that the Robinson projection would keep most sizes and shapes accurate and would also keep distances accurate.

5. Each map has different characteristics. One accurately shows oceans and distances. Another accurately shows land shapes and sizes.

Reviewing Key Terms

Sentences should show the meaning of each word through context.

Critical Thinking

1. Students should explain that the modern world has been thoroughly explored and accurately mapped. It has even been photographed from space. Hundreds of years ago, people had only explored their immediate areas.

2. Students should explain that many mapmakers have tried to solve the problem of representing a globe on a flat map.

Review and Activities

Reviewing Main Ideas

1. (a) What two questions do geographers always ask about a place? (b) What do geographers use to help answer the questions?

2. Explain how geographers locate any spot on the Earth.

3. You read in the newspaper that geographers are part of a team of people planning a new highway in your area. List and describe three geography themes that the team might use.

4. If you had to make a map, how would you show the Earth so that the size and shape of its features and the distances between them were accurate?

5. An ocean navigator uses one particular map to determine the best route from New Hampshire to Florida. An official who must solve an argument about which country owns a certain piece of land uses a different kind of map. Why do these two people use different maps?

Reviewing Key Terms

Use each key term below in a sentence that shows the meaning of the term.

1. geography	**7.** meridian	**13.** projection
2. latitude	**8.** Prime Meridian	**14.** compass rose
3. parallel	**9.** plain	**15.** cardinal direction
4. degree	**10.** globe	**16.** key
5. Equator	**11.** scale	
6. longitude	**12.** distortion	

Critical Thinking

1. Recognizing Cause and Effect Explain why today's maps are more accurate than maps drawn hundreds of years ago.

2. Expressing Problems Clearly Explain why there are so many different types of map projections.

Graphic Organizer

Choose a place that interests you. It might be a place you know very well or a place you have never seen. Fill in the web chart on the right. Write the name of the place in the center oval. If you know the place well, list facts or information under each theme. If you don't know the place, list questions that would fit each theme.

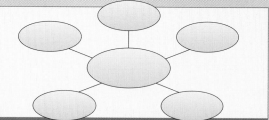

Graphic Organizer

Student answers should reflect understanding of the five themes of location (absolute and relative), place, human-environment interaction, movement, and regions. Questions listed should fit these themes.
Sample answers for Washington, D.C., are shown.

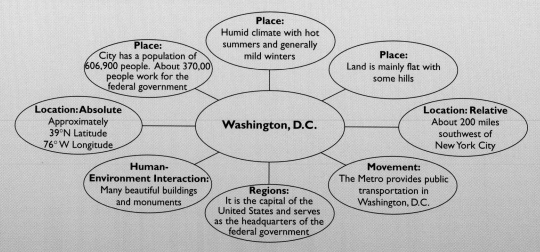

Place: Humid climate with hot summers and generally mild winters

Place: City has a population of 606,900 people. About 370,00 people work for the federal government

Place: Land is mainly flat with some hills

Location: Absolute Approximately 39°N Latitude 76° W Longitude

Washington, D.C.

Location: Relative About 200 miles southwest of New York City

Human-Environment Interaction: Many beautiful buildings and monuments

Regions: It is the capital of the United States and serves as the headquarters of the federal government

Movement: The Metro provides public transportation in Washington, D.C.

Map Activity

Place Location

The Globe
For each place listed below, write the letter from the map that shows its location.

1. Prime Meridian
2. Equator
3. North Pole
4. South Pole
5. Europe
6. Africa
7. South America
8. North America

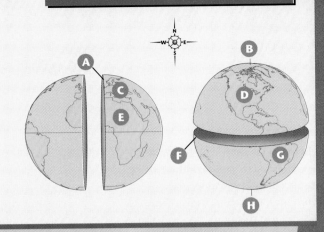

Map Activity

1. A	4. H	7. G
2. F	5. C	8. D
3. B	6. E	

Skills Review

(a) Students' responses should reflect either identifying the problem, thinking about the problem, or putting the problem into words. (b) Response should indicate how a clear statement of a problem can lead to a solution.

Writing Activity

Writing a Paragraph
Write a paragraph describing ways that you have seen people use maps. You may include such things as road maps, maps for seats in a sports arena or areas in a museum, or even hand-drawn maps to a friend's house.

Writing Activity

Students' answers may include road maps; maps of a department store or a mall; maps of a recreation area; hiking or trail maps of a wilderness area; or political, physical (natural features), climate, product, population, or historical maps.

Internet Activity

Use a search engine to find the **National Geographic Society** site. Click on the passport, then click on **Map Machine**. Choose **Political Maps** or **Physical Maps**. Click on the different regions to see the maps. With a partner, make a physical or a political map of the region of your choice.

Skills Review

Turn to the Skills Activity. Review the steps for expressing problems clearly. Then complete the following: (a) Name one strategy you can use to help you express problems clearly. (b) How can expressing problems clearly help you to solve problems?

How Am I Doing?

Answer these questions to help you check your progress.

1. Can I list the five themes of geography and describe how they are used?

2. Do I understand the advantages and disadvantages of different ways of showing the Earth's surface?

3. What information from this chapter can I use in my book project?

Internet Activity

If students are having difficulty finding this site, you may wish to have them use the following URL, which was accurate at the time this textbook was published:
> **http://www.nationalgeographic.com/**

You might also guide students to a search engine. Four of the most useful are Infoseek, AltaVista, Lycos, and Yahoo. For additional suggestions on using the Internet, refer to the Prentice Hall Social Studies' Educator's Handbook "Using the Internet," in the *Prentice Hall World Explorer Program Resources.*

For additional links to world history and culture topics, visit the Prentice Hall Home Page at:
> **http://www.phschool.com.**

How Am I Doing?

Point out to students that this checklist is just a quick reminder of what they learned in the chapter. If their answer to any of the questions is *no* or if they are unsure, they may need to review the topic.

Resource Directory

Teaching Resources

Chapter Tests Forms A and B are in the Tests booklet, pp. 2–7.

Program Resources

Writing Process Handbook includes Outlining Your Material, p. 25, to help students with the Writing Activity.

Media and Technology

Color Transparencies Color Transparency 171 (Graphic organizer web template)
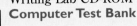**Prentice Hall Writer's Solution** Writing Lab CD-ROM
Computer Test Bank
Resource Pro™ CD-ROM

Lesson Objectives

1 Identify five important world rivers or mountains around which to plan a world tour.

2 Explain and apply the five themes of geography in context.

3 Use interdisciplinary skills to create a descriptive brochure, including a language chart and calculated geographic distances.

Lesson Plan

1 Engage

Warm-Up Activity

Tell students to imagine that they have been asked to plan a school tour for new students. Ask them to identify what they would include in the tour. If necessary, prompt students with questions such as *What are the tour's goals? What school features should be included in the tour? Why? How should each tour stop be described? How long should the tour last? What written material should students receive during the tour?*

Activating Prior Knowledge

Talk with students about travel planning. Ask any students who have traveled by air or helped plan a trip to share their experiences.

Invite students to list some important world rivers and mountains, naming either individual peaks or mountain ranges. Ask whether they have seen pictures or read books about any of these places.

INTERDISCIPLINARY ACTIVITY SHOP

A Five-Theme Tour

As discussed in Chapter 1, geographers use five themes to organize their study of the world and its people: location, place, human-environment interaction, movement, and regions. As you use this book, you will also be a geographer. You will gather, organize, and analyze geographic information. The five themes can help you. Before you use them, however, it helps to thoroughly know what they mean. A good way to explore the themes is through real-life examples.

Purpose

In this activity, you will plan a world tour. Your destination is either the world's mountains or the world's rivers. As you plan your tour, you will also explore the five geography themes.

Decide Where You Will Go

First, select the mountain tour or the river tour. Then, use a physical map of the world to choose five places you will visit along the way. Research each place so you can describe its relative location. That is, you will be able to write down descriptions such as "The Nile River in northeast Africa flows through Sudan and Egypt." This is an example of the theme of location, which answers the question "Where is this place?"

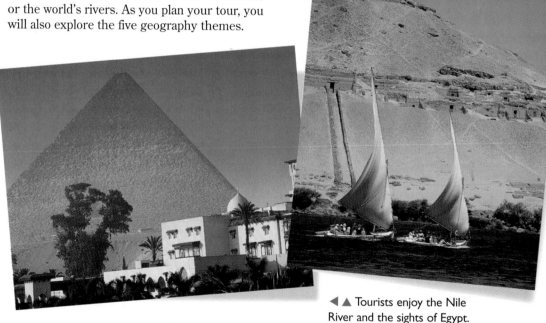

◄▲ Tourists enjoy the Nile River and the sights of Egypt.

Resource Directory

Teaching Resources

📁 **Activity Shop: Interdisciplinary** in the Activities and Projects booklet, p. 7, provides a structure that helps students complete the interdisciplinary activity.

Describe the Places on Your Tour

Use the theme of place to write an exciting description of each place on your tour. The theme of place answers the question "What is this place like?" Include both physical and human characteristics. Physical characteristics are the natural features of the Earth. Things related to people are human characteristics. Your research will help you focus what makes your places unique.

Next, focus on the theme of human-environment interaction. This theme answers the questions: "How do people use this place? How and why have people changed this place?" For each place on your tour, gather information that answers these two questions. Add the information to your descriptions.

Plan a Travel Route

The theme of movement answers the question "How has this place been affected by the movement of people, goods, and ideas?" To explore this theme, choose just one place. Do research to plan a travel route from your community to that place.

Call or visit a travel agent to find the number of miles for each section of the journey. Add the distances together to find the total number of miles for the trip.

Learn About the Language

The theme of regions answers the question "How is this place similar to and different from other regions?" To help you learn about this theme, focus on the same one special place. Do research to find out what languages people speak there. Then find other places in the world where people speak the same languages. This activity will show you one type of region—a language region. Your place belongs to a group of places that share something similar: the same language.

Do additional research to make a chart of some common words in the languages spoken in your place. For instance, you might find the words for "hello," "good-bye," "thank you," and "please." These are words a visitor will need to know.

Create a Travel Brochure

Now, use the information you have gathered to create a brochure about the places you will visit on your tour. The brochure will tell everyone about your plans. Include the descriptions you wrote for each place on the tour. Also include your travel route and language chart. Decorate the brochure with drawings or magazine pictures.

ANALYSIS AND CONCLUSION

Write a summary that tells which type of tour you planned—mountains or rivers. Be sure to answer the following questions in your summary.

1. How did the process of planning your tour help you learn about the five themes?

2. Which of the five themes do you think are most important in your tour?

2 Explore

Have volunteers take turns reading sections of the Activity Shop aloud. Elicit questions after each section. Ask students to name and explain the five themes of geography (location, place, human-environment interaction, movement, regions). Confirm that students can identify five world mountains or rivers. (Possible answers: Rivers: Nile, Ganges, Amazon, Mississippi, Danube; Mountains: Himalaya, Rockies, Andes, Alps, Pyrenees)

3 Teach

Organize the class into groups of four students. Be sure each group adopts clearly defined roles for group members such as researcher, writer, artist, mathematician, or mapmaker. Students may help each other while completing their main tasks. Direct groups to record members' assignments and follow progress on a master chart, checking off each task as it is completed.

4 Assess

Evaluate students' tour stops, distance calculations, and descriptions for accuracy, and all the tour materials for quality of research, creativity, and clarity. Assess students' understanding of the geography themes by evaluating their responses to the section questions.

Answers to . . .

ANALYSIS AND CONCLUSION

1. Students' responses may vary, accept any reasonable explanation.

2. Students should support their choices with facts or examples.

Earth's Physical Geography

To help you plan instruction, the chart below shows how teaching resources correspond to chapter content. Use the resources to vary instruction, add activities, or plan block schedules. Where appropriate, resources have **suggested time allotments** for students. Time allotments are approximate.

Managing Time and Instruction

	Geography: Tools and Concepts Teaching Resources Binder		World Explorer Program Resources Binder	
	Resource	**mins.**	**Resource**	**mins.**
1 SECTION 1 Our Planet, the Earth	**Chapter and Section Support** Reproducible Lesson Plan, p. 15 Ⓢ Guided Reading and Review, p. 16 Ⓢ Section Quiz, p. 17 **Social Studies and Geography Skills,** Using Latitude and Longitude, p. 11	20 25 30	**Outline Maps** The World: Physical, p. 2 The World: Political, p. 5 **Nystrom Desk Atlas** Ⓣ Primary Sources and Literature Readings **Writing Process Handbook** Outlining Your Material, p. 8	20 20 40 25
SKILLS ACTIVITY Using Special Geography Graphs	**Social Studies and Geography Skills,** Understanding Climate Graphs, p. 65	30		
2 SECTION 2 Land, Air, and Water	**Chapter and Section Support** Reproducible Lesson Plan, p. 18 Ⓢ Guided Reading and Review, p. 19 Ⓢ Section Quiz, p. 20 Critical Thinking Activity, p. 31	20 25 30	**Outline Maps** The World: Tectonic Plate Boundaries, p. 2 **Environmental and Global Issues** Topic: Water, pp. 43–48	20 30
3 SECTION 3 Climate and What Influences It	**Chapter and Section Support** Reproducible Lesson Plan, p. 21 Ⓢ Guided Reading and Review, p. 22 Ⓢ Section Quiz, p. 23 **Social Studies and Geography Skills,** Understanding Latitude and Longitude, p. 10	20 25 30	**Outline Maps** The World: Political, p. 5	20
4 SECTION 4 How Climate Affects Vegetation	**Chapter and Section Support** Reproducible Lesson Plan, p. 24 Ⓢ Guided Reading and Review, p. 25 Ⓢ Section Quiz, p. 26 Ⓢ Vocabulary, p. 28 Reteaching, p. 29 Enrichment, p. 30 Ⓢ Chapter Summary, p. 27 **Tests** Forms A and B Chapter Tests, pp. 8–13 **Social Studies and Geography Skills,** Reading a Climate Map, p. 26	20 25 20 25 25 15 40 30	**Outline Maps** The World: Political, p. 5	20
ACTIVITY SHOP: LAB The Earth's Seasons	Activity Shop: Lab, p. 6	30		

Block Scheduling Folder
PROGRAM TEACHING RESOURCES

Activities and Projects

Block Scheduling Program Support

Interdisciplinary Links

Resource Pro™ CD-ROM

Media and Technology

Media and Technology

Resource	mins.
(◖▶) /◿ Ⓢ World Video Explorer	20
/◿ Planet Earth CD-ROM	20
▭ Color Transparencies 1, 3, 98, 99, 105, 106	20
/◿ Planet Earth CD-ROM	20
▭ Color Transparencies 4, 5, 31, 32, 33, 103, 104, 116, 120, 121	20
▭ Color Transparencies 6, 7, 9, 31, 32, 53, 54, 55, 56, 60, 110, 115, 120, 123	20
/◿ Planet Earth CD-ROM	20
▭ Color Transparencies 1, 2, 6, 7, 8, 9, 10, 11, 123	20
⌒ Ⓢ Guided Reading Audiotapes	20
▭ Color Transparency 172 (Graphic organizer tree map template)	20
/◿ The Writer's Solution CD-ROM	30
⊟ Computer Test Bank	30

Ⓣ Teaming Opportunity
This resource is especially well-suited for teaching teams.

Ⓢ Spanish
This resource is also in Spanish support.

/◿ CD-ROM

/◿ Laserdisc

▭ Transparency

⊟ Software

(◖▶) Videotape

⌒ Audiotape

Assessment Opportunities

From Guiding Questions to Assessment A series of Guiding Questions serves as an organizing framework for this book. The Guiding Question that relates to this chapter is below. Section Reviews and Section Quizzes provide opportunities for assessing students' insights into these Guiding Questions. Additional assessments are listed below.

GUIDING QUESTION

- *What is the Earth's geography like?*

ASSESSMENTS

Section 1

Students should be able to simulate the change of seasons using simple props to represent the Earth and the sun.

▶ **RUBRIC** See the Assessment booklet for a rubric on assessing a simulation.

Section 2

Students should be able to create a web of the Earth's major landforms.

▶ **RUBRIC** See the Assessment booklet for a rubric on assessing graphic organizers.

Section 3

Students should be able to write a short paragraph distinguishing climate from weather.

▶ **RUBRIC** See the Assessment booklet for a rubric on assessing a writing assignment.

Section 4

Students should be able to create a map of the natural vegetation that grows throughout a country of their choice.

▶ **RUBRIC** See the Assessment booklet for a rubric on assessing a map produced by a student.

Activities and Projects

Mental Mapping

Let's Get Physical Ask students to discuss what they would see on a physical map. Their answers should include features such as bodies of water, landmasses, mountains, deserts, and forests.

Have students count off by five. Assign all students who are "number ones" to draw a physical map of their town, city, or county. Ask all the "twos" to draw a physical map of their state, the "threes" to draw a physical map of the United States, the "fours" a map of North America, and the "fives" a map of the world.

Then have students gather in groups that include at least one of each number to compare maps. Have them discuss the ways their maps are similar and different (they should mostly note differences in level of detail).

Links to Current Events

Global Warming Ask students to do research to find out more about global warming. Have the class as a whole prepare a bulletin board exhibit or large-format book that answers these questions:
- What is global warming?
- What evidence do we have that global warming is taking place?
- What do scientists believe is causing global warming?
- What effects do scientists believe global warming will have?
- What can be done to decrease global warming?

Encourage students to illustrate their display with illustrations clipped from magazines or other materials.

Hands-On Activities

Finding Out About Climates Have students use a globe to discuss the world's climates. Have them locate the Equator and the poles. Then ask them what kind of climates they would find in those areas. Point out that mountains and large bodies of water also influence climate. Have them locate examples.

Ask students to locate places on the globe they think might have a climate similar to where they live.

Students may have misconceptions about the climate in some areas. For example, they might think that all of South America is tropical. Point out factors that can be observed on a globe (for example, that a large part of South America is as far from the Equator as the United States is) to challenge such misconceptions.

Vegetation Have students make a vegetation map of the world using natural materials such as moss and grass to show the kinds of vegetation. They might add sand and salt to identify deserts, forests, tundra, and polar regions. You may choose to have the class as a whole make one large map or assign smaller groups the task of making their own maps. *Average*

Weather Broadcast Invite volunteers to create a weather map to be used as a visual aid in a television weather report. Their map should include information about atmosphere, landforms, and water. Ask them to give an oral presentation explaining their weather map. *Challenging*

Outer Space Display a photograph of the Earth taken from outer space. Have students imagine they are astronauts viewing the scene in the photograph from their spaceships or from the moon. Ask them write a journal entry or series of journal entries describing what they see. *Basic*

Climates Around the World Ask students whose families are from other countries to describe the climates of those countries. Encourage students to explain how the climate affects the way people dress and build their houses. You may want to ask students to make a bulletin board display of maps, photographs, and other items to illustrate. *English Language Learners*

F.Y.I.

This page can help you extend your own and students' understanding of the concepts in this chapter. You may want to browse through some of the suggestions in the **Bibliography. Interdisciplinary Links** can connect social studies understandings to areas elsewhere in the curriculum through the use of other Prentice Hall products. **National Geography Standards** reflected specifically in this chapter are listed for your convenience. Some hints about appropriate **Internet Access** are also provided. **School to Careers** provides insights into the practical uses of some of the concepts in this chapter as they might pertain to various careers.

BIBLIOGRAPHY

FOR THE TEACHER

Farndon, John. *Dictionary of the Earth.* Dorling Kindersley, 1995.

Pringle, Laurence. *Antarctica: The Last Unspoiled Continent.* Simon & Schuster, 1992.

Smith, Miranda. *Living Earth.* Dorling Kindersley, 1996.

FOR THE STUDENT

Easy
Jordan, Tanis. *Angel Falls: A South American Journey.* Kingfisher, 1995.

Average
McVey, Vicki. *The Sierra Club Book of Weather-Wisdom.* Sierra Club/Little Brown, 1991.

Roop, Peter and Connie, ed. *Off the Map: The Journals of Lewis and Clark.* Walker, 1993.

van Rose, Susanna. *The Earth Atlas.* Dorling Kindersley, 1994.

Challenging
Macquitty, Miranda. *Desert.* Knopf, 1994.

LITERATURE CONNECTION

Jacobs, Francine. *A Passion for Danger: Nansen's Arctic Adventures.* Putnam, 1994.

Thaxter, Celia; Loretta Krupinski, adaptor and illustrator. *Celia's Island Journal.* Little Brown, 1992.

Zak, Monica. *Save My Rainforest.* Volcano, 1992.

INTERDISCIPLINARY LINKS

Subject	Theme: Exploration
MATH	Middle Grades Math: Tools for Success Course 1, Lesson 3-10, **Great Expectations: Astronaut** Course 1, Chapter 10, **Investigation: How's the Weather?**
SCIENCE	Prentice Hall Science *Exploring Planet Earth,* Lesson 4-1, **The Continents** *Exploring Earth's Weather,* Lesson 2-1, **What Causes Climate?**
LANGUAGE ARTS	Choices in Literature *It's Up to You,* **The Old Man and His Mountain** Prentice Hall Literature *Bronze,* **A Boy and a Man**

NATIONAL GEOGRAPHY STANDARDS

Students explore the 18 National Geography Standards throughout *Geography: Tools and Concepts.* Chapter 2, however, concentrates on investigating the following standards: 1, 2, 5, 9, 10, 11, 12, 13, 14, 15, 16, 17, 18. For a complete list of the standards, see the *Teacher's Flexible Planning Guide.*

SCHOOL TO CAREERS

In Chapter 2, Earth's Physical Geography, students learn about the physical characteristics of the Earth. Additionally, they address the skill of understanding special graphs used in geography. Understanding physical geography can help students prepare for careers in many fields such as mining, weather forecasting, farming, and so on. Using graphs is particularly useful for economists, managers, journalists, and others. The curriculum presented in this book, as in all eight titles of Prentice Hall's *World Explorer* program, is designed to prepare students not only for careers but also for good citizenship—of the world as well as of this country.

INTERNET ACCESS

Many social studies teachers and students use Internet browsers, or search engines, to investigate particular topics. For the best results, use narrow rather than broad topics. Try these for Chapter 2: plate tectonics, weather, Pangaea, climate. Finding age-appropriate sites is an important consideration when using the Internet. For links to age-appropriate sites in world studies and geography, visit the Prentice Hall Home Page at: **http://www.phschool.com**

CHAPTER 2

Earth's Physical Geography

Connecting to the Guiding Questions

As students complete this chapter, they will focus on the physical conditions that determine and alter the geography of the Earth as well as the complex interactions of atmosphere, landforms, and water that determine weather and climate. Thus, the content in this chapter corresponds to this Guiding Question:

● What is the Earth's geography like?

Using the Picture Activities

Encourage students to examine the photo of the Earth from space.

• Students will probably be able to identify continents by their shapes. Clouds may be cited as indications of rain.

• Encourage students to explain their choices.

Heterogeneous Groups

The following Teacher's Edition strategies are suitable for heterogeneous groups.

Interdisciplinary Connections
Language Arts   p. 28
Math   p. 35
Science   p. 40

Critical Thinking
Drawing
Conclusions   pp.33, 41
Recognizing Cause
and Effect   pp.39, 46

SECTION 1
Our Planet, the Earth

SECTION 2
Land, Air, and Water

SECTION 3
Climate and What Influences It

SECTION 4
How Climate Affects Vegetation

PICTURE ACTIVITIES

Before we had satellites in space, people could only imagine how the Earth truly looked. Now, satellites let people see the Earth's land and water beneath a swirling mix of clouds. The following activities will help you get to know your planet.

Be a global weather forecaster

Weather forecasters use satellite pictures like the one above to see weather patterns. The white areas in the picture are clouds. What land areas do you recognize? How do you recognize them? On the day this picture was taken, what areas seem cloudier? Swirling patterns may indicate storms. Do you see any storm patterns?

Become an Earth expert

Watch especially for one of these topics as you read this chapter: Beneath the Earth's Surface, On the Earth's Surface, and Beyond the Earth's Atmosphere. Which one would you like to be an expert on?

Resource Directory

Media and Technology

 Forces That Shape the Earth, from the World Video Explorer, enhances students' understanding of plate tectonics, earthquakes, and volcanoes.

 Weather and Climate, from the World Video Explorer, enhances students' understanding of the forces that create weather and climate.

Chapter 4

Chapter 5

Our Planet, the Earth

BEFORE YOU READ

Reach Into Your Background

What is spring like where you live? What is winter like? How long do these seasons last

where you live? If you can answer these questions, consider yourself an amateur geographer. You have noticed the changes in your region at different times of the year.

Questions to Explore

1. How does the Earth move in space?

2. Why do seasons change?

Key Terms

orbit   low latitudes
revolution   high latitudes
axis   middle latitudes
rotation

Key Places

Tropic of Cancer
Tropic of Capricorn
Arctic Circle
Antarctic Circle

"The Sky Father opened his hand. Within every crease there lay innumerable grains of shining maize [corn]. In his thumb and forefinger he took some of the shining grains and placed them in the sky as brilliant stars to be a guide to humans when the bright sun was hidden."

This is part of an ancient myth of the Pueblos, who lived in what today is the southwestern United States. They used the story to explain the appearance of the night sky.

The Earth and the Sun

The Earth, the sun, the planets, and the twinkling stars in the sky are all part of a galaxy, or family of stars. We call our galaxy the Milky Way because the lights from its billions of stars look like a trail of spilled milk across the night sky. Our sun is one of those stars. Although the sun is just a tiny speck in the Milky Way, it is the center of everything for the Earth.

▼ Thousands of years ago, Native Americans laid this wheel out in Wyoming's Bighorn Mountains. They may have used it to track the movements of the stars.

Lesson Objectives

1 Diagram how the Earth moves in space and its relation to the sun.

2 Describe how day and night are related to the rotation of the Earth.

3 Analyze the connection between the Earth's tilt and orbit around the sun and seasonal changes on the Earth.

Lesson Plan

1 Engage

Warm-Up Activity

Ask students to orient themselves so that they can point to the east, where the sun rises, and to the west, where the sun sets. (You may wish to have a directional compass on hand to confirm students' observations.)

Activating Prior Knowledge

Have students read Reach Into Your Background in the Before You Read box. Ask students whether the type of clothing they wear, the activities they engage in, or the foods they eat change from season to season.

Teaching Resources

📁 **Reproducible Lesson Plan** in the Chapter and Section Resources booklet, p. 15, provides a summary of the section lesson.

📁 **Guided Reading and Review** in the Chapter and Section Resources booklet, p. 16, provides a structure for mastering key concepts and reviewing key terms in the section. Available in Spanish in the Spanish Chapter and Section Resources booklet, p. 10.

Program Resources

📁 Material in the **Primary Sources and Literature Readings** booklet extends content with a selection related to the concepts in this chapter.

📁 **Outline Maps** The World: Physical, p. 2; The World: Political, p. 5

2 Explore

After students read the section, have them describe the Earth's position in the solar system. Encourage them to include answers to the following questions in their descriptions. Why does a model of the solar system include moving planets? If the speed of the Earth's rotation were slower, how would it affect the cycle of day and night? How would a different slant to the axis of the Earth change the temperature of the surface of the Earth?

Activity

Interdisciplinary Connections

Language Arts Ask students why the Pueblo image of innumerable grains of corn in the Sky Father's palm is effective. Have them think of other metaphors that express the vastness of the universe, or the change from day into night. Students can also draw pictures or make a book of images. *Visual*

Answers to ...

CHART STUDY

Days will get longer. The east coast of North America gets daylight first.

Predict What causes day to change into night?

Understanding Days and Nights The sun may be about 93 million miles (150 million km) away, but it still provides the Earth with heat and light. The Earth travels around the sun in an oval-shaped path called an **orbit**. It takes $365\frac{1}{4}$ days, or one year, for the Earth to complete one **revolution**, or circular journey, around the sun.

As the Earth revolves around the sun, it is also spinning in space. The Earth turns around its **axis**—an imaginary line running through it between the North and South poles. Each complete turn, which takes about 24 hours, is called a **rotation**. As the Earth rotates, it is daytime on the side facing the sun. It is night on the side away from the sun.

Understanding Seasons At certain times of the year, days are longer than nights, and at other times, nights are longer than days. This happens, in part, because the Earth's axis is at an angle. At some points in the Earth's orbit, the tilt causes a region to face toward the sun for more hours than it faces away from the sun. Days are longer. At other times, the region faces away from the sun for more hours than it faces toward the sun. Days are shorter.

The Earth's tilt and orbit also cause changes in temperatures during the seasons. The warmth you feel at any time of year depends on how directly the sunlight falls upon you. Some regions receive a great deal of fairly direct sunlight, while other regions receive no direct sunlight. Special latitude lines divide up these regions of the world. You can see them on the diagram on the next page.

How Night Changes Into Day

Chart Study This diagram shows how places on the Earth move from night into day. Today, it takes almost 24 hours for the Earth to make one complete rotation. But when the Earth first formed millions of years ago, it spun 10 times faster. A full cycle of day and night on the Earth lasted just over two hours.
Critical Thinking As time passes, the Earth spins more and more slowly. What will eventually happen to the length of a day? Find North America on the globe. Which coast gets daylight first?

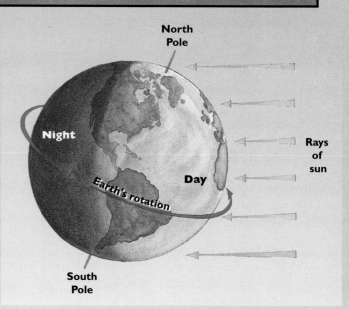

Resource Directory

Program Resources

Nystrom Desk Atlas

Media and Technology

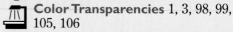

Planet Earth CD-ROM includes satellite maps of the whole Earth that allow students to visually explore any region.

Color Transparencies 1, 3, 98, 99, 105, 106

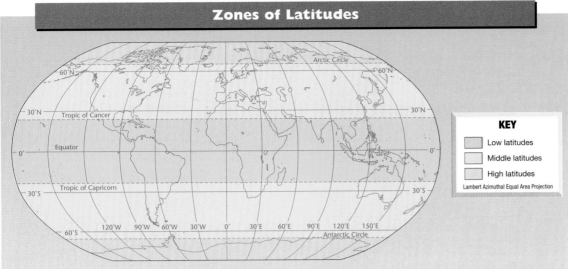

Zones of Latitudes

KEY
Low latitudes
Middle latitudes
High latitudes
Lambert Azimuthal Equal Area Projection

Map Study If you travel far enough north or south, you will reach a place where it stays light all night in the summer and dark all day in the winter. As you approach the Equator, days and nights are more equal in length. **Location** Use the key to find the low latitudes. What is the climate like in this region? Why?

Looking at Latitudes

Look at the diagram on the next page. In some places on the Earth, the sun is directly overhead at particular days during the year. One place is the Equator, an imaginary latitude line that circles the Earth at 0°, exactly halfway between the North Pole (90°N) and the South Pole (90°S). On about March 21 and September 23, the sun is directly over the Equator. On those days, all over the Earth, days are almost exactly as long as nights. People call these days the spring and fall equinoxes.

Two other imaginary latitude lines lie $23\frac{1}{2}°$ north and $23\frac{1}{2}°$ south of the Equator. At $23\frac{1}{2}°$N is the Tropic of Cancer. Here, the sun shines directly above on June 20 or 21. This is the first day of summer, or the summer solstice (SOHL stiss), in the Northern Hemisphere. At $23\frac{1}{2}°$S is the Tropic of Capricorn. Here, the sun shines directly above on December 21 or 22. This is the first day of winter, or the winter solstice, in the Northern Hemisphere. The seasons are reversed in the Southern Hemisphere. When would the summer solstice occur there?

The area between the Tropic of Cancer and the Tropic of Capricorn is called the **low latitudes,** or the tropics. Any location in the low latitudes receives direct sunlight at some time during the year. In this region, it is almost always hot.

Two other latitude lines set off distinct regions. To the north of the Equator, at $66\frac{1}{2}°$N, is the Arctic Circle. To the south of the Equator, at $66\frac{1}{2}°$S, is the Antarctic Circle. The regions between these circles and the poles are the **high latitudes,** or the polar zones. The high latitudes receive no direct sunlight. It is very cool to bitterly cold.

LINKS TO SCIENCE

Midnight Sun Earth's axis is at an angle of $23\frac{1}{2}°$, which makes the Earth seem to "lean." When the North Pole (0°N) leans toward the sun, it never sets. At the same time, the South Pole (0°S) leans away from the sun, so the South Pole, the sun never rises. This lasts for six months. When the South Pole leans toward the sun, this pole has six months of continuous sunlight. Sunlight at the poles falls at an angle, so the poles receive very little heat.

Teaching Resources

📁 **Using Latitude and Longitude** in the Social Studies and Geography Skills booklet, p. 11, provides additional skill practice.

3 Teach

Have students make a model of the Earth with clay, a round balloon, or a ball. Have them indicate the locations of the poles, the Equator, and the Southern and Northern hemispheres. Then have students use their models to demonstrate the Earth's rotation and revolution. This activity should take about 20 minutes.

4 Assess

See the answers to the Section Review. You may also use students' models as an assessment.

Acceptable use of the model includes positioning the poles opposite one another, the Equator equidistant from the poles, and labeling the hemispheres correctly.

Commendable use of the model demonstrates the tilt and rotation of the Earth in relation to a point designated as the sun.

Outstanding use of the model includes correctly demonstrating the tilt of the Earth's axis in relation to the sun throughout its orbit.

Answers to ...

MAP STUDY

very warm or hot, because these areas are close to the Equator

1. Key term definitions appear in the Glossary. Page numbers here indicate first use of the term in the text. (a) orbit, p. 28 (b) revolution, p. 28 (c) axis, p. 28 (d) rotation, p. 28 (e) low latitudes, p. 29 (f) high latitudes, p. 29 (g) middle latitudes, p. 30

2. (a) latitude line at $23\frac{1}{2}°$N
(b) latitude line at $23\frac{1}{2}°$S
(c) latitude line at $66\frac{1}{2}°$N
(d) latitude line at $66\frac{1}{2}°$S

3. The Earth revolves around the sun as it travels in its orbit. The Earth rotates, or turns on its own axis, every 24 hours.

4. The tilt of the Earth's axis remains the same as the Earth revolves around the sun, so the two hemispheres receive differing amounts of direct sunlight during the year.

5. The tilt of the Earth's axis results in fairly direct sunlight at some times of the year and indirect sunlight at other times. The differences in sunlight result in different seasons.

6. High latitudes are very cool to bitterly cold. Middle latitudes have temperate conditions with periods of cool and periods of warm temperatures. Low latitudes are almost always hot.

7. Plant and animal life would change because there would no longer be seasonal cycles.

8. Students' storybooks should mention the Earth's orbit, revolution, and the relationship of the Earth's turning on its axis to the seasons of the year.

Answers to ...

CHART STUDY

summer

Seasons of the Northern Hemisphere

Summer On June 21 or 22, the sun's direct rays are over the Tropic of Cancer. The Northern Hemisphere receives the greatest number of sunlight hours. It is the beginning of summer there.

Spring On March 20 or 21, the sun's rays shine strongest near the Equator. The Northern and Southern Hemispheres each receive almost equal hours of sunlight and darkness. It is the beginning of spring in the Northern Hemisphere.

Sun

Autumn On September 22 or 23, the sun's rays shine strongest near the Equator. Again, the Northern and Southern Hemispheres each receive almost equal hours of sunlight and darkness. It is the beginning of fall in the Northern Hemisphere.

Winter Around December 21, the sun is over the Tropic of Capricorn in the Southern Hemisphere. The Northern Hemisphere is tilted away from the sun and it is the beginning of winter there.

Chart Study As the Earth moves around the Sun, summer changes to fall and fall changes to winter. But the warmest and coldest weather does not start as soon as summer and winter begin. Why? Oceans and lakes also affect the weather, and they warm up and cool off slowly. **Critical Thinking** Australia lies in the Southern Hemisphere. What is the season in Australia when it is winter in the United States?

Two areas remain: the **middle latitudes,** or the temperate zones. At some times of the year, these areas receive fairly direct sunlight. At other times, they receive fairly indirect sunlight. So, the middle latitudes have seasons: spring, summer, winter, and fall. Each lasts about three months and has distinct patterns of daylight, temperature, and weather.

SECTION 1 REVIEW

1. Define (a) orbit, (b) revolution, (c) axis, (d) rotation, (e) low latitudes, (f) high latitudes, (g) middle latitudes.

2. Identify (a) Tropic of Cancer, (b) Tropic of Capricorn, (c) Arctic Circle, (d) Antarctic Circle.

3. The Earth revolves and the Earth rotates. Explain the difference between the two.

4. Why are seasons different in the Northern and Southern hemispheres?

5. What causes the Earth to have seasons?

6. Describe conditions in the high, middle, and low latitudes.

Critical Thinking

7. Drawing Conclusions What would happen to plant and animal life if the Earth did not tilt on its axis? Why?

Activity

8. Writing to Learn Write a storybook for a young child explaining the relationship between the Earth and the sun.

Resource Directory

Teaching Resources

Section Quiz in the Chapter and Section Resources booklet, p. 17, covers the main ideas and key terms in the section. Available in Spanish in the Spanish Chapter and Section Resources booklet, p. 11.

Land, Air, and Water

Lesson Objectives

1. Identify the materials the Earth is made of and the landforms it contains.

2. Describe forces that shape the land, such as volcanoes, earthquakes, weathering, and erosion.

3. Investigate the theory of plate tectonics and its role in understanding the Earth.

4. Analyze the role water plays in the Earth's geography.

BEFORE YOU READ

Reach Into Your Background

Think of one of your favorite outdoor activities, such as skiing, cycling, or hiking. Tell how the shape of the land helps you enjoy it.

Questions to Explore

1. What forces shape the land?
2. What are the Earth's major landforms?

Key Terms

landform
mountain
hill
plateau
plain
plate tectonics
plate
weathering
erosion
atmosphere

Key Places

Ring of Fire
Pangaea

Listen to the words of Megumi Fujiwara, a Japanese medical student who lived through the Great Hanshin Earthquake in 1995.

"Early that morning, I had awakened hearing explosions and feeling my body rising. I knew immediately that it was an earthquake and expected the shaking to last only a moment. It didn't, and after landing back on my futon [bed], I lay frozen, listening to windows rattling and breaking [and] seeing objects flying above. Then everything blacked out. I awoke some time later, inhaling dust and unable to see anything. [I] found myself outside at ground level, rather than in my second-story apartment. Open sky had replaced my ceiling."

Fujiwara was lucky. The Great Hanshin Earthquake killed 5,500 people when it struck Kobe (KOH bay), Japan, on January 17, 1995.

Forces Inside the Earth

Japan knows about earthquakes because it is part of what geographers call the "Ring of Fire." About 90 percent of the world's earthquakes and many of the world's active volcanoes occur on the Ring, which circles the Pacific Ocean. Earthquakes and volcanoes are two forces that shape

Lesson Plan

1 Engage

Warm-Up Activity

Have students sort photos of landscapes by the different landforms, such as mountains, hills, seashores, plains, and plateaus, and make a poster collage. As they complete the chapter, they can return to their posters and label the landforms represented.

Activating Prior Knowledge

Have students read Reach Into Your Background in the Before You Read box. Encourage students to describe how activites such as skiing or biking change as land changes from flat to hilly.

SKILLS MINI LESSON

Previewing

You may **introduce** the skill by indicating to students that previewing a reading selection is a bit like using a menu in a restaurant or watching the "Coming Attractions" at a theatre. Previewing provides clues about the content to come. Have students **practice** and **apply** the skill by asking them to make a list of the headings and subheadings in the section. Then ask them to predict what information they will find in reading the text. Ask them how changing the order of the items on their list might affect their prediction. After completing the section, return to the list and have the students evaluate their earlier predictions.

2 Explore

After students read the section, have them discuss the following questions. What do geographers who study volcanoes and earthquakes learn about the Earth? Why is it important to study what's happening under the ocean? What leads scientists to think that South America and Africa once fit together like puzzle pieces? How are the massive plates of the Earth's surface able to move?

3 Teach

Have students trace the continents to make a puzzle map of the world. Have them experiment with moving the continents in the directions indicated. This activity should take about 30 minutes.

4 Assess

See the answers to the Section Review. You may also assess students' use of their puzzle maps.

Acceptable use includes accurate placement of the continents as they are now.

Commendable use includes an ability to reconstruct the movement of the plates.

Outstanding use includes an ability to reconstruct, using the reference map, the current movements of the plates.

Answers to . . .
Map Study

Accept any reasonable answer—it looks as though North and South America would fit around West Africa. Australia could have been attached to Asia. It also looks as though Europe, Asia, and Africa once fit together more closely.

and reshape the Earth. They provide clues about the Earth's structure, and they are one reason why the Earth's surface constantly changes.

What Is the Earth Made Of? To understand events like volcanoes and earthquakes, you must study the Earth's structure. Pictures of the Earth show a great deal of water and some land. The water covers about 75 percent of the Earth's surface in lakes, rivers, seas, and oceans. Only 25 percent of the Earth's surface is land.

In part, continents are unique because of their **landforms,** or shapes and types of land. **Mountains** are landforms that rise usually more than 2,000 feet (610 m) above sea level. They are wide at the bottom and rise steeply to a narrow peak or ridge. **Hills** are lower and less steep than mountains, with rounded tops. A **plateau** is a large, mostly flat area that rises above the surrounding land. At least one side of a plateau has a steep slope. **Plains** are large areas of flat or gently rolling land. Many are along coasts. Others are in the interiors of some continents.

Pangaea: The Supercontinent For hundreds of years, as geographers studied the Earth's landforms, they asked "where" and "why" questions. When they looked at the globe, they thought they saw a relationship between landforms that were very far apart.

Predict Why do scientists think the Earth once had only one, large landmass?

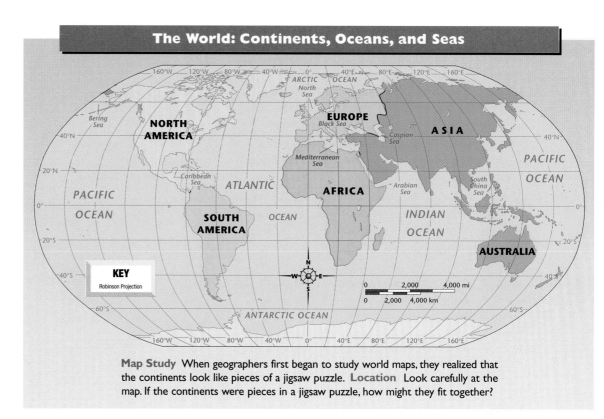

The World: Continents, Oceans, and Seas

KEY
Robinson Projection

Map Study When geographers first began to study world maps, they realized that the continents look like pieces of a jigsaw puzzle. **Location** Look carefully at the map. If the continents were pieces in a jigsaw puzzle, how might they fit together?

The Movement of the Continents

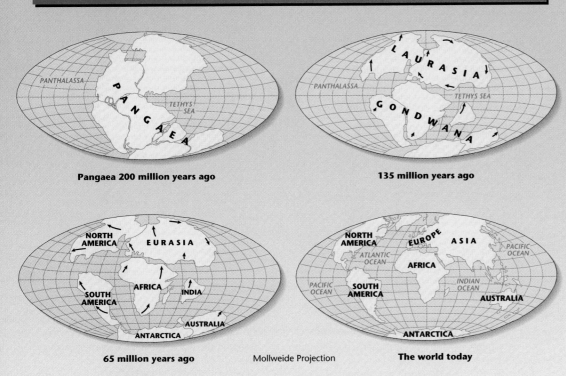

Pangaea 200 million years ago

135 million years ago

65 million years ago   Mollweide Projection   **The world today**

Map Study The first animals to walk on land lived on Pangaea. Birds and dinosaurs first appeared on Laurasia and Gondwana, and dinosaurs died not long after the continents began to separate. Humans did not appear until two million years ago. **Movement** If you were a scientist trying to prove the theory of plate tectonics, what clues would you look for?

Today, geographers theorize that millions of years ago the Earth had only one huge landmass. They called it Pangaea (pan JEE uh). Scientists reasoned that about 200 million years ago, some force made Pangaea split into several pieces, and it began to move apart. Over millions of years, the pieces formed separate continents.

But why did the continents separate? To explain this question, geographers use a theory called **plate tectonics.** It says the outer skin of the Earth, called the crust, is broken into huge pieces called **plates.** The continents and oceans are the top of the crust. Below the plates is a layer of rock called magma, which is hot enough to be fairly soft. The plates float on the magma, altering the shape of the Earth's surface. Continents are part of plates, and plates shift over time. We cannot see them move because it is very slow and takes a long time. When geographers say a plate moves quickly, they mean it may shift two inches (five cm) a year.

Teaching Resources

📁 **Critical Thinking Activity** in the Chapter and Section Resources booklet, p. 31, helps students apply the skill of distinguishing fact from opinion.

Media and Technology

💿 **Planet Earth** CD-ROM includes satellite maps of the whole Earth that allow students to visually explore any region.

Background

Biography

One Big Landmass Alfred Lothar Wegener (1880–1930) studied astronomy and taught meteorology. Even though his education focused on the sky, Wegener was interested in the shapes of continental landmasses. In 1912, Wegener proposed that a single large landmass broke apart to form the continents we see today. As evidence, he pointed to closely related fossil organisms and similar rock strata that occur on the continents. Geologists rejected his ideas. Forty years later, precise dating of rocks on the opposite sides of the Atlantic Ocean indicated that Wegener's ideas were not only plausible, but likely.

Activity

Critical Thinking

Drawing Conclusions *Suitable as a whole class activity.* Scientists have discovered the bones of a dinosaur called a *Mesosaurus* in locations such as eastern South America and West Africa. Ask students how this information might help scientists conclude that the continents once formed one large landmass.

Answers to ...

MAP STUDY

Accept any reasonable answer using fossils or rock formations as clues.

Colonists settling in the green hills of Guatemala in 1543 chose a site in a valley surrounded by volcanic peaks for the capital of the region. Not surprisingly, Antigua, Guatemala was troubled by the shaking and shifting of the earth. It withstood serious earthquakes in 1581, 1590, 1651, 1751, and 1773, as well as other minor tremors. The architectural history of Antigua shows the development of building styles intended to withstand earthquakes. Buildings have thick stone walls; high windows; strong, shallow arches; and short towers incorporated into walls for added strength. Despite the architectural innovations, Antigua was virtually destroyed by the earthquake of 1773.

The World: Plate Boundaries

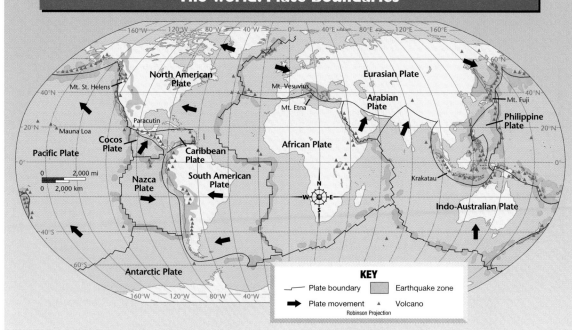

KEY

⌇ Plate boundary	▨ Earthquake zone
➤ Plate movement	▲ Volcano

Robinson Projection

Map Study The Earth's plates move very slowly—a fast moving plate moves no faster than your hair grows. When plates move away from each other, they create oceans and valleys. When they push into one other, they create mountains and volcanoes. **Movement** Based on the direction the plates are moving, name the areas where you think oceans are getting bigger.

A New Island For thousands of years, magma from underwater volcanoes built up until it rose above sea level to create the Hawaiian islands. Today, a new island, named Loihi (low EE hee), is forming. Already two miles (3.2 km) high, it has 3,000 feet (914 m) to go before it breaks the ocean's surface. Loihi erupts almost all the time. It causes earthquakes and tidal waves that threaten the other islands.

Volcanoes, Earthquakes, and Shifting Plates Look at the map of plate boundaries on this page. It shows that plates move in different directions. In some places, plates move apart, and magma leaks out through cracks in the crust. In the oceans, over time, the cooling rock builds up to form lines of underwater mountains called ridges. On either side of the line, the plates move away from each other.

In other places, the plates push against one another, forcing one plate under the other. Tremendous pressure and heat builds up. Molten rock races upward, exploding onto the surface and producing a volcano.

Along plate boundaries, there are many weak places in the Earth's crust. When plates push against one another, the crust cracks and splinters from the pressure. The cracks are called faults. When the crust moves along faults, it releases great amounts of energy in the form of earthquakes. These movements can cause dramatic changes.

Forces on the Earth's Surface

Forces like volcanoes slowly build up the Earth; other forces slowly break it down. Often, the forces that break the Earth down are not as dramatic as volcanoes, but the results can last just as long.

Weathering is a process that breaks rocks down into tiny pieces. Three things cause weathering: wind, rain, and ice. Slowly but surely, they wear away the Earth's landforms. Hills and low, rounded mountains show what weathering can do. The Appalachian Mountains in the eastern United States once were as high as the Rocky Mountains of the western United States. Wind and rain weathered them into much lower peaks. Weathering helps create soil, too. Tiny pieces of rock combine with decayed animal and plant material to form soil.

Once this breaking down has taken place, small pieces of rock may be carried to new places by a process called **erosion.** Weathering and erosion slowly create new landforms.

Air and Water: Two Ingredients for Life

The Earth is surrounded by a thick layer of special gases called the **atmosphere.** It provides life-giving oxygen for people and animals and life-giving carbon dioxide for plants. The atmosphere also acts like a blanket. It holds in the amount of heat from the sun that makes life possible. Winds, as you can see in the map below, help to distribute this heat around the globe.

About 97 percent of the Earth's water is found in its oceans. This water is salty. Fresh water, or water without salt, makes up only a tiny percentage of all the Earth's water. Most fresh water is frozen at the

Predict What two things do people, other animals, and plants need to survive?

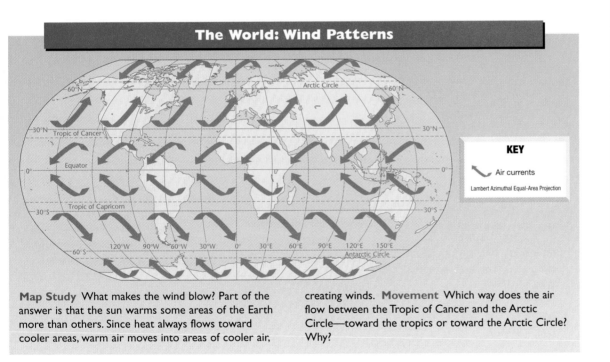

The World: Wind Patterns

KEY

Air currents

Lambert Azimuthal Equal-Area Projection

Map Study What makes the wind blow? Part of the answer is that the sun warms some areas of the Earth more than others. Since heat always flows toward cooler areas, warm air moves into areas of cooler air, creating winds. **Movement** Which way does the air flow between the Tropic of Cancer and the Arctic Circle—toward the tropics or toward the Arctic Circle? Why?

1. Key term definitions appear in the Glossary. Page numbers here indicate first use of the term in the text. (a) landform, p. 32 (b) mountain, p. 32 (c) hill, p. 32 (d) plateau, p. 32 (e) plain, p. 32 (f) plate tectonics, p. 33 (g) plate, p. 33 (h) weathering, p. 35 (i) erosion, p. 35 (j) atmosphere, p. 35

2. (a) chain circling the Pacific Ocean of many of the world's active volcanoes (b) single landmass that scientists theorize existed millions of years ago

3. Weak places in the Earth's crust crack and splinter from pressure, causing earthquakes, or break apart, allowing liquid rock from beneath the surface to rise as volcanoes.

4. wind, rain, and ice

5. It makes it possible for life to exist on the Earth.

6. Answers will vary, but students should note interlocking shapes of continents and fossil evidence.

7. Answers will vary. However, students should note that forces such as plate tectonics and weathering will change a region over time.

Answers to ...
CHART STUDY

through rivers and streams

The Water Cycle

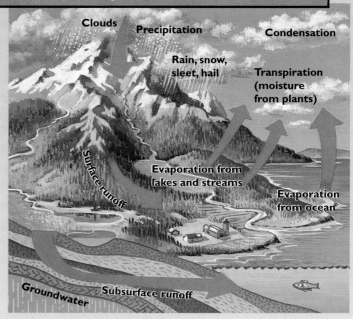

Chart Study Ocean water is too salty to drink or to irrigate crops. However, the oceans are a source of fresh water. How does this happen? When water evaporates from the ocean's surface, salt is left behind. The water vapor rises and forms clouds. The rain that falls to the Earth is fresh. **Critical Thinking** Once rain has fallen, how does water return to the ocean?

Clouds · Precipitation · Condensation · Rain, snow, sleet, hail · Transpiration (moisture from plants) · Evaporation from lakes and streams · Evaporation from ocean · Surface runoff · Groundwater · Subsurface runoff

North and South poles. People need fresh water for many things. This fresh water comes from lakes, rivers, and rain. Also, much fresh water, called groundwater, is stored in the soil itself. The diagram above shows the movement of all the water on the Earth's surface, in the ground, and in the air. The Earth does have enough water for people. However, some places have too much water and other places have too little.

SECTION 2 REVIEW

1. Define (a) landform, (b) mountain, (c) hill, (d) plateau, (e) plain, (f) plate tectonics, (g) plate, (h) weathering, (i) erosion, (j) atmosphere.

2. Identify (a) Ring of Fire, (b) Pangaea.

3. Why are there earthquakes and volcanoes?

4. What forces on the Earth's surface break down rocks?

5. Why is the atmosphere important?

Critical Thinking

6. Distinguishing Fact From Opinion What facts support the theory of plate tectonics?

Activity

7. Writing to Learn Suppose you were able to see the region you live in 10,000 years from now. Describe how the landforms might look. Explain what might have caused those changes.

Resource Directory

Teaching Resources

Section Quiz in the Chapter and Section Resources booklet, p. 20, covers the main ideas and key terms in the section. Available in Spanish in the Spanish Chapter and Section Resources booklet, p. 13.

Climate and What Influences It

Reach Into Your Background
Thunderstorms can knock down power lines and trees. Hurricanes can destroy whole communities. What is the worst weather you have experienced? How did you feel? How did you stay safe?

Questions to Explore
1. What is climate?
2. How do landforms and bodies of water affect climate?

Key Terms
weather
temperature
precipitation
climate

Key Names and Places
Gulf Stream
Peru Current
California Current
St. Louis
San Francisco

I n late May 1996, a tornado's furious winds tore down the movie screen of a drive-in theater in St. Catherine's, Ontario, Canada. Ironically, the week's feature movie was *Twister,* a film about tornadoes.

Richard and Daphne Thompson spend their time tracking tornadoes in Oklahoma. Daphne Thompson recalls one particular storm: "The car was hit by 50- to 70-mile-per-hour gusts," she says. "Tumbleweeds were blowing so hard one left a dent in the car."

Weather or Climate?

These two stories show that weather like tornadoes can be dangerous. Or is it "climate" like tornadoes? What is the difference between weather and climate?

Every morning, most people check the temperature outside before they get dressed. But in some parts of India, people have very serious reasons for watching the **weather,** or the day-to-day changes in the air. In this region, it rains only during one period of the year. No one living there wants the rainy days to end too soon. That rain must fill the wells with enough fresh water to last through the coming dry spell.

▼ Tornadoes can easily flatten buildings. Tornado winds are the most powerful and violent winds on the Earth.

Interpreting Diagrams
You might want to **introduce** the skill by pointing out to students that diagrams can often present complicated concepts in an easy-to-follow style. Direct students' attention to the Water Cycle diagram. Work with students as they **practice** the skill by having them finger trace the path of water once it leaves clouds as precipitation. Ask students how the diagram shows that the Earth's water is recycled. Encourage students to **apply** the skill by having them write two questions that can be answered using the diagram. Have students exchange and answer one another's questions.

2 Explore

Once students have read the section, ask them to discuss the following questions. Why does the sun rise earlier during the summer months than during the winter months? What makes some months colder than others? What is the deciding factor between rain and snow?

3 Teach

Have students keep a weather record on daily weather conditions such as temperature, precipitation, and wind direction. Have them record observations each day for one week. Use these weather records as the basis for a discussion about weather and climate in your region. This activity should take 10 minutes each day, and 15 minutes for discussion at the end of the week.

4 Assess

See the answers to the Section Review. You may also use students' weather records as an assessment.

Acceptable records include information on temperature and precipitation.

Commendable records include more detailed information, including a description based on personal observation each day.

Outstanding records indicate a recognition of weather patterns.

Answers to ...
MAP STUDY

tropical wet, tropical wet and dry; arid

The World: Climate Regions

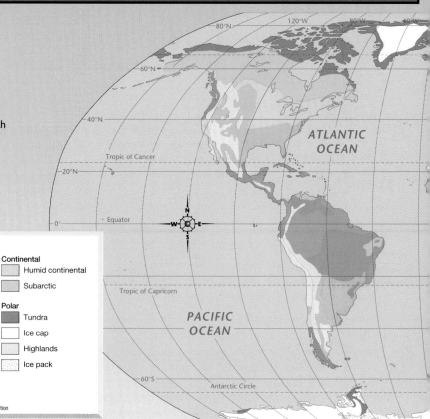

Map Study Many factors, including nearness to the Equator and to bodies of water, affect climate.
Regions What are the two major climate regions of South America? What is the major climate region of North Africa?

KEY

Tropical
- Tropical wet
- Tropical wet and dry

Dry
- Semiarid
- Arid

Mild
- Mediterranean
- Humid subtropical
- Marine west coast

Continental
- Humid continental
- Subarctic

Polar
- Tundra
- Ice cap
- Highlands
- Ice pack

Robinson Projection

Predict What do you think influences the climate of an area?

Weather is measured primarily by temperature and precipitation. **Temperature** is how hot or cold the air feels. **Precipitation** is water that falls to the ground as rain, sleet, hail, or snow.

Climate is not the same as weather. The **climate** of a place is the average weather over many years. Weather is what people see from day to day. A day is rainy or it is dry. Climate is what people know from experience happens from year to year.

Latitude, Landforms, and Climate   The Earth has many climate regions. Some climates are hot enough that people rarely need to wear a sweater. In some cold climates, snow stays on the ground most of the year. And there are places on the Earth where between 30 and 40 feet (9 and 12 meters) of rain fall in a single year. Geographers know climates are different in the low, middle, and high latitudes, because latitude affects temperature. Major landforms such as mountains also affect climates in neighboring areas. Wind and water also play a role.

Resource Directory

Teaching Resources

📁 **Reproducible Lesson Plan** in the Chapter and Section Resources booklet, p. 21, provides a summary of the section lesson.

📁 **Guided Reading and Review** in the Chapter and Section Resources booklet, p. 22, provides a structure for mastering key concepts and reviewing key terms in the section. Available in Spanish in the Spanish Chapter and Section Resources booklet, p. 14.

Media and Technology

🖳 **Color Transparencies** 6, 7, 9, 31, 32, 53, 54, 55, 56, 60, 110, 115, 123

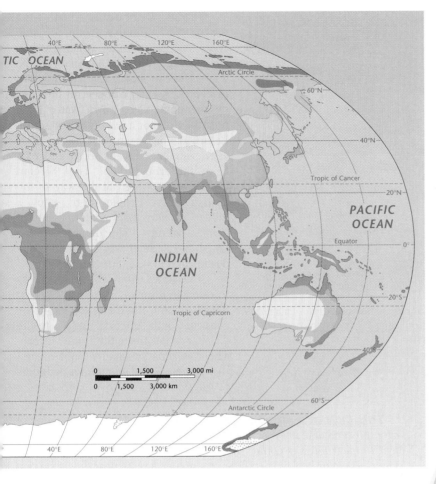

Wind and Water

Without wind and water, the Earth would overheat. If you sit in the sun for a while on a hot day, you will feel warmer and warmer. The same thing could happen to the tropical regions of the Earth if wind and water did not help spread the sun's heat.

The Blowing Winds   In part, the Earth's rotation creates our winds. Because of it, air moves in an east-west direction, as the map at the end of the last section shows. Two other factors make air move in a north-south direction: (1) Hot air rises and circulates toward regions where the air is not as hot. (2) Cold air sinks and moves toward regions where the air is warmer. As a result, hot, moist air from the Equator rises in the atmosphere, then moves toward the North Pole or the South Pole. Cold, dry air from the poles moves toward the Equator. This movement helps keep the Earth from overheating.

Ozone Alert! The higher you rise from the Earth's surface, the colder it gets. So warm air rises, carrying pollutants such as dust and exhaust. They spread out in the upper atmosphere and blow away. But if temperatures increase as you go higher, warm air cannot rise. Pollution stays at the surface, producing hazardous air conditions. People must limit using such machines as automobiles and lawnmowers.

Interdisciplinary Connections

Science Conduct the following demonstration for students. Fill one large beaker or measuring cup with warm water. In another container, melt ice to make ice water. Add food coloring to the ice water. Use a straw to place some of the ice water on top of the warm water. Have students observe what happens. Then repeat the demonstration, placing warm water on top of the ice water. Ask students to identify which of the trials demonstrated a current. (cold onto warm) Have them use what they know about the densities of hot and cold water to explain their observations.

Relief and Precipitation

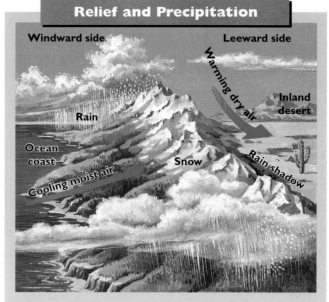

Chart Study As moist air blowing from the ocean rises up a mountain, it cools and drops its moisture. **Critical Thinking** Describe the climate on a mountain's leeward side—or side away from the wind.

Ask Questions What would you like to know about the raging storms that are part of the Earth's climate?

Ocean Currents: Hot and Cold The Earth's rotation also creates ocean currents, which are like fast-moving rivers in the oceans. Like winds, ocean currents travel great distances. As you can see on the map on the next page, warm water from near the Equator moves north or south. In the Atlantic Ocean, the Gulf Stream, a warm current, travels north and east from the tropics. The Gulf Stream carries warm water all the way to the British Isles. People there enjoy a milder climate than people living in similar latitudes. The diagram to the left shows another way in which warm ocean currents can affect climate.

Cold water from the poles flows toward the Equator. The Peru Current moves north from Antarctica, along the coast of South America, and on to the Galapagos Islands in the Pacific Ocean. These islands sit on the Equator, but the current is cold enough for penguins to live there.

The Ocean's Cooling and Warming Effects Bodies of water affect climate in other ways, too. Have you gone to a beach on a hot day? You learned it is cooler by the water. That is because water takes longer to heat or cool than land. So in summer, a place near the ocean or a lake will be cooler than an area farther away. In the winter, it will be warmer.

For example, consider two places in the United States—San Francisco, California, and St. Louis, Missouri. Both cities have an average annual temperature of about 55°F (13°C). Their climates, however, are quite different. San Francisco borders the Pacific Ocean. The California Current passes by the city, carrying cool water from the waters off Alaska. In winter, the ocean current is warmer than the air, so the current gives off warmth and the air temperature rises. A San Franciscan traveling to St. Louis in December would find it much colder there than at home. In summer, the current is colder than the air, so the current absorbs heat, making the air temperature fall. A San Franciscan probably would find the summer months in St. Louis uncomfortably warm.

Raging Storms Wind and water can make climates milder, but they also can create storms. Some storms cause great destruction. Hurricane Andrew, for example, struck south Florida in the early morning hours of August 24, 1992, and left 160,000 people homeless. Julius Keaton recalls what happened:

"I heard one window break, so I jumped up and put a
mattress against it. But I guess that storm really
wanted to get in, 'cause it blew out another window and
beat down the front door."

Hurricanes are wind and rain storms that form over the tropics
in the Atlantic Ocean. The whirling winds at the center of a hurricane travel over 73 miles (122 km) per hour and can reach speeds
of more than 100 miles (160 km) an hour. Hurricanes produce huge
waves called storm surges, which flood over shorelines and can destroy
homes and towns. Typhoons are similar storms that take place in the
Pacific Ocean.

Hurricanes and typhoons affect large areas. One single hurricane
can threaten islands in the Caribbean Sea, the east coast of Mexico,
and the southern coast of the United States. Other storms are just as
dangerous, but they affect smaller areas. Tornadoes, for example, are
swirling funnels of wind that can reach 200 miles (320 km) per hour. The
winds and the vacuum they create in their centers can wreck almost

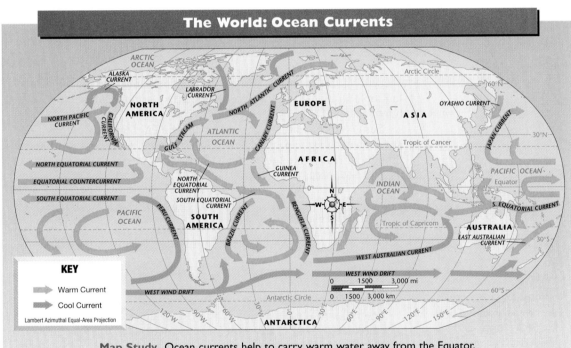

The World: Ocean Currents

Map Study Ocean currents help to carry warm water away from the Equator,
and cold water away from the poles. The warm water helps warm up cool parts
of the Earth, while the cold water cools down warm areas. **Regions** Which
ocean currents affect the coasts of North America?

Using Route Maps
To **introduce** the skill, tell students that route maps can show how people or goods move from one location to another. Then direct students' attention to the ocean currents map, locating the Equator on the map. Have students **practice** the skill by following the currents with a finger. Students can work in pairs, challenging each other to identify the regions each current passes. For example: "If a bottle floated along the Canary Current past Portugal, what continent would it flow past next?" (Africa) Encourage students to **apply** the skill by naming the current that might have carried European settlers to North America or to South America.

Activity column

Activity

Journal Writing

Doldrums In some areas of the ocean, winds that carry sailing ships are nor-mally light and unpredictable. Seas can remain calm for weeks or even months at a time. Encourage students to picture themselves as passen-gers on a sailing ship caught in the Doldrums. Suggest that they write a series of journal entries expressing their feel-ings and concerns about being nearly motionless at sea. If students are keeping an Explorer's Journal, as described in the opening two pages of this book, you may wish to do this writing activity as a part of that journal.

Activity

Critical Thinking

Drawing Conclusions
Suitable as a whole class or an individual activity. Point out to students that marine animals such as eels, turtles, and whales migrate. Often, the paths of migration match the paths of ocean currents. Have students draw conclu-sions on why this is so.

Answers to . . .
MAP STUDY

the North Pacific Current, the Alaska Current, the California Current, the Labrador Current.

1. Key term definitions appear in the Glossary. Page numbers here indicate first use of the term in the text. (a) weather, p. 37 (b) temperature, p. 38 (c) precipitation, p. 38 (d) climate, p. 38

2. (a) a warm current in the Atlantic Ocean (b) a cool current in the Pacific Ocean (c) a Pacific Ocean current that is cool in the summer and warm in the winter (d) U.S. city that has an average annual temperature of about 55°F (e) U.S. city near the Pacific Ocean that experiences the California Current

3. Weather is the day-to-day condition of the air in terms of temperature and precipitation. Climate is the average weather condition that occurs over many years in a region.

4. Hot air masses form in the low latitudes and rise and move to higher latitudes where air is not as hot. Cold air from the higher latitudes sinks and moves to the lower latitudes where air is not as cold.

5. Climates on the coastal side of mountains tend to be moist. Climates on the inland side of mountains tend to be dry.

6. Ocean currents from the tropics are warm and travel north and east. By doing so, the currents make the climate milder in some areas, as compared with other areas of the same latitude.

7. Students' responses should reflect an organized presentation of data.

Answers to . . .

MAP STUDY

areas near the Equator

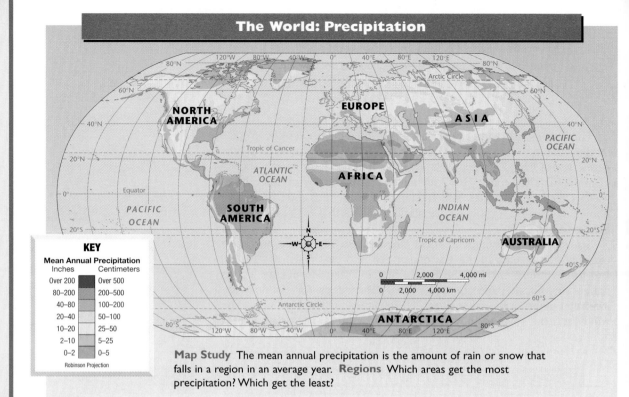

The World: Precipitation

KEY

Mean Annual Precipitation

Inches	Centimeters
Over 200	Over 500
80–200	200–500
40–80	100–200
20–40	50–100
10–20	25–50
2–10	5–25
0–2	0–5

Robinson Projection

Map Study The mean annual precipitation is the amount of rain or snow that falls in a region in an average year. **Regions** Which areas get the most precipitation? Which get the least?

everything in their path. However, tornadoes only average about one-half mile in diameter. Therefore, they affect a more limited area than hurricanes.

Some storms are less severe. In winter, blizzards dump huge amounts of snow on parts of North America. And severe rainstorms and thunderstorms strike the continent most often in spring and summer.

SECTION 3 REVIEW

1. Define (a) weather, (b) temperature, (c) precipitation, (d) climate.

2. Identify (a) Gulf Stream, (b) Peru Current, (c) California Current, (d) St. Louis, (e) San Francisco.

3. Explain the difference between weather and climate.

4. How does latitude affect climate?

5. How do mountains affect neighboring climates?

Critical Thinking

6. Recognizing Cause and Effect Explain how currents from the tropics affect climates far away.

Activity

7. Writing to Learn Check a newspaper's local weather forecasts for the last several weeks. Make a chart. Then write a paragraph about your climate. Use what you know about your region's climate to describe the weather as normal or abnormal for this time of year.

Resource Directory

Teaching Resources

Section Quiz in the Chapter and Section Resources booklet, p. 23, covers the main ideas and key terms in the section. Available in Spanish in the Spanish Chapter and Section Resources booklet, p. 15.

How Climate Affects Vegetation

BEFORE YOU READ

Reach Into Your Background
Make a list of some plants and trees native to your area. How much rain and sunlight do they seem to need? How do they react to unusual weather?

Questions to Explore
1. Where are the Earth's major climate regions?
2. What kinds of vegetation grow in each climate region?

Key Terms
vegetation
canopy
tundra
vertical climate

Key Place
Great Plains

Suppose you live in Arizona. You may walk past cactus plants on the way to school. In Minnesota, you may see leafy trees that change color in the fall. In Georgia, you may see Spanish moss draped along bald cypress trees. All these differences are related to climate.

Climate and Vegetation

A climate must provide plants with water, sunlight, and certain nutrients, or elements, plants use as food. Also, plants have features, called *adaptations,* that enable them to live in their particular climate. That means that over a very long time, small, accidental changes in a few individual plants made them better able to survive in a particular place.

How do geographers use such information? They can predict the kinds of plants they will find in a climate. Geographers discuss five broad types of climates: tropical, dry, moderate, continental, and polar. Each has its unique **vegetation,** or plants that grow there naturally.

Tropical Climates In the low latitudes, you will find two types of tropical climates. Both are hot and wet. A tropical wet climate has two seasons—one with a great deal of rain and one with a little less rain. A tropical wet and dry climate also has two seasons: one with much rain and one with very little rain. The vegetation associated with these climates is tropical rain forest.

▼ Cacti have waxy skins that hold water in. Prickly spines protect a cactus from being eaten by animals that want its water.

Teaching Resources

📁 **Reproducible Lesson Plan** in the Chapter and Section Resources booklet, p. 24, provides a summary of the section lesson.

📁 **Guided Reading and Review** in the Chapter and Section Resources booklet, p. 25, provides a structure for mastering key concepts and reviewing key terms in the section. Available in Spanish in the Spanish Chapter and Section Resources booklet, p. 16.

Media and Technology

📽 **Color Transparencies** 1, 2, 6, 7, 8, 9, 10, 11, 123

💿 **Planet Earth** CD-ROM includes satellite maps of the whole Earth that allow students to visually explore any region.

Lesson Objectives

1 Identify, compare, and contrast the major climate regions of the Earth.

2 Describe the kinds of vegetation found in different climate regions.

3 Analyze how temperature, precipitation, and elevation affect climate in a region.

Lesson Plan

1 Engage
Warm-Up Activity

Ask students what they think would be different about their lives if they lived in a different climate region. Would the school building or their homes be constructed differently? Would they wear different clothes? Eat different foods? Play different games or sports? Ask them to describe what they think might be the advantages or disadvantages of living in a different climate.

Activating Prior Knowledge

Have students read Reach Into Your Background in the Before You Read box. Ask them to name or describe the plants, bushes, vines, and trees that they see around them. How do they stay alive? How do they propagate? Do they show signs of seasonal change?

2 Explore

Direct students to read the section. Suggest that, as they read, they keep in mind the following questions. Why can some plants survive better in one climate than in another? Are there plants that can survive in all climates? Why do climates change? Why is the study of fossils useful when investigating climate and change? What might happen to a climate region if there was a big change in the landforms of the region, such as might happen in an earthquake or a volcano?

3 Teach

Have students create a chart with a column for each of the climate regions discussed in the text: *tropical climate; dry climate; moderate climate; humid continental climate; subarctic continental climate;* and *polar climate*. Have them fill in the chart with facts they draw from the section. Suggest that they include information from the rainfall and temperature maps. Use the completed chart as a resource for a discussion of the similarities and differences in different regions. This activity should take about 30 minutes.

Answers to ...
MAP STUDY

Vegetation and climate areas often match—for example, arid areas often are covered by desert or desert scrub. The ice caps near the poles have no vegetation, probably because it is too cold for plants to grow.

Predict What kinds of adaptations would the vegetation of dry climates need to develop?

Because growing conditions are so perfect—there is so much light, heat, and rain—thousands of kinds of plants grow in a rain forest. Some trees rise 130 feet (40 meters) into the air. Their uppermost branches create a **canopy.** Little sunlight can break through this dense covering of leafy branches. Other types of trees, which are adapted to the shade, grow to lower heights. Thousands of kinds of vines and ferns thrive in the rain forest.

Dry Climates   Arid and semiarid climates are very hot but receive very little rain. Since there is so little moisture, vegetation in dry regions is sparse. Plants grow far apart in sandy, gravelly soil. Their shallow roots are adapted to absorb scarce water before it evaporates in the heat. Some plants have small leaves, which lose little moisture into the air through evaporation. Other plants flower only when it rains so that as many seeds survive as possible.

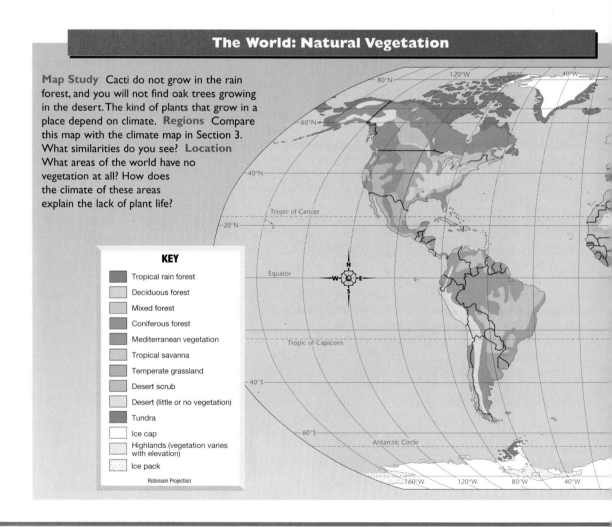

The World: Natural Vegetation

Map Study Cacti do not grow in the rain forest, and you will not find oak trees growing in the desert. The kind of plants that grow in a place depend on climate. **Regions** Compare this map with the climate map in Section 3. What similarities do you see? **Location** What areas of the world have no vegetation at all? How does the climate of these areas explain the lack of plant life?

KEY

- Tropical rain forest
- Deciduous forest
- Mixed forest
- Coniferous forest
- Mediterranean vegetation
- Tropical savanna
- Temperate grassland
- Desert scrub
- Desert (little or no vegetation)
- Tundra
- Ice cap
- Highlands (vegetation varies with elevation)
- Ice pack

Robinson Projection

Resource Directory

Teaching Resources

Reading a Climate Map in the Social Studies and Geography Skills booklet, p. 26, provides additional skill practice.

Program Resources

Outline Maps The World: Political, p. 5

Moderate Climates Moderate climates are found in the middle latitudes. There are three types: Mediterranean, marine west coast, and humid subtropical. In all three climate types, rain is moderate. There are seasonal changes, but temperatures hardly ever fall below freezing.

Moderate climates have a wide variety of vegetation. Forests of deciduous trees, which lose their leaves in the fall, grow here. So do tall shrubs, low bushes—or scrub—wildflowers, and a variety of grasses. The Mediterranean climate receives most of its rain in winter and summers are hot and dry. In this climate, plants have leathery leaves, which hold in moisture during the dry summers. Of the three moderate climates, the humid subtropical climate has the most precipitation, heat, and humidity. It supports many types of vegetation. Most marine west coast climates are mountainous and are cooled by ocean currents. Therefore, they support more forests than grasses.

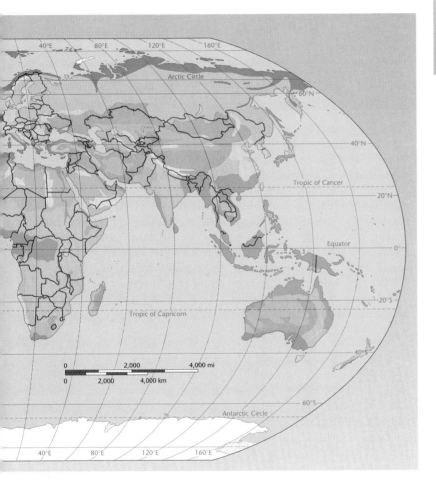

To Be a Leader
In the 1970s, Michael Stewartt was a charter airplane pilot in Alaska. Every day he flew over its vast forests, where he could see the damage to national forests from clear-cut logging. Lawmakers should see this for themselves, he thought. So, Stewartt founded Lighthawk, an environmental plane service that took people on educational "tours" in the air. Lighthawk continues today. It also creates plans for change.

4 Assess

See the answers to the Section Review. You can also use students' completed charts as an assessment.

Acceptable charts include three factually correct entries in each column.

Commendable charts include parallel entries in each column, that is, information about temperature in all climate areas.

Outstanding charts show an understanding of the important factors that determine climate.

Background

Global Perspective

Life in a temperate climate region may include hundreds of coexisting species of plants and animals. In contrast, a tropical region may be home to tens of thousands of species. For example, the country of Ecuador, no larger than the state of Colorado, has over 1,300 species of birds. There are about 700 species of birds in all of the United States and Canada.

Antarctica (right) is an "icy desert"—a world of permanent ice and snow. In contrast, Oregon (below) is a world of constant green, teeming with life. **Critical Thinking** How do you think humans could adapt to living in each of these environments?

LINKS ACROSS TIME

Plant Fossils In ancient rocks in Wyoming, scientists have found fossils of palm trees. Centuries ago, sediments such as sand or ash buried the plants quickly. Over thousands of years, the buildup continued. Slowly, the plants turned to rock. Scientists study fossils to learn about ancient climate and vegetation. Scientists also learn how climate and vegetation have changed over time.

Continental Climates In a humid continental climate, summer temperatures are moderate to hot, but winters can be very cold. This kind of climate supports grasslands and forests. Grasses tend to be tall. The first European settlers on the Great Plains of the United States noted that the grass there was high enough to hide a horse and its rider! Certain areas in this climate region support large deciduous forests. In areas where winters are colder, coniferous forests are found. Coniferous trees have needles, not leaves, and have cones to produce seeds. These adaptations provide protection through the winter.

Regions with subarctic continental climates are much drier, with cool summers and cold winters. Grasses are much shorter. Some subarctic continental areas have huge coniferous forests. Others, however, have few trees.

Polar Climates and Their Vegetation The polar climates of the high latitudes are cold all year around. The **tundra,** which lies along the Arctic Circle, has short, cold summers and long, even colder winters. No trees grow here. Low shrubs bloom during brief summers. Mosses and strange plants called lichens (LY kuhns) grow on the surfaces of rocks. In the northern regions of the tundra, it is even colder and precipitation is very scarce. Only low grasses, mosses, lichens, and a few flowering plants grow.

A Vertical Climate

The climate at the top of Mount Everest, in Nepal in Southeast Asia, is like Antarctica's. But Mount Everest is near the Tropic of Cancer, far from the South Pole. Why is it so cold at the top of the mountain? A mountain is an example of **vertical climate,** where the climate changes according to the mountain's height.

Picture yourself on a hike up a mountain in a moderate climate. Grasslands surround the base of the mountain, and temperatures are warm. You begin to climb and soon enter a region with less precipitation than below. There are short grasses, like those in a continental climate. As you climb higher, you move through deciduous forests. It is cooler and drier here. Slowly the forests change to coniferous trees.

As you continue to climb, you find only scattered, short trees. Finally, there are only low shrubs and short grasses. Soon it is too cold and dry even for them. Mainly you see only the mosses and lichens of a tundra. And at the mountain top, you find an icecap climate, where no vegetation grows.

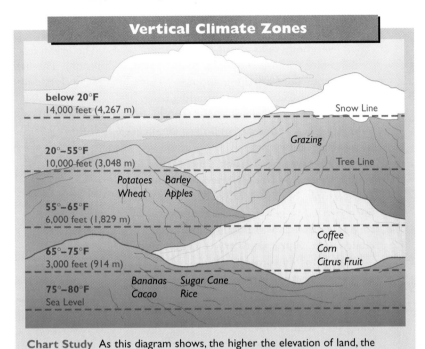

Vertical Climate Zones

below 20°F
14,000 feet (4,267 m)

Snow Line

Grazing

Tree Line

20°–55°F
10,000 feet (3,048 m)

Potatoes Barley
Wheat Apples

55°–65°F
6,000 feet (1,829 m)

Coffee
Corn
Citrus Fruit

65°–75°F
3,000 feet (914 m)

Bananas Sugar Cane
Cacao Rice

75°–80°F
Sea Level

Chart Study As this diagram shows, the higher the elevation of land, the cooler it gets. **Critical Thinking** If you lived in mountains like these, what actions would you take to adapt to your surroundings?

SECTION 4 REVIEW

1. Define (a) vegetation, (b) canopy, (c) tundra, (d) vertical climate.

2. Identify (a) Great Plains, (b) Antarctica.

3. Why do polar climates have sparse vegetation?

4. What climate region has the most varied vegetation? Why?

5. How are continental climates different from moderate climates?

Critical Thinking
6. Drawing Conclusions Choose a climate region. Explain why certain kinds of plants do *not* grow there.

Activity
7. Writing to Learn Research three different cities. Find out what climate and vegetation regions they are in. Write an essay explaining how climate and vegetation affects everyday life in these cities.

📁 **Spanish Glossary** in the Spanish Chapter and Section Resources, pp. 49–53, provides key terms translated from English to Spanish as well as definitions in Spanish.

📁 **Chapter Summary** in the Chapter and Section Resources booklet, p. 27, provides a summary of chapter content. Available in Spanish in the Spanish Chapter and Section Resources booklet, p. 18.

📁 **Cooperative Learning Activity** in the Activities and Projects booklet, pp. 24–27, provides two student handouts, one page of teacher's directions, and a scoring rubric for a cooperative learning activity on making a relief map.

Media and Technology

🎧 **Guided Reading Audiotapes** (English and Spanish)

Section 4 Review

1. Key term definitions appear in the Glossary. Page numbers here indicate first use of the term in the text.
(a) vegetation, p. 43
(b) canopy, p. 44 (c) tundra, p. 46 (d) vertical climate, p. 47

2. region of the United States that supports grasslands and forests

3. Vegetation is scarce in polar regions because the temperatures are so cold.

4. Tropical climates have the most varied vegetation because the temperature is always warm and nutrients and water are plentiful.

5. Moderate climates have a wide variety of vegetation. Deciduous trees grow here, as do shrubs, wildflowers, and grasses. Continental climates have grasslands and forests. Certain areas support deciduous forests. Other areas support coniferous forests.

6. Student answers will vary, but should be supported with information from the section. For example, in polar climates, trees do not grow, nor do wildflowers or tall grasses. The climate is too cold to support such vegetation.

7. Student answers will vary. However, examples should incorporate information from the section regarding climate and vegetation.

Answers to . . .

CHART STUDY

Accept any reasonable answer, such as: dressing more warmly the higher on the mountain you live, planting crops that will grow at each elevation, or herding animals if you live so high that crops won't grow.

1. Define a climate graph and explain how it is used.

2. Create a climate graph from supplied information.

3. Read a climate graph in context.

Lesson Plan

1 Engage

Warm-Up Activity

Ask students what information they usually want about the weather (temperature and likelihood of precipitation). Then **introduce** the skill by reading the opening paragraphs to students. Point out that climate graphs answer the questions most people have about weather.

Activating Prior Knowledge

Invite students to list on the chalkboard all the graph types they know. Have other students draw an example of each listed graph type. Ask students how these graphs might be used to show climate data. Render their suggestions on the chalkboard in graph form.

Using Special Geography Graphs

"**E**verybody talks about the weather," Mark Twain is supposed to have said, "but nobody does anything about it." The great humorist was both right and wrong. People have always talked about the weather. Where we live and what we do are all affected by weather and climate.

Because weather is such a big part of life, people have tried to do something about it. For example, hundreds of years ago people in Europe tried to get rid of thunderstorms by ringing church bells. Today, people "seed" clouds with chemicals to try to cause rainfall.

Trying to "do something" about the weather is not very successful. Geographers have managed to do one thing very well, however. That is to gather information about weather and climate. One of the ways geographers do this is by making a climate graph. It usually shows average precipitation and average temperature.

Get Ready

A climate graph is really two graphs in one. Look at the climate graph on this page, for the city of São Paulo, Brazil.

The graph has two parts: a line graph and a bar graph. The line graph shows temperature. The scale for temperature is along the graph's left side. The bar graph shows precipitation. The scale for average precipitation in inches is along the right side of the graph. Finally, along the bottom of the graph is the scale for months of the year.

A good way to learn more about climate graphs is to make one of your own. You will need:

- a sheet of graph paper
- a lead pencil
- two different colored pencils

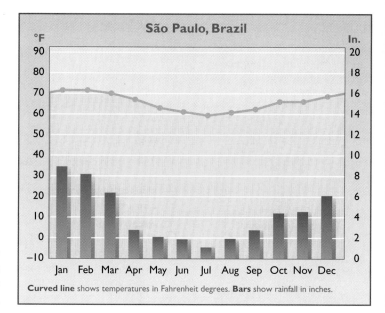

Curved line shows temperatures in Fahrenheit degrees. **Bars** show rainfall in inches.

Resource Directory

Teaching Resources

Understanding Climate Graphs in the Social Studies and Geography Skills booklet, p. 65, provides additional skill practice.

► During which months do you think most thunderstorms occur in South Carolina?

Try It Out

A. Draw a grid. Use the graph paper and the lead pencil to draw a large square. Divide the square into 10 horizontal rows and 12 vertical rows.

B. Label the grid. At the top of the graph, write the name of the city. Using the lead pencil, copy the labels on the climate graph as shown on the next page. Put labels for Fahrenheit temperature on the left side of the graph. Put labels for precipitation in inches on the right side. Finally, put labels for the months of the year along the bottom of the graph.

C. Make a line graph. The data on this page is for Charleston, South Carolina. Use the temperature data to plot a line graph. Use the climate graph on the opposite page as a model. Plot your line graph with one of the colored pencils.

D. Make a bar graph. Now use the data for precipitation to make a bar graph. Use the climate graph on the opposite page as a model. Plot your bar graph with the other colored pencil.

Charleston, South Carolina

	Temperature (Fahrenheit)	Precipitation (inches)
January	48	3.5
February	51	3.5
March	58	4.5
April	65	3.0
May	73	4.0
June	78	6.5
July	82	7.0
August	81	7.0
September	76	5.0
October	67	3.0
November	58	2.5
December	51	3.0

Apply the Skill

Use the steps below to practice reading your climate graph.

1 **Compare differences in temperature.** (a) Which months have the highest temperatures in Charleston? (b) Which months have the lowest?

2 **Compare differences in precipitation.** (a) Which months have the highest precipitation? (b) Which months have the lowest?

3 **Describe the climate.** Temperature and precipitation are two major factors that determine a climate. Using the information presented in the climate graph, how would you describe Charleston's climate?

Review and Activities

Reviewing Main Ideas

1. The Earth's rotation causes the cycle of day and night, and a cycle of cooling and heating of the air. Rotation of the Earth moves air in an east–west direction.

2. Latitudes closer to the Equator experience less variance in the amount of direct sunlight they receive throughout the year. Because of the tilt of the Earth's axis, the higher latitudes are tilted toward the sun during the summer, when they receive more direct sunlight, and away from the sun during the winter, when they receive less direct sunlight.

3. As the Earth's plates move apart, magma oozes out and forms new land. As plates meet, they can grind against each other, causing earthquakes, or volcanoes. The slow pressure of plates pressing together can push up mountains.

4. During weathering, rock is broken down into tiny pieces by wind, rain, and ice. During erosion, the broken-down rock is carried away by wind, rain, and ice.

5. Climate is determined by precipitation as well as temperature. Places with the same average temperatures may have different climates because one is drier than the other.

6. Both are too cold for vegetation to survive.

7. (a) Major climate regions included in this chapter are tropical, dry, moderate, continental, and polar (b) Answers may vary, but students should include basic concepts for each region:

Tropical: wide variety of plants, from tall trees to vines and ferns. Dry: sparse vegetation that grows far apart and has shallow roots. Moderate: wide variety of deciduous trees, shrubs, grasses, and wildflowers. Continental: either grasses and mixed forests or short grasses and (sometimes) coniferous forests. Polar: low shrubs, mosses, lichens, and few flowering plants.

Reviewing Key Terms

Sentences should show the meaning of each word through context.

Reviewing Main Ideas

1. How do the rotation and revolution of the Earth affect wind?
2. Why are the seasons at higher latitudes different from seasons at latitudes near the Equator?
3. How do plate tectonics shape the Earth?
4. What is the difference between weathering and erosion?
5. Why can two places have the same average temperatures but still have different climates?
6. How are climates closer to the poles similar to the tops of vertical climates?
7. (a) List five major climate regions in the world. (b) Then choose one of them and describe plants that live there.

Reviewing Key Terms

Use each key term below in a sentence that shows the meaning of the term.

1. orbit
2. revolution
3. axis
4. rotation
5. plate tectonics
6. weathering
7. erosion
8. atmosphere
9. weather
10. temperature
11. precipitation
12. climate
13. vegetation
14. tundra
15. vertical climate

Critical Thinking

1. **Identifying Central Issues** How does water affect a region's landforms and climate?
2. **Recognizing Cause and Effect** Why is the Earth continually changing form?

Graphic Organizer

Copy the chart on a separate sheet of paper. Select three climates from tropical, dry, moderate, continental, or polar. Write one term in each box of column 1. In column 2, write temperature, precipitation, plus other important information.

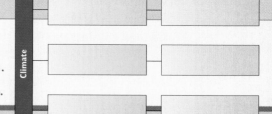

Graphic Organizer

Students' responses will vary. Sample answer:

Climate		
	Tropical	hot and wet; ideal for thousands of kinds of plants
	Dry	very hot; little rain; vegetation in dry regions is sparse; plants grow far apart
	Polar	cold all year around; short, cold summers; long, very cold winters; no trees; low shrubs bloom during brief summer

Map Activity

Place Location

North America
For each place listed below, write the letter on the map that shows its location. Use the Atlas at the back of the book to complete the exercise.

1. Tropic of Cancer
2. Appalachian Mountains
3. Rocky Mountains
4. Arctic Circle
5. Great Plains

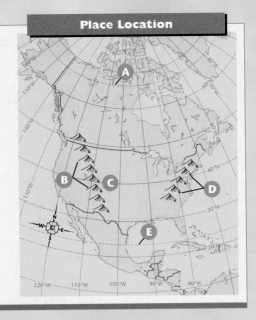

Writing Activity

Writing a News Report
Choose a well-known natural disaster such as Hurricane Andrew or the eruption of Mount St. Helens. Find out where it happened, why it happened, and what were the immediate and long-term effects. Then, write a news report that explains the natural disaster in geographic terms.

Skills Review

Turn to the Skills Activity.
Review the steps for understanding special geography graphs. Then complete the following: (a) What two kinds of information are included in a climate graph? (b) How does a line graph help geographers describe a climate?

Internet Activity

Use a search engine to find the **Weather Map** site. Look at the satellite map and click on your state or town to determine today's weather. Make a chart showing the temperature, humidity, wind, pressure, and weather throughout the day. What does the chart tell you about today's weather patterns?

How Am I Doing?

Answer these questions to help you check your progress.

1. Do I know how the Earth's movements through space create day, night, and seasons?
2. Do I understand the forces that shape the Earth?
3. Can I explain the influences on the Earth's weather and climate?
4. Do I know why the Earth's climates support a variety of vegetation?
5. What information from this chapter can I use in my book project?

Internet Activity

If students are having difficulty finding this site, you may wish to have them use the following URL, which was accurate at the time this textbook was published:

http://www.mit.edu:8001/ usa.html

You might also guide students to a search engine. Four of the most useful are Infoseek, AltaVista, Lycos, and Yahoo. For additional suggestions on using the Internet, refer to the Prentice Hall Social Studies' Educator's Handbook "Using the Internet," in the *Prentice Hall World Explorer Program Resources.*

For additional links to world history and culture topics, visit the Prentice Hall Home Page at:
http://www.phschool.com

How Am I Doing?

Point out to students that this checklist is just a quick reminder of what they learned in the chapter. If their answer to any of the questions is *no* or if they are unsure, they may need to review the topic.

Critical Thinking

1. Answers will vary. Students should refer to patterns of precipitation and the effects of weathering and erosion on local landforms. Specific mention of mountains and large bodies of water are likely.

2. Answers will vary. Students may refer to forces from within the Earth that change its form, such as the movement of tectonic plates, earthquakes, and volcanoes. They may also cite the effects of weathering and erosion and mention the more dramatic changes that can be caused by storms.

Map Activity

1. E   3. B   5. C
2. D   4. A

Skills Review

(a) temperature and precipitation (b) The graph shows changes over time.

Writing Activity

Students' news reports will vary, but should answer where, what, and when, as well as give a simple description of the cause of the disaster.

Resource Directory

Teaching Resources

📁 **Chapter Tests** Forms A and B are in the Tests booklet, pp. 8–13.

Program Resources

📁 **Writing Process Handbook** includes Locating Information, pp. 17-18, to help students with the Writing Activity.

Media and Technology

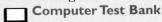 **Color Transparencies**
Color Transparency 172 (Graphic organizer tree map template)
 Prentice Hall Writer's Solution Writing Lab CD-ROM
💾 **Computer Test Bank**

💿 **Resource Pro™ CD-ROM**

The Earth's Seasons

Lesson Objectives

1. Describe the relationship between the sun and the moon.

2. Demonstrate how the relationship between the sun and the moon creates the seasons.

Lesson Plan

1 Engage

Warm-Up Activity

Write the following headings on the chalkboard: *Fall, Winter, Summer,* and *Spring.* Ask students to name their favorite season and list some of its features in the chart. Explain that many of these features—snow, temperature, flowers, and so on—arise from the relationship between the Earth and the sun.

Activating Prior Knowledge

Invite students to describe the physical relationship between the Earth and the sun. Have them explain how this relationship causes the seasons. Record some responses on the chalkboard.

2 Explore

Direct students to read the directions carefully before beginning. Pair students to discuss the relationships shown in Steps one to four. Point out that other factors such as wind currents and distance from the ocean also affect seasonal climates. Ask students to look at the climate region map in the Activity Atlas and to suggest how and why the seasons vary throughout the United States.

We take seasons for granted. Summer always follows spring, and winter follows fall. Anywhere in the United States, you can usually tell when the seasons begin to change. Two factors cause seasons. One is the way the Earth revolves, or travels, around the sun. The other is the angle of the Earth's axis.

Purpose

In this activity, you will make a model that shows how the revolution of the Earth around the sun causes the seasons.

Materials

- masking tape
- marker
- lamp
- globe

Procedure

STEP ONE

Make a model of the Earth's path around the sun. Use masking tape to mark a spot on the floor for the "sun." Following the diagram, use the tape to mark the Earth's orbit around the sun. Next, label the tape where each season begins. Now, tape the globe firmly to its frame. Because the Earth's rotation does not

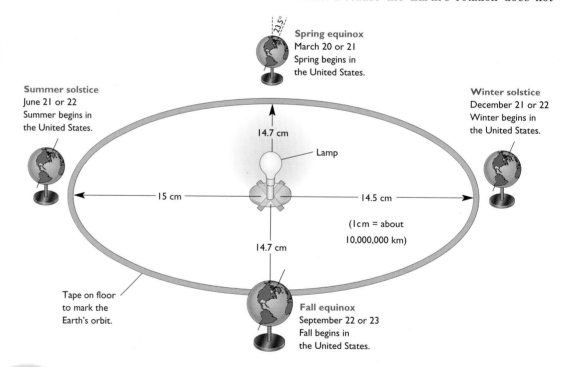

Spring equinox
March 20 or 21
Spring begins in
the United States.

Summer solstice
June 21 or 22
Summer begins in
the United States.

Winter solstice
December 21 or 22
Winter begins in
the United States.

14.7 cm

Lamp

15 cm

14.5 cm

(1cm = about 10,000,000 km)

14.7 cm

Tape on floor
to mark the
Earth's orbit.

Fall equinox
September 22 or 23
Fall begins in
the United States.

Resource Directory

Teaching Resources

Activity Shop: Lab in the Activities and Projects booklet, p. 6, provides a structure that helps students complete the lab activity.

affect the seasons, the globe can remain in place. Put a lamp on the mark for the sun. Remove the shade and turn on the lamp.

STEP TWO

Show winter in the United States. Move the globe to the spot in the orbit where the season is winter in the United States. Be sure that the Earth's axis matches the position in the diagram. Notice that at other times of the year the Earth will be farther from the sun. Something besides distance must cause the season to be winter.

Let the globe sit for five minutes. Study how the sun's light hits the globe. Then, feel it by placing one hand on the Northern Hemisphere and the other on the Southern Hemisphere. Because of the tilt of the Earth's axis, the Northern Hemisphere gets less direct sunlight from the sun than the Southern Hemisphere. That means that the Northern Hemisphere receives less energy from the sun. So temperatures are cooler in the United States than in the Southern Hemisphere.

STEP THREE

Show spring in the United States. Place the globe on the floor at the spot where it is spring in the United States. Line up the Earth's axis correctly. Let the globe sit for five minutes. Place one hand on the Northern Hemisphere and the other on the Southern Hemisphere. Both hemispheres should feel about the same. Notice how the sun's light strikes the Earth. All parts of the Earth get about the same amount of energy.

STEP FOUR

Show summer in the United States. Place the globe at the spot where the season is summer in the United States. Notice that the Earth is farther from the sun than it was in winter. Line up the axis correctly. Let the globe sit for five minutes. Study the effect of the sun on both the Northern and Southern hemispheres. This time, because of the tilt of the axis, the Northern Hemisphere gets more direct sunlight from the sun, and therefore energy, than the Southern Hemisphere. Now, it is summer in the United States.

STEP FIVE

Show fall in the United States. Place the globe on the floor at the spot where it is fall in the United States. Line up the axis correctly. Let the globe sit for five minutes. Study both the Northern and the Southern hemispheres. Again, both hemispheres should feel about the same because all parts of the Earth get about the same amount of energy.

Observation

1. Which affects the seasons more—the angle at which the sun's rays hit the Earth or its distance from the sun? Explain your answer.

2. Which season does the Southern Hemisphere have when it is winter in the Northern Hemisphere?

3. When will you have about the same amount of daylight as night—January 8, July 20, or September 22? Explain your answer.

1. If the Earth was not tilted on its axis, how do you think the seasons would be affected? Explain your answer.

2. In a science fiction story, the Earth's orbit is disturbed. The planet travels in a straight line, not around the sun. How would this affect the seasons?

Earth's Human Geography

To help you plan instruction, the chart below shows how teaching resources correspond to chapter content. Use the resources to vary instruction, add activities, or plan block schedules. Where appropriate, resources have suggested time allotments for students. Time allotments are approximate.

Managing Time and Instruction

		Geography: Tools and Concepts Teaching Resources Binder		World Explorer Program Resources Binder	
		Resource	mins.	Resource	mins.
1	**SECTION 1** Where Do People Live?	**Chapter and Section Support** Reproducible Lesson Plan, p. 33 ⓢ Guided Reading and Review, p. 34 ⓢ Section Quiz, p. 35 **Social Studies and Geography Skills,** Reading a Population Density Map, p. 62	20 25 30	**Outline Maps** The World: Political, p. 5 **Nystrom Desk Atlas** Ⓣ Primary Sources and Literature Readings **Writing Process Handbook** Focusing Your Research, p. 16	20 40 25
	SKILLS ACTIVITY Using Distribution Maps	**Social Studies and Geography Skills,** Reading a Population Distribution Map, p. 33	30		
2	**SECTION 2** A Growing Population	**Chapter and Section Support** Reproducible Lesson Plan, p. 36 ⓢ Guided Reading and Review, p. 37 ⓢ Section Quiz, p. 38 Critical Thinking Activity, p. 46 **Social Studies and Geography Skills,** Reading a Natural Vegetation Map, p. 25	20 25 30 30	**Environmental and Global Issues** Topic: Population, pp. 49–53	30
3	**SECTION 3** Why People Migrate	**Chapter and Section Support** Reproducible Lesson Plan, p. 39 ⓢ Guided Reading and Review, p. 40 ⓢ Section Quiz, p. 41 ⓢ Vocabulary, p. 43 Reteaching, p. 44 Enrichment, p. 45 ⓢ Chapter Summary, p. 42 **Tests** Forms A and B Chapter Tests, pp. 14–19	20 25 20 25 25 15 40	**Environmental and Global Issues** Topic: Urbanization, pp. 54–58 Ⓣ Interdisciplinary Explorations *A Nation of Immigrants* *Urban Planning and SimCity*	30 40 40
	LITERATURE *My Side of the Mountain* by Jean Craighead George			Ⓣ Primary Sources and Literature Readings	40

Block Scheduling Folder
PROGRAM TEACHING RESOURCES

Activities and Projects

Block Scheduling Program Support

Interdisciplinary Links

Resource Pro™ CD-ROM

Media and Technology

From Guiding Questions to Assessment A series of Guiding Questions serves as an organizing framework for this book. The Guiding Question that relates to this chapter is below. Section Reviews and Section Quizzes provide opportunities for assessing students' insights into these Guiding Questions. Additional assessments are listed below.

Media and Technology

Resource	mins.
◖◗ ⦿ ⓢ World Video Explorer	20
⦿ Planet Earth CD-ROM	20
⊐ Color Transparencies 9, 12, 25, 27, 41, 43, 56, 58, Historical Map Set 8	20
⦿ Planet Earth CD-ROM	20
⊐ Color Transparencies 25, 27, 28, 29, 124	20
⦿ Planet Earth CD-ROM	20
⊐ Color Transparencies 1, 2, 13, 14, 15, 16, 19, 23, 24	20
⌢ ⓢ Guided Reading Audiotapes	20
⊐ Color Transparency 171 (Graphic organizer web template)	20
⦿ The Writer's Solution CD-ROM	30
⊟ Computer Test Bank	30

T **Teaming Opportunity**
This resource is especially well-suited for teaching teams.

S **Spanish**
This resource is also in Spanish support.

⦿ **CD-ROM**

⦿ **Laserdisc**

⊐ **Transparency**

⊟ **Software**

◖◗ **Videotape**

⌢ **Audiotape**

GUIDING QUESTION

• *Where do the world's people live?*

ASSESSMENTS

Section 1

Students should be able to write a short paragraph distinguishing population distribution from population density.

▶ **RUBRIC** See the Assessment booklet for a rubric on assessing a writing assignment.

Section 2

Students should be able to create a bar graph that shows life expectancy in selected countries.

▶ **RUBRIC** See the Assessment booklet for a rubric on assessing a bar graph.

Section 3

Students should be able to write a glossary of the key terms in the section.

▶ **RUBRIC** See the Assessment booklet for a rubric on assessing a glossary.

Activities and Projects

Mental Mapping

Where Is Everyone? Ask students to name the seven continents and write them on the chalkboard. (Africa, Antarctica, Asia, Australia, Europe, North America, South America)

Explain that population density describes the average number of people per square mile (or kilometer). A country that has crowded cities but lots of desert or mountains might have a low population density.

Ask students which continents they think have the densest populations. Have them rank-order the continents.

You may wish to save their rankings so they can adjust them after doing research. The ranking, starting with the most densely populated, is: Asia (191 people per square mile), Europe (142), Africa (56), North America (46.2), South America (41), and Australia (5). Since Antarctica has no permanent settlements, its population density ranks last.

Links to Current Events

Charting Growth Have students refer to an almanac or another source to find the world population over the last 50 years. They should obtain figures at ten year intervals. Have students make bar graphs or line graphs to show the changes in the Earth's population. Suggest that some students choose individual countries and chart the population growth in these countries over the same period. Display all the charts together. Give the class a chance to examine them and discuss which countries' populations are growing at a faster or slower pace than that of the world at large.

Hands-On Activities

Big Cities Post a world map on a cork or foam backing. Provide three different colors of map pins and information about the populations of the world's largest cities. You might provide pages from an almanac or encyclopedia. Another good source is the book *Why in the World* by George J. Demko. Ask students to locate cities from the list of cities you provide and color-code them according to population by using the map pins.

For example, blue pins might be used to identify cities with a population of eight million or more; green pins for a population of five to eight million; and yellow pins for a population of two to five million.

After students have pinned the cities, ask them what patterns they notice about the locations of large cities.

Interviews Have students interview people who have immigrated to your area or whose parents did. These may be people who came from a different country or who moved from another area of the United States. Interviewers should ask why people moved, what was hard about leaving, what things they brought with them, what they miss the most about their former home, what they like about their new home, and what they had to change or adjust to in their new home. Ask students to describe their interviews to the class. *Average*

Welcoming Committee Ask students what they would like to have known or what they think someone else their age

would like to know as newcomers to their community. What are the things about their community they think newcomers would especially enjoy? What would students want to offer newcomers as a welcome gift? Have students write their ideas. Then invite them to form a welcoming committee to provide information, advice, and perhaps a small gift to newcomers to their school community. *English Language Learners*

Immigration Policy Are immigrants a threat or an asset? Should the government limit certain types of immigration and encourage others? Do immigrants take jobs—or create businesses? Have students

research different issues in immigration policy and summarize them for the rest of the class. Encourage them to avoid taking a position themselves, but to concentrate on presenting fairly some of the positions that have been taken by others. Some students may wish to research the immigration policies of other industrialized nations and compare them with those of the United States. *Challenging*

F.Y.I.

This page can help you extend your own and students' understanding of the concepts in this chapter. You may want to browse through some of the suggestions in the **Bibliography. Interdisciplinary Links** can connect social studies understandings to areas elsewhere in the curriculum through the use of other Prentice Hall products. **National Geography Standards** reflected specifically in this chapter are listed for your convenience. Some hints about appropriate **Internet Access** are also provided. **School to Careers** provides insights into the practical uses of some of the concepts in this chapter as they might pertain to various careers.

BIBLIOGRAPHY

FOR THE TEACHER
Atkin, Beth S. *Voices from the Fields: Children of Migrant Farmworkers Tell Their Stories.* Joy Street/Little Brown, 1993.

Lowe, Jacques. *Looking at Photographs: People.* Chronicle Books, 1995.

Sandler, Martin, W. *Immigrants.* HarperCollins, 1995.

Winckler, Suzanne and Mary M. Rodgers. *Population Growth.* Lerner, 1991.

FOR THE STUDENT
Easy
Margolies, Barbara A. *Kanu of Kathmandu: A Journey in Nepal.* Four Winds, 1992.

Average
Copsey, Susan Elizabeth and Anabel Kindersley. *Children Just Like Me.* Dorling Kindersley, 1995.

Graff, Nancy Price. *Where the River Runs: A Portrait of a Refugee Family.* Little Brown, 1993.

Morris, Ann. *Dancing to America.* Dutton, 1994.

Challenging
Blashfield, Jean F. *Too Many People?* Childrens Press, 1992.

LITERATURE CONNECTION
Strete, Craig Kee. *The World in Grandfather's Hands.* Clarion, 1995.

Whelan, Gloria. *Goodbye, Vietnam.* Knopf, 1992.

INTERDISCIPLINARY LINKS

Subject	Theme: Populations
MATH	Course 1, Lesson 5-7, **Graphing Functional Data** Course 2, Lesson 6-7, **Interpreting Graphs**
SCIENCE	Prentice Hall Science *The Nature of Science,* Lesson 3-3, **Exploring the Earth**
LANGUAGE ARTS	Choices in Literature *Communication Explosion,* **The Secret Among the Stones** *Deciding What's Right,* **The Leader in the Mirror** Prentice Hall Literature *Copper,* **The Giants of Easter Island**

NATIONAL GEOGRAPHY STANDARDS

Students explore the 18 National Geography Standards throughout *Geography: Tools and Concepts.* Chapter 3, however, concentrates on investigating the following standards: 2, 5, 6, 9, 10, 11, 12, 13, 17, 18. For a complete list of the standards, see the *Teacher's Flexible Planning Guide.*

SCHOOL TO CAREERS

In Chapter 3, Earth's Human Geography, students learn about the population of the Earth. Additionally, they address the skill of using distribution maps. Understanding population can help students prepare for careers in many fields such as demography, urban planning, politics, and so on. Using distribution maps is a skill particularly useful for marketers, urban planners, and pollsters. The curriculum presented in this book, as in all eight titles of Prentice Hall's *World Explorer* program, is designed to prepare students not only for careers but also for good citizenship—of the world as well as of this country.

INTERNET ACCESS

Many social studies teachers and students use Internet browsers, or search engines, to investigate particular topics. For the best results, use narrow rather than broad topics. Try these for Chapter 3: population, migration, immigration, urbanization. Finding age-appropriate sites is an important consideration when using the Internet. For links to age-appropriate sites in world studies and geography, visit the Prentice Hall Home Page at: **http://www.phschool.com**

Earth's Human Geography

Connecting to the Guiding Questions

As students complete this chapter, they will focus on where most of the world's population lives and on significant changes in population patterns. Students will compare the movements of people and will correlate population growth, population density, and their challenges to the environment. Content in this chapter thus corresponds to this Guiding Question:

● Where do the world's people live?

Using the Picture Activities

Use the photo of the crowded city to help students grasp the concept of population and the characteristics of dense population centers.

- Students should be able to list locations such as Africa, Asia, Puerto Rico, and so on.

- Students may create names such as Crowdopolis or Denseville.

Heterogeneous Groups

The following Teacher's Edition activities are suitable for heterogeneous groups.

Cooperative Learning
Immigration Bulletin
Board   p. 66

SECTION 1
Where Do People Live?

SECTION 2
A Growing Population

SECTION 3
Why People Migrate

PICTURE ACTIVITIES

Many people live in New York City, Los Angeles, and other large American cities. To learn more about these people, carry out the following activities.

Study the picture
Look at this crowd of people hurrying along a busy New York City street. Many have come from other countries. List some places you think people in New York City might be from.

Rename the city
With a population of over seven million, New York City has more people than many small countries. The city has enough business and industry to be a country. What would you name the crowded "country" of New York City? Why?

Resource Directory

Media and Technology

Where People Live, from the World Video Explorer, enhances students' understanding of the geographic factors that influence population distribution.

Chapter 6

Where Do People Live?

BEFORE YOU READ

Reach Into Your Background

Would you like to live in a city or in the country? List some interesting things you could do if you lived far from a city. List the things you would enjoy most about city life.

Questions to Explore

1. Where do most of the world's people live?
2. How is the world's population changing?

Key Terms

population
population distribution
demographer
population density

Key Places

Nile River valley

Imagine that you go to school in Tokyo, the capital of Japan. Every day you ride the Tokyo "bullet train" to school. What is it like? You probably must stand up for your two-hour ride. Every day more and more people jam the train. Often the car is so crowded that special station guards push people inside so the doors can close behind them.

This is not an exaggeration. The country of Japan is smaller than California. But it is home for 125 million people. Over 26.5 million of them live in Tokyo and its suburbs. Public transportation, roads, and living space are extremely crowded.

What Is Population Distribution?

The world's **population,** or total number of people, is spread unevenly over the Earth's surface. Some places have large numbers of people. In other places, the population is very small. **Population distribution** describes the way the population is spread out over the Earth.

▲ At rush hour in Tokyo, white-gloved guards jam two more passengers onto an already full train.

Teaching Resources

📁 **Reproducible Lesson Plan** in the Chapter and Section Resources booklet, p. 33, provides a summary of the section lesson.

📁 **Guided Reading and Review** in the Chapter and Section Resources booklet, p. 34, provides a structure for mastering key concepts and reviewing key terms in the section. Available in Spanish in the Spanish Chapter and Section Resources booklet, p. 21.

Program Resources

📁 Material in the **Primary Sources and Literature Readings** booklet extends content with a selection related to the concepts in this chapter.

📁 **Outline Maps** The World: Political, p. 5

Nystrom Desk Atlas

Section 1

Lesson Objectives

1. Describe factors that cause large populations in some parts of the world and limit population in other parts.

2. Explain how population density is measured, and name a city, a country, and a continent with a dense population.

3. Summarize how the geography of a country helps determine the size of its population.

Lesson Plan

1 Engage

Warm-Up Activity

Briefly tell students the story of Robinson Crusoe, who was shipwrecked on a desert island. Then have the students imagine that they are shipwrecked on a desert island. Have them make a geography "survival chart" telling what kind of climate would help Crusoe live comfortably on the island. Encourage them to think about what landforms and vegetation would be best. Direct students to list additional geographical features they think might make the island an easier place in which to live.

Activating Prior Knowledge

Have students read Reach Into Your Background in the Before You Read box. Have students record their lists and then, as a class, indicate which things would make survival easier and which might make survival more difficult.

2 Engage

Have students read the section, looking for answers to the following questions: What are some important characteristics about the places where people live? How do climate and landforms affect where people live? In what ways do fertile soil, natural resources, and fresh water affect population in an area? Why does the United States have a large population? Why does Canada have a small population?

3 Teach

Have students create charts similar to the following.

Populous Continent	
Favorable Climate and Landforms	Unfavorable Climate and Landforms

Not Populous Continent	
Favorable Climate and Landforms	Unfavorable Climate and Landforms

Ask students to fill in the charts with facts from the section. Use their completed charts to discuss the factors that seem to affect population distribution. This activity should take about 20 minutes.

Answers to . . .

MAP STUDY

Most students would suggest that population density would be low in such areas, because of the lack of flat land on which to settle and to farm.

LINKS TO SCIENCE

Rising Ocean Levels
Suppose world temperatures rose enough to melt Earth's glaciers and polar ice caps. A recent government report said the oceans are rising, although this may be only temporary. However, some scientists say ocean levels may rise $1\frac{1}{2}$ feet by 2100. Cities like San Francisco, Sydney, and Rio de Janeiro, which lie along ocean coastlines, would flood.

The reasons population is distributed as it is may seem unclear. Scientists called demographers try to figure it out. **Demographers** study the populations of the world. They examine such things as rates of birth, marriage, and death. And they look at the reasons why people choose to live in certain areas.

Why Is Population Distribution Uneven? To answer this question, demographers start with the idea that people are choosy. Recall an important fact about the Earth's surface. Many of the Earth's landforms are rugged mountains, hot deserts, and dry land with little vegetation. Few people can live in these places.

Many factors make a location a good place for people to live. Most major civilizations of world history began along bodies of water. Rivers and lakes form natural "roads" for trade and travel. Also, rivers and lakes supply fresh water for drinking and farming. People also prefer areas of flat, fertile soil. There they can grow food and build easily. Therefore, plains and valleys are easy to settle. Flat coastal areas make it easy for people to trade by ship with other countries. Look at the maps on this page and the opposite page to see how landforms affect where people live.

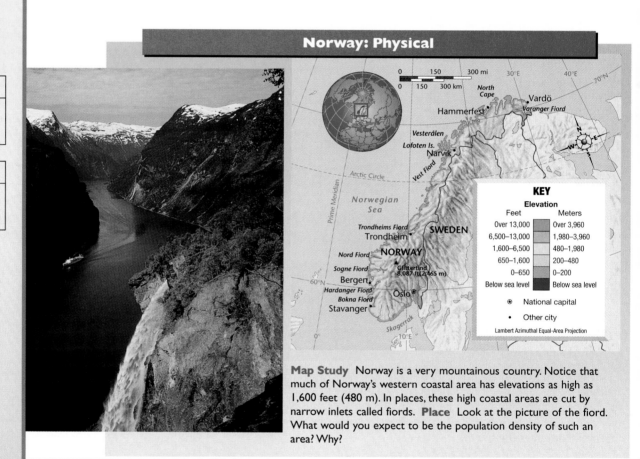

Map Study Norway is a very mountainous country. Notice that much of Norway's western coastal area has elevations as high as 1,600 feet (480 m). In places, these high coastal areas are cut by narrow inlets called fiords. **Place** Look at the picture of the fiord. What would you expect to be the population density of such an area? Why?

Resource Directory

Teaching Resources

📁 **Reading a Population Density Map** in the Social Studies and Geography skills booklet, p. 62, provides additional skill practice.

Media and Technology

💿 **Planet Earth** CD-ROM includes Thematic Maps: Population Density which enhances students' understanding of where people live.

📽 **Color Transparencies** 9, 12, 25, 27, 41, 43, 56, 58, Historical Map Set 8

Other factors affect where people live. People prefer areas where the climate is not too hot or too cold, and where there is adequate rainfall. These places make it easier to raise food crops and animals. People also prefer places with natural resources to build houses and make products. For instance, few trees grew on the America's Great Plains. Few people settled there at first. They went on to other regions.

Continents Populous and Not Populous These reasons explain why more than 81 percent of the Earth's people—about 4.5 billion—live in Asia, Europe, and North America. These continents total only about 35 percent of the world's land. However, they have fertile soil, plains, valleys, and other favorable landforms. They also have fresh water, rich natural resources, and good climates.

Other continents have smaller populations partly because it is harder to live there. For example, Australia is about three million square miles, about as large as the continental United States. Only about 18 million people live in Australia, however. About the same number of people live in just the state of New York. Australia's environment is mostly desert or dry grassland. There are few rivers and little rainfall. As a result, most people live along the coasts, where conditions are better.

In Africa, too, landforms and climates limit population. Africa has about 15 percent of the world's land. But it has only 12 percent of the world's population. Africa has two of the world's largest deserts, one in the

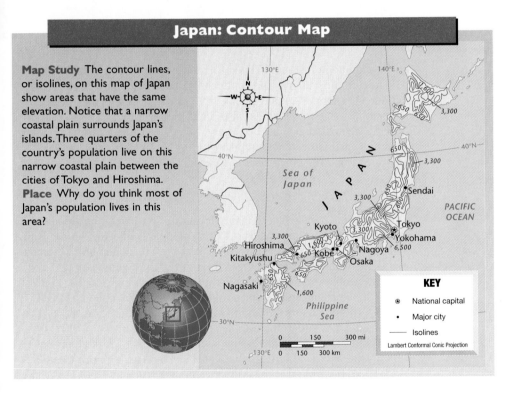

Japan: Contour Map

Map Study The contour lines, or isolines, on this map of Japan show areas that have the same elevation. Notice that a narrow coastal plain surrounds Japan's islands. Three quarters of the country's population live on this narrow coastal plain between the cities of Tokyo and Hiroshima.
Place Why do you think most of Japan's population lives in this area?

4 Assess

See the answers to the Section Review. The students' charts can also be valuable assessment tools.

Acceptable charts include two supporting facts for each column.

Commendable charts include several supporting entries and some indication of the benefits associated with some climates and landforms.

Outstanding charts include several supporting entries and some indication of the benefits associated with some climates and landforms, as well as the disadvantages associated with others

Background

Daily Life

Living in Antarctica Antarctica has no population, yet people live here! The United States, Britain, Australia, and other countries have set up long-term research stations on the continent. As many as 1200 researchers live in Antarctica during the summer. In winter, the population drops to 250. These men and women must be totally self-sufficient. During the harsh winters, no supply planes or medical personnel can reach the camps. In one case, a Russian doctor had to remove his own appendix!

Using Isolines
To **introduce** the skill, point out to students that on an elevation map, isolines connect locations of equal elevation. Direct students' attention to the isoline map of Japan. Work with students as they **practice** the skill by having them answer questions such as

Where is the highest elevation? If the map shows isolines that are close together, what can you say about the land? To help students **apply** the skill, ask them to write a description of how elevation affects population in Japan. Encourage them to support their descriptions with details from the isoline map.

Answers to ...
MAP STUDY

This area, which contains most of Japan's largest cities, is located near water and is flat compared to the country's mountainous interior.

In many countries, people can choose to live in very different places. For example, these photographs show apartments in Boston's Back Bay (above), houses in a Texas suburb (above right), and farms dotting the rich land near Lancaster, Pennsylvania (right). **Critical Thinking** What factors might cause people to choose homes in the city, the suburbs, or the country?

north and one in the south. Then there are broad bands of land that get little rain. In the center of the continent, along the Equator, there is a vast rain forest. Therefore, many people in Africa live along its narrow coasts.

Landforms and climates also limit South America's population. About 309 million people live there. Most live along the continent's Atlantic coast. Other regions have soaring mountains, vast dry plains, and thick rain forests. Fewer people live in these areas.

What Is Population Density?

How many people live on your street or in your neighborhood? The average number of people who live in a square mile (or square kilometer) is called population density. In every city and country, population density varies from one area to another. In a country with a high density, people are crowded together. Japan has one of the highest population densities in the world. Almost all of its 125 million people live on only 16 percent of the land. In Tokyo alone, there are more than 1,000 people per square mile (5,380 people per sq km).

In contrast, Canada has a low population density. It is about seven persons per square mile (less than three persons per sq km). Canada is bigger than the United States. But only about 28 million live there. Many factors affect Canada's population. For instance, its cool climate has a short growing season. This limits farming.

Studying Population Density How do demographers measure population density? They divide the number of people living in a place by the number of square miles (or sq km) of that place. For example, California's population is 31,430,697 people. Its land area is 155,973 square miles (403,814 sq km). Therefore, California's average population density is 201.5 persons per square mile (404.0 persons per sq km).

Remember that population density is an *average*. People are not evenly distributed over the land. New York City has a very dense population. However, New York state has many fewer people per square mile. Even in the city, some areas are more densely populated than others.

On a world population density map, different colors show how world population is distributed. Darker colors show areas with heavy population. Find this map on pages 6 and 7. Find the most densely populated areas of each continent. Now, find these places on the world physical map on pages 2 and 3. Compare the landforms to the population density. Notice that people tend to live on level areas near bodies of water.

Find the Nile River valley in Egypt. This region is very densely populated. In some areas the population density is about 5,000 people per square mile (1,900 per sq km). This is one of the highest population densities in the world. Why do so many people live here? If you think it is because the Nile is a great source of water and the land around it is flat and fertile, you are right. The land beyond the river is desert. Life there is difficult.

Some people do live in areas most of us would find uncomfortable. The Inuit and the Sami people live in frozen Arctic regions. Herders in desert regions of Africa and Asia survive in places that would challenge most people. Over many generations, these people have developed ways of life suited to their environments.

READ ACTIVELY

Connect Would you rather live in a place where the population density was high or low? Explain why.

SECTION 1 REVIEW

1. Define (a) population, (b) population distribution, (c) demographer, (d) population density.

2. Identify Nile River valley.

3. How do the physical characteristics of a country tend to affect its population distribution?

4. Why is it important to understand that population density is an average?

Critical Thinking

5. Making Comparisons A large percentage of the world's population lives on a small percentage of the world's land. How do the population distributions in Japan and Canada reflect this fact?

Activity

6. Writing to Learn You are a demographer studying your community. Make a list of questions to ask and possible sources for answers. Include in your list some population issues that are important to your community.

SKILLS MINI LESSON

Using the Writing Process

You can **introduce** the skill by listing for students the steps involved in the writing process: prewriting, drafting, revision, proofreading, and publishing. To help students **practice** and **apply** the skill, direct them to write a few paragraphs explaining why populations are more dense in some areas, less dense in others. Work with students as they prewrite, gathering information about the geography of locations with dense populations. Have them draft their paragraphs, then exchange them with a partner for review. After review, have students revise and proofread their paragraphs. Allow students to publish their writing by posting their paragraphs on a bulletin board.

Section 1 Review

1. Key term definitions appear in the Glossary. Page numbers here indicate first use of the term in the text. (a) population, p. 55 (b) population distribution, p. 55 (c) demographer, p. 56 (d) population density, p. 58

2. region in Egypt with one of the world's densest populations

3. Answers will vary. Students may suggest that people tend to live in places with good climates, landforms, vegetation, and adequate fresh water supplies.

4. Students should suggest that the actual population density may vary greatly within an area or region. For example, the heavy density of the Nile Valley population contrasts with the sparse population in Egypt's vast desert. Average density thus gives a truer picture of an area's population.

5. The population in Japan is densely concentrated in its major cities, which comprise only a small part of Japan's total land area. Canada's population is concentrated along its southern border, in several large cities. The vast northern area of Canada has a small population.

6. Answers will vary but may include questions about the population's size and where most residents live as well as questions about the geography of the area—rivers, mountains, lakes, and so on. Answers may be found at the local library, historical society or state geological department.

A Growing Population

BEFORE YOU READ

Reach Into Your Background

If you called a hospital in your community, you could find out how many babies were born last week. Multiply that number by all the hospitals in the world. Then, add the number of babies who were not born in hospitals. That's one way to find out how much the world's population increased in seven days.

Questions to Explore

1. How fast is the world's population growing?

2. What challenges are created by the world's growing population?

Key Terms

birthrate
death rate
life expectancy
Green Revolution

Imagine that all the years from A.D. 1 to the year A.D. 2000 took place in just 24 hours. Now you have an imaginary clock to measure how fast the world's population grew. The list below shows that the Earth's population doubled several times in those 24 hours.

12:00 AM	200 million people in the world
7:48 PM	Population doubles to 400 million
10:12 PM	Population doubles to 800 million
11:00 PM	Population doubles to 1.6 billion
11:36 PM	Population doubles to 3.2 billion
11:59 PM	Population will double to 6.4 billion

How large was the world population at 12:00 AM (A.D. 1)? At 10:12 PM? During the 24 hours, how many times has the world's population doubled? How long did it take for the world population to double the first time? The last time?

Population Growth Is Worldwide

The example above makes it easy to see that world population has grown rapidly. Even more important, the rate of growth has increased greatly in modern times. For example, in 1960 the world population was 3 billion. By 2000—only 40 years later—it will climb to 6.4 billion people.

Population Birthrate and Death Rate During different historical periods, populations grew at different rates. Demographers want to understand why. They know that population growth depends on the birthrate and the death rate. The **birthrate** is the number of live births each year per 1,000 people. The **death rate** is the number of deaths each year per 1,000 people. By comparing birthrates and death rates, demographers can figure out population growth.

For centuries, the world population grew slowly. In those years, farmers worked without modern machinery. Food supplies often were scarce. Many thousands died of diseases. As a result, although the birthrate was high, the death rate was even higher. The **life expectancy,** or the average number of years that people live, was short. A hundred years ago in the United States, men and women usually lived less than 50 years.

Reasons for Population Growth Today Today, things have changed. The birthrate has increased dramatically. The death rate has slowed. As a result, populations in most countries have grown very fast. In some countries, the population doubles in less than 20 years. People live longer than ever. In the United States, for example, the average life expectancy for women is about 80 years and for men about 73 years.

Two scientific developments have made this possible. First, new farming methods have greatly increased the world's food supply. Starting in the 1950s, scientists developed new varieties of important food crops and new ways to protect crops against insects. Scientists developed new fertilizers to enrich the soil so farmers can grow more crops. Scientists also discovered ways to raise crops with less water. These changes in agriculture are called the Green Revolution.

The second set of scientific advancements came in medicine and health. Today, new medicines and types of surgery treat health problems that used to kill people, such as heart disease and serious injuries from accidents. Researchers also have created vaccines and antibiotics to fight diseases such as smallpox, polio, and measles. As a result, many more babies are born healthy, and people live many more years.

Better Health Care for the Young

A mother and baby await medical help at the Kenyatta National Hospital in the East African country of Kenya. **Critical Thinking** How has modern medical care helped to increase the world's population growth?

LINKS TO SCIENCE

Hydroponics How can you grow a plant without soil? People called hydroponics farmers grow plants in water and necessary nutrients. The techniques are used where there is no soil, such as on ships. Today some groceries sell hydroponic vegetables. Some scientists say hydroponics may help feed the world's rapidly growing population.

2 Explore

As students read this section, have them think about these key questions: Why was population growth slower in past centuries? What factors have contributed to the world's recent rapid population growth? How does rapid population growth affect the environment today in many parts of the world?

3 Teach

Have the class discuss the impact of rapid population growth on the environment. Ask students to name several factors that affect population growth and to write a description telling how each factor works to increase or decrease population growth. Ask them to indicate which factor they feel is the most serious and give reasons for their opinions.

Teaching Resources

📁 **Reading a Natural Vegetation Map** in the Social Studies and Geography Skills booklet, p. 25, provides additional skill practice.

Program Resources

📁 **Environmental and Global Issues** Topic: Population, pp. 49–53

Media and Technology

💿 **Planet Earth** CD-ROM includes Thematic Maps: Population Total, and Population Growth which enhance students' understanding of human population issues.

Answers to . . .

BETTER HEALTH CARE FOR THE YOUNG

by reducing the number of babies that die as well as by preventing and fighting diseases that kill older people

4 Assess

See the answers to the Section Review. The students' descriptions of factors leading to population growth can also be used as an assessment tool.

Acceptable descriptions list life expectancy, birthrate, and death rate as major factors in population growth.

Commendable descriptions list the three main factors and indicate how each affects population growth.

Outstanding descriptions indicate how advances in science and technology have affected population growth.

Background

Biography

Thomas Malthus In 1798, English writer Thomas Malthus (1766–1834) published a book on population. Malthus expressed concern that the world's population was growing too fast. He believed that future generations would not be able to raise enough food to keep up with population growth. He predicted widespread misery and starvation unless population growth slowed. Malthus's ideas remain influential today.

Answers to ...

GRAPH STUDY

The United States and Italy have the highest life expectancies. Egypt, India, and Brazil have the lowest life expectancies.

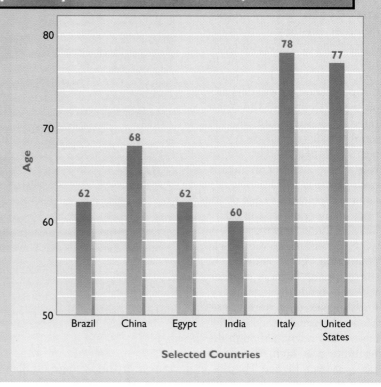

Life Expectancy in Selected Countries, 1995

Graph Study Life expectancy, or the number of years a newborn baby can expect to live, has soared in many countries since 1900. In some countries, however, life expectancy remains low. Which countries on this chart have the highest life expectancies? Which have the lowest? **Critical Thinking** What has contributed to the rise in life expectancy over the last few years?

READ ACTIVELY

Ask Questions What would you like to learn about the problems of population growth?

The Challenges of Population Growth

Today, food supplies have increased and people live longer. Even so, the people in many countries still face very serious problems. Growing populations use resources much faster than stable populations. Some nations, like those in Southwest Asia, face shortages of fresh water and energy. In Asia and Africa, food supplies cannot keep up with the growing population. Often, these countries do not have enough money to purchase imported food.

Population growth puts pressure on all aspects of life. The population of many countries is increasing so fast that many people cannot find jobs. There are not enough schools to educate the growing number of children. Decent housing is scarce and expensive. Public services like transportation and sanitation are inadequate.

A recent study by the World Bank describes the situation.

“Today, South Asia is home to a quarter of the world's population, but it accounts for 39 percent of the world's poor [people] . . . . Out of every 12 children born, at least one is expected to die before reaching the age of one.”

Resource Directory

Teaching Resources

Critical Thinking Activity in the Chapter and Section Resources booklet, p. 46, helps students apply the skill of recognizing cause and effect.

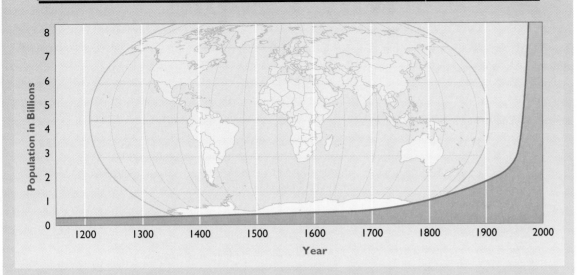

World Population Growth, A.D. 1150–2000

Population in Billions: 8, 7, 6, 5, 4, 3, 2, 1, 0

Year: 1200, 1300, 1400, 1500, 1600, 1700, 1800, 1900, 2000

Graph Study For hundreds of years, the world's population rose very slowly. Recently, however, the rate of growth has skyrocketed. **Critical Thinking** How does the graph show the slow growth of the world's population? How does it show the rapid increase in the rate of growth?

Rapid population growth also affects the environment. For instance, forests in areas of India and Pakistan are disappearing. People cut the trees to use the wood for building and for fuel. Cutting forests affects the supply of clean air. Before, tree roots held soil in place. Now heavy rainfall may wash away the soil.

Look at the population changes indicated in the graph on this page. It shows how rapidly change has occurred in the last 300 years. The Earth's resources must now be shared by six times as many people than in earlier times. All the Earth's people must work to meet this challenge.

SECTION 2 REVIEW

1. **Define** (a) birthrate, (b) death rate, (c) life expectancy, (d) Green Revolution.

2. Why has the world's population increased so dramatically in the last four or five decades?

3. How have science and technology contributed to the growing population?

Critical Thinking

4. **Drawing Conclusions** The world's population has been growing at a fast rate. What are some of the dangers of a rapidly increasing population?

Activity

5. **Writing to Learn** World hunger is one of the major concerns caused by the rapid population growth. Write one or two suggestions to help solve this problem.

Teaching Resources

📁 **Section Quiz** in the Chapter and Section Resources booklet, p. 38, covers the main ideas and key terms in the section. Available in Spanish in the Spanish Chapter and Section Resources booklet, p. 24.

SECTION 3

Why People Migrate

1 List several reasons why people migrate to new places.

2 Explain how the "push-pull" theory describes the process of immigration.

3 Analyze urbanization as a factor in the migration of people in many different lands.

Lesson Plan

1 Engage

Warm-Up Activity

Ask students how many of them have lived in another city, state, or country. Then ask whether they remember what it was like when their families moved. What things did they find familiar? What things were new or different? Did they feel at home in the new place at first? Ask them to describe how they made friends at school and with neighbors.

Activating Prior Knowledge

Have students read Reach Into Your Background in the Before You Read box. Invite students to discuss how they react when children from other cities, towns, or countries move into their neighborhood? Have them describe what they can do to make the newcomers feel welcome.

BEFORE YOU READ

Reach Into Your Background

There may have been a time in your life when you or your family moved to a new home. Or perhaps a close friend moved away from your neighborhood. You probably felt a little sad and uncertain then. Imagine how you would feel if you moved to another country!

Questions to Explore

1. Why do people migrate?
2. What are some important population issues?

Key Terms

migration
immigrant
"push-pull" theory
urbanization
rural area
urban area

Key Places

Cuba
Vietnam
Jakarta

Roberto Goizueta heads Coca-Cola, one of the largest companies in the world. Yet when he came to the United States from Cuba in 1960, he had nothing. This is how he describes his escape from Cuba:

▼ On July 4, 1996—Independence Day—hundreds of people celebrate receiving their citizenship in El Paso, Texas.

"When my family and I came to this country [the United States], we had to leave everything behind . . . our photographs hung on the wall, our wedding gifts sat on the shelves."

Like millions of others who came to the United States, Roberto Goizueta has helped the nation become a land of prosperity.

Migration: The Movement of People

For centuries people have moved from one place to another. This is called **migration. Immigrants** are people who leave one country and move to another. From 1881 to 1920, almost 23.5 million Europeans moved to the United States. Since the late 1970s, more than 773,700 people migrated here from the country of

Resource Directory

Teaching Resources

📁 **Reproducible Lesson Plan** in the Chapter and Section Resources booklet, p. 39, provides a summary of the section lesson.

📁 **Guided Reading and Review** in the Chapter and Section Resources booklet, p. 40, provides a structure for mastering key concepts and reviewing key terms in the section. Available in Spanish in the Spanish Chapter and Section Resources booklet, p. 25.

Media and Technology

📺 **Color Transparencies** 1, 2, 13, 14, 15, 16, 19, 23, 24

💿 **Planet Earth** CD-ROM includes Thematic Maps: Population Urbanization which helps students understand human migration.

Vietnam. Over 818,000 million came from El Salvador and other Central American countries, and over 3.5 million came from Mexico. More than 919,000 immigrants came from the Dominican Republic, Haiti, Jamaica, and Trinidad.

Demographers use the **"push-pull" theory** to explain immigration. It says people migrate because certain things in their lives "push" them to leave. Often, the reasons are economic. Perhaps people cannot buy land or find work. Or changes in a government may force people to leave.

For instance, in 1959 there was a revolution in Cuba. Some Cubans lost land and businesses. Many fled to America to find safety and a better life. In the last century, many Scandinavians moved to Minnesota and Wisconsin. They wanted their own land, which was scarce in Scandinavia. Some also left to escape religious persecution.

What about the "pull" part of the theory? The hope for better living conditions "pulls" people to a country. Cubans settled in Florida because it was near their former home. It already had a Spanish-speaking population. Also, Florida's climate and vegetation are similar to Cuba's. Scandinavians were "pulled" by the United States government's offer of free land for immigrants willing to set up farms. They also moved to a familiar place. The long, cold winters in Minnesota and Wisconsin were similar to those in northwestern Europe.

Connect Did you or any members of your family or your ancestors immigrate to the United States? Why did they come here?

Cuba and Florida: Climate Regions

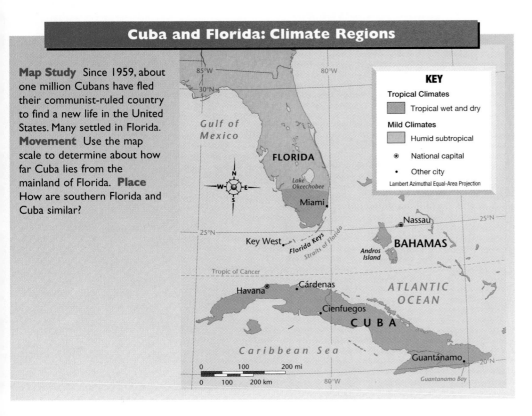

Map Study Since 1959, about one million Cubans have fled their communist-ruled country to find a new life in the United States. Many settled in Florida. **Movement** Use the map scale to determine about how far Cuba lies from the mainland of Florida. **Place** How are southern Florida and Cuba similar?

KEY

Tropical Climates
- Tropical wet and dry

Mild Climates
- Humid subtropical
- ⊛ National capital
- • Other city

Lambert Azimuthal Equal-Area Projection

Program Resources

Environmental and Global Issues
Topic: Urbanization, pp. 54–58
Interdisciplinary Explorations
A Nation of Immigrants
Urban Planning and SimCity

2 Explore

The United States is often called "a nation of immigrants." As students read the section, ask what evidence they can find to support this statement. What peoples came here from other parts of the world in the 1800s? What peoples arrived in the United States during the 1900s? What were some reasons for their migration?

3 Teach

Have students create a two-column chart, *The "Push-Pull" of Migration*. Have students fill in each column of their chart with facts from the section. When they have completed their charts, have them rank the items in each column by numbering them from most to least important. This activity should take about 20 minutes.

4 Assess

See the answers to the Section Review. You may also use students' completed charts as an assessment.

Acceptable charts list three correct entries in each column.

Commendable charts list three entries in each column and a ranking that places survival "pushes" at the top of the list.

Outstanding charts include an indication of the cause-and-effect relationships between push and pull factors.

Answers to ...
MAP STUDY

Movement Cuba lies about 150 miles (240 km) from Florida's mainland. **Place** Southern Florida and Cuba both have a tropical wet and dry climate.

Cooperative Learning

Immigration Bulletin Board Have students form teams and prepare a bulletin board display on immigration to the United States. One team can research the major periods of American immigration and prepare an immigration time line for display. Another team can obtain copies of photos or make drawings of city immigrant families and Western settlers. A third group can indicate on a world outline map the countries from which these immigrants came.

LINKS ACROSS TIME

Settlement of Polynesia Not all people end up in a location by choice. Thousands of years ago people settled in Polynesia, a group of islands in the Pacific Ocean. Scholars theorize that these people left eastern Asia in search of new land. Then violent storms blew them off course. Ocean currents carried these people to the islands they now call home.

Irish Immigrants in the United States Demographers use the push-pull theory to explain the great Irish immigration in the 1840s and 1850s. In those years, 1.5 million people left Ireland for the United States. Why did so many Irish people come to America? Ireland was a farming nation. In the 1840s, disease destroyed its main crop—potatoes. Hunger and starvation pushed people to migrate. Also, England ruled Ireland very harshly. There were very few ways for Irish people to improve their lives. These things also pushed people to move. Job opportunities pulled Irish families to the United States.

Vietnamese Come to the United States The push-pull theory also explains Vietnamese immigration. These people came from southeastern Asia to the United States. After many years of war between North and South Vietnam, peace came in 1975. North Vietnam had won. Soon, it extended its communist form of government to South Vietnam. This was a serious change for many South Vietnamese. Thousands left the country. They were not welcome in nearby Asian countries. But the United States and the South Vietnamese had been allies during the war. The United States accepted the immigrants. That pulled the Vietnamese here.

An Irish-American President

John Fitzgerald Kennedy was elected President of the United States in 1960. His great-grandfather migrated to the United States from Ireland. Like many other immigrants to this country, Irish Americans have made many important contributions. President Kennedy is shown here delivering a speech at the University of California, Berkeley, in 1962.

Background

Global Perspectives

Immigration Is Worldwide People have migrated to many other countries besides the United States. In the late 1800s, for example, half a million people came to Canada from the Ukraine (then a part of Russia). Later, people from Poland, Italy, Germany, and the Netherlands migrated to Canada. In South America, Italians, Germans, and Spaniards settled in Argentina, Brazil, Chile, and Uruguay. China was the homeland of many immigrants who moved to Indonesia, Malaysia, and other Southeast Asian countries.

Other Kinds of Immigration Sometimes, people are forced to migrate. Australia was colonized by the English. Some were convicts serving their sentences in Australia. When their sentences were done, they stayed. War also forces people to migrate. In the mid-1990s, war broke out among three ethnic groups in the former Yugoslavia, in Eastern Europe. Many refugees fled to escape the warfare. Also, victorious soldiers of one group often forced entire communities of other groups to leave. Millions of immigrants flooded into countries in Eastern and Western Europe.

Other people leave their countries for a few years to help their families. Young men from Morocco and Turkey often go to Europe to find work. They leave their families behind. For a few years they work hard and save their money. Then they return home.

The World Becomes More Urban

Migration also occurs within a country. This happens in the United States. Americans migrate more than citizens of any other country, but most move from one state to another. Recently, the population has shifted from the northeastern states to the southern and southwestern states. People may be searching for better job opportunities or a better climate. This growth in urban areas of southern states has put great stress on services. Southwestern cities, for example, are developing new ways to ensure an adequate supply of fresh water.

Drawing Conclusions To **introduce** the skill, indicate to students that they can use what they know in concert with what they learn to draw conclusions about events in the world around them. Help students **practice** the skill by asking them to name the main reasons for which people migrate to another country. List their responses on the chalkboard. Then, help students use these facts to make a generalized statement, a conclusion, that explains migration. Encourage students to **apply** the skill by listing reasons for migration from rural areas to cities and by using the reasons to draw a conclusion about rural-urban migration. Remind students that their conclusions must be supported by relevant facts.

Ask Questions What questions would you like to ask someone who plans to migrate to a city from a rural area?

One of the biggest challenges to today's nations is people migrating to cities from farms and small villages. In recent years, the population of major cities has grown tremendously. The movement of people to cities and the growth of cities is called **urbanization.** What pushes people from rural areas? What pulls people to cities?

Growing Cities, Growing Challenges Cities in Indonesia are an example. In the past, most Indonesians were farmers, fishers, and hunters. They lived in **rural areas,** or villages in the countryside. Recently, more and more Indonesians have moved to **urban areas,** or cities and nearby towns. Its urban population is increasing rapidly. For example, in 1978, about 4.5 million people lived in the capital of Jakarta. By 1994, its population was about 11 million. That is an increase of 138 percent. And demographers estimate that by 2015 the population will have risen to about 21 million.

Jakarta is not unique. In South America, too, large numbers of people are moving from rural to urban areas. São Paulo, Brazil, is now the largest city in South America. The city has hundreds of tall office buildings, stores, banks, businesses, and small factories. In 1991, its population was 15.4 million. By 2015, it is expected to be 21 million.

The problem in cities like São Paulo is that too many people are coming too fast. Cities cannot keep up. They cannot provide housing,

World Urban and Rural Populations, 1800–2000

Graph Study In countries all over the world, city populations have soared, while rural populations have fallen. What percentage of the world's population lived in cities in 1800? What percentage of the world's population will live in cities in 2000? **Critical Thinking** Based on the graph, what do you predict will happen to the world's rural and urban populations by the year 2050?

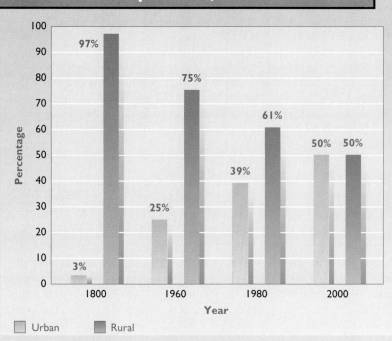

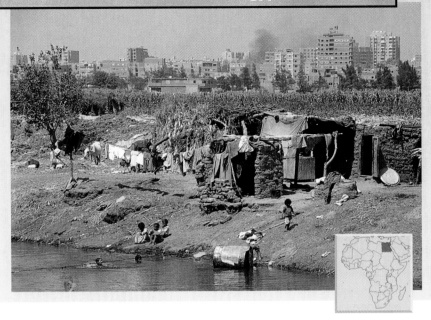

Across the world, growing cities face special challenges. Sometimes, there is not enough housing for newcomers to the cities. Sometimes, newcomers cannot afford the housing that is available. Until they find better housing, many newcomers build whatever shelters they can. These shelters are in Cairo, Egypt's capital.

jobs, schools, hospitals, and other services that people need. The country as a whole also suffers. With fewer farms, there is less food.

If you visited São Paulo, you would see why some migrants have a hard life. Schoolrooms are crowded. The city's four million cars and buses pollute the air. Traffic noise echoes day and night. Traffic jams and crowds often make it a struggle to get around.

With so many daily problems, why do immigrants flock to São Paulo and other big cities? Most are seeking a better life for their families. They are looking for jobs, decent houses, and good schools. Above all, most want more opportunities for their children.

READ ACTIVELY

Visualize Visualize what it would be like to move to a city like São Paulo, Brazil.

SECTION 3 REVIEW

1. **Define** (a) migration, (b) immigrant, (c) "push-pull" theory, (d) urbanization, (e) rural area, (f) urban area.

2. **Identify** (a) Cuba, (b) Vietnam, (c) Jakarta.

3. What are some of the reasons why people migrate from place to place?

4. Why have some immigrants left their homelands to live in the United States?

Critical Thinking

5. **Making Comparisons** What is the difference between migration within a country and migration from one country to another?

Activity

6. **Writing to Learn** When too many people migrate from rural to urban areas, it can mean hardships. List suggestions and ideas to help people decide whether to migrate to the city.

📁 **Chapter Summary** in the Chapter and Section Resources booklet, p. 42, provides a summary of chapter content. Available in Spanish in the Spanish Chapter and Section Resources booklet, p. 27.

📁 **Cooperative Learning Activity** in the Activities and Projects booklet, pp. 28–31, provides two student handouts, one page of teacher's directions, and a scoring rubric for a cooperative learning activity on making a relief map.

Media and Technology

🎧 **Guided Reading Audiotapes** (English and Spanish)

---

1. Key term definitions appear in the Glossary. Page numbers here indicate first use of the term in the text. (a) migration, p. 64 (b) immigrant, p. 64 (c) "push-pull" theory, p. 65 (d) urbanization, p. 68 (e) rural area, p. 68 (f) urban area, p. 68

2. (a) island nation in the Caribbean Sea south of Florida (b) capital and largest city in Egypt (c) country in Southeast Asia

3. Students' answers should indicate that people migrate to escape starvation, to find freedom, to escape wars and religious persecution, to find jobs and better lives, or to work and save money abroad and then return home.

4. Students may supply examples such as the following. Cubans came to the United States to escape Castro's harsh rule and to enjoy freedom here. Scandinavians came for farmland.

5. Answers will vary, but should include the fact that migration within a country usually involves people moving from farms and rural areas to cities. Migration to another country often involves moving to a land with a different culture in search of a better life.

6. Answers will vary, but students may suggest that families need to leave their friends and relatives behind to move. They may want to learn whether there are jobs and decent places to live there.

Lesson Objectives

❶ Describe a distribution map and explain how it is used.

❷ Create a distribution map from supplied information.

❸ Read a distribution map in context.

Lesson Plan

1 Engage

Warm-Up Activity

Darken the classroom, except for the lit area at your desk. Then have students listen as you **introduce** the skill by reading the opening paragraphs. With the lights on again, ask students whether the light at your desk helped them locate you in the room. Point out that light helps geographers study population distribution in a similar way (except in areas where electricity is uncommon).

Activating Prior Knowledge

Have students use their existing knowledge and a dictionary to define the terms *population* and *distribution*. Then invite students to write a question that could be answered by a population distribution map. (Possible question: Where in my state do the most people live?)

Using Distribution Maps

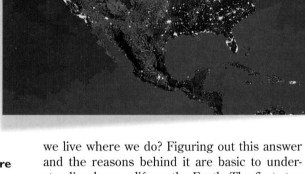

Imagine yourself in a spaceship, floating high above the Earth. Although there is no day or night in space, you can see day and night on the planet beneath you. Half the Earth is lit by the sun, and half of it is in darkness. As you begin to glide over the night side, the Earth comes between you and the sun. Looking out of the spacecraft, you see that in many places there are small smudges of light spaced across the dark land. Some huge areas are brightly lit.

You are seeing the lights of human settlement. They include firelight, street lights, floodlights in parking lots, and the combined effect of millions of lights in homes. Where there are people, there is light. The distribution of the light reflects the distribution of people on the planet. The term geographers use to refer to where people live on the planet is population distribution. Floating over the Earth, you are looking at a living population distribution map of the Earth.

Get Ready

Why do geographers study population distribution? People live all over the world, yet population is concentrated in certain places. Consider this. Nearly six billion people live in the world. Yet all of us, standing close to each other, could easily fit into the state of Connecticut! Why do we live where we do? Figuring out this answer and the reasons behind it are basic to understanding human life on the Earth. The first step is to find out where we do live. A population distribution map shows this best.

To see how population distribution maps are made and used, make and use one of your own. You will need paper, a pen, and a ruler.

Try It Out

A. Draw a map of your school. Use a large sheet of paper. Use the ruler to draw straight lines. Show and label classrooms, hallways, and so on.

B. Make a key for your map. Use stick figures as symbols. Each figure will represent five people. See the example on the next page.

Resource Directory

Teaching Resources

📁 **Reading a Population Distribution Map** in the Social Studies and Geography Skills booklet, p. 33, provides additional skill practice.

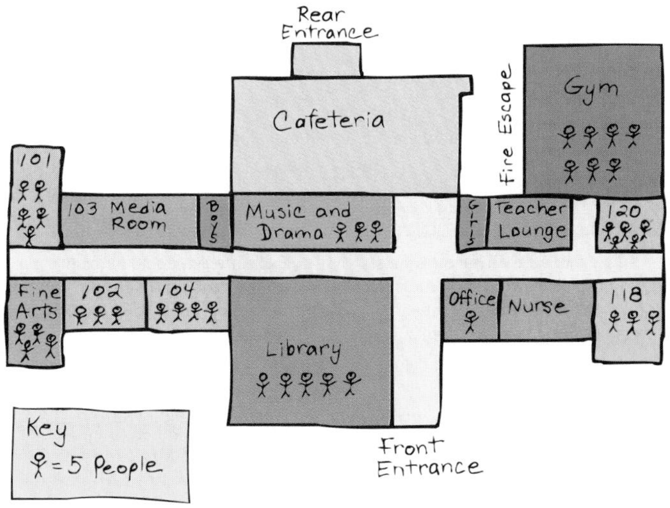

C. **Add stick-figure symbols to your map.** Remember to put the symbols where the people are. Put the right number of symbols to show how many people are in each room. If there are 24 students and 1 teacher in your classroom, for example, you would draw 5 stick-figure symbols on the part of the map that shows your classroom.

D. **Give your map an appropriate title.** You have just made a population distribution map. It answers the same two questions that any such map does: Where are the people? How many people are in each place? Your map also provides clues about another question. Why is the population distributed in the way it is? See if you can answer this question about your school map.

Apply the Skill

Now that you see how population distribution maps are made and what questions they answer, you can learn a great deal from one of Mexico. Use the map here to answer these questions.

1. **Read the map key.** Look at the key to get a sense of what the map is about. How is population represented on the map? How many people does each symbol stand for?

2. **Answer the "where" and "how many" questions that population distribution maps can answer.** Where do most of the people of Mexico live?

3. **Answer the "why" question that population distribution maps can address.** Why do you think the population of Mexico is distributed the way it is? Think about physical factors such as climate and landforms as well as historical factors.

4. **Think about distribution maps generally.** This map shows population distribution. Other maps show the distribution of such things as natural resources, technology, and wealth. Find another type of distribution map and share it with the class.

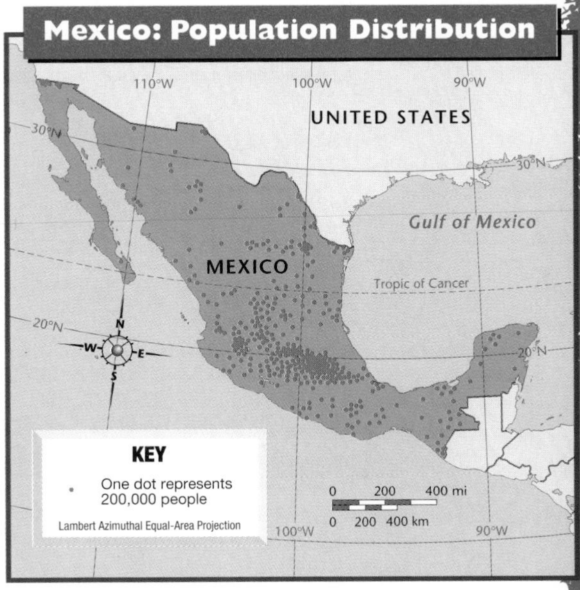

2 Explore

Discuss the text under Get Ready. Write the question *Why do we live where we do?* on the chalkboard. Clarify that some places in the world are home to very few people. With students, compare the posted question to those written earlier. Then have students read the rest of the skills activity.

3 Teach

Confirm that students have the materials described in Try It Out. As they **practice,** monitor students' progress and answer questions. Establish a rule for populations not divisible by five, for example rounding to the nearest multiple of five or using partial stick figures. Finally, discuss why your school's population is distributed as it is. (People are more likely to be in classrooms because that is where the classes are.)

4 Assess

Urge students to **apply** the skill to the map in the final activity section. **Assess** their oral replies to the text questions for accuracy and completeness.

Answers to . . .

Apply the Skill

1. with dots = numbers of people; 200,000
2. in the center
3. Possible answer: The climate is most favorable to crop growing and other industries. The landforms are stable and allow for transportation.
4. Accept examples of any type of distribution map.

Reviewing Main Ideas

I. People tend to settle in regions where the climate, landforms, vegetation, water supply, and other geographic features provide a comfortable environment.

2. (a) Asia, Europe, and North America; South America, Africa, Australia, and Antarctica (b) Sample response: In Asia and Australia, populations are concentrated along rivers and ocean coasts; interior desert regions are sparsely settled. Answers will vary.

3. People look for flat, fertile land, access to water, and mild climate. People avoid mountainous, rocky, less fertile land where transportation is difficult and the climate severe.

4. Nearly all of Egypt's fertile soil and fresh water are found here.

5. a decrease in the death rate, vaccines, better diet, and the Green Revolution

6. Sample response: People are moving from rural to urban areas to find jobs, homes, and opportunities to improve their lives. Jakarta, Indonesia, and São Paulo, Brazil, are two of these cities.

7. "Push" factors include wars, lack of jobs, changes in governments, the search for a better life, religious persecution, and the inability to own land. "Pull" factors include the promise of better living conditions, similar climate and vegetation, the promise of land, and more freedom.

Reviewing Key Terms

Sentences should show the meaning of each word through context.

Critical Thinking

I. Africa has two huge deserts, dry grasslands without fertile soil or enough rainfall for farming, as well as limited fresh water and natural resources.

2. In many countries, farmers and other people living in rural areas are moving their families to towns and large cities. Those countries are becoming urbanized.

Reviewing Main Ideas

I. How does geography affect where people settle?

2. (a) List the three continents with the most population and the four continents with the least population. (b) Choose one continent in each group and describe its landforms. Explain how those landforms affect population.

3. What kind of region is most attractive to new settlers? Which is least attractive?

4. Why does the Nile River valley of Egypt have such a high population density?

5. What factors caused a rapid increase in human population?

6. Explain why people in many parts of the world are moving from rural areas to cities. Name two of these cities.

7. What are some conditions that push people to leave their country and pull them to migrate to another country?

Reviewing Key Terms

Use each key term below in a sentence that shows the meaning of the term.

I. population
2. population distribution
3. population density
4. urbanization
5. rural
6. urban
7. Green Revolution
8. life expectancy
9. birthrate
10. death rate
11. migration
12. immigrants
13. demographer
14. "push-pull" theory

Critical Thinking

I. Recognizing Cause and Effect How have Africa's landforms and climate limited its population?

2. Identifying Central Issues Explain the meaning of this statement: "Today, many countries of the world are becoming more urban." What does this statement tell about the movement of people in those countries?

Graphic Organizer

Copy the chart below onto a sheet of paper. Then fill the empty boxes with other effects that are the result of population growth.

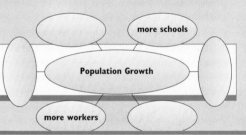

Graphic Organizer

Sample entries are shown below.

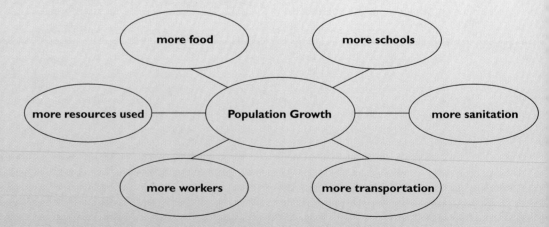

Map Activity

Place Location

Continents

For each place listed below, write the letter from the map that shows its location.

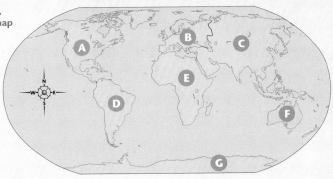

1. Asia
2. Antarctica
3. Africa
4. South America
5. North America
6. Europe
7. Australia

Writing Activity

Writing to Learn

Find out how the population of your state has changed in the last 50 years. Write a paragraph that explains the main reasons why people migrated from your state.

Internet Activity

Use a search engine to find the **U.S. Census Bureau.** Click on **Just for Fun,** then click on **data map.** Click on your state. Find out the population of your state for 1990. Choose **Subject A-Z** and explore other data such as frequently occurring first names and birthrate. With the data you have explored, make a graph of census data for your state.

Skills Review

Turn to the Skills Activity.

Review the steps for using distribution maps. Then complete the following: (a) What can you learn from a population distribution map? (b) Would you learn more if you compared a population distribution map with a landform map or a climate map? Explain your answer.

How Am I Doing?

Answer these questions to help you check your progress.

1. Do I understand why the world's population is distributed unevenly?

2. Can I identify the continents with the highest population density? The continents where fewer people live?

3. Can I describe how the Earth's landforms and climates affect where people live?

4. Do I understand why many people move from rural to urban areas?

5. What information from this chapter can I use in my book project?

Internet Activity

If students are having difficulty finding this site, you may wish to have them use the following URL, which was accurate at the time this textbook was published:

http://www.census.gov/

You might also guide students to a search engine. Four of the most useful are Infoseek, AltaVista, Lycos, and Yahoo. For additional suggestions on using the Internet, refer to the Prentice Hall Social Studies' Educator's Handbook "Using the Internet," in the *Prentice*

Hall World Explorer Program Resources.

For additional links to world history and culture topics, visit the Prentice Hall Home Page at:
http://www.phschool.com

How Am I Doing?

Point out to students that this checklist is just a quick reminder for them of what they learned in the chapter. If their answer to any of the questions is *no* or if they are unsure, they may need to review the topic.

My Side of the Mountain

BY JEAN CRAIGHEAD GEORGE

BEFORE YOU READ

Reach Into Your Background

Has your electricity ever gone out during a storm or a power failure? Suppose you had no electricity at all, or your home had no heating system. Without modern technology, how would you cope with the natural world around you?

Most people would have a hard time. But Sam Gridley, the fictional hero of the novel *My Side of the Mountain,* decided to live close to nature. He went to the Catskill Mountains in New York state and built a treehouse in a tall hemlock tree. His only companion was his falcon, Frightful. This excerpt tells how Sam managed during his first winter in the mountains.

Questions to Explore

1. What did Sam learn about nature as he lived alone in a forest in winter?

2. What skills did Sam need to survive alone in the wilderness?

hemlock (HEM lahk) *n.* pine trees with drooping branches and short needles

copse (kahps) *n.* a thicket of small trees or shrubs

READ ACTIVELY

Connect What would you do to pass the time if you did not have television, radio, or other electronic gadgets?

I lived close to the weather. It is surprising how you watch it when you live in it. Not a cloud passed unnoticed, not a wind blew untested. I knew the moods of the storms, where they came from, their shapes and colors. When the sun shone, I took Frightful to the meadow and we slid down the mountain on my snapping-turtle-shell sled. She really didn't care much for this.

When the winds changed and the air smelled like snow, I would stay in my tree, because I had gotten lost in a blizzard one afternoon and had to hole up in a rock ledge until I could see where I was going. That day the winds were so strong I could not push against them, so I crawled under the ledge; for hours I wondered if I would be able to dig out when the storm blew on. Fortunately I only had to push through about a foot of snow. However, that taught me to stay home when the air said "snow." Not that I was afraid of being caught far from home in a storm, for I could find food and shelter and make a fire anywhere, but I had become as attached to my hemlock house as a brooding bird to her nest. Caught out in the storms and weather, I had an urgent desire to return to my tree, even as The Baron Weasel returned to his den, and the deer, to their copse.

◀ Sunrise over Mongaup Pond in the Catskill Mountains, New York

We all had our little "patch" in the wilderness. We all fought to return there.

I usually came home at night with the nuthatch that roosted in a nearby sapling. I knew I was late if I tapped the tree and he came out. Sometimes when the weather was icy and miserable, I would hear him high in the trees near the edge of the meadow, yanking and yanking and flicking his tail, and then I would see him wing to bed early. I considered him a pretty good barometer, and if he went to his tree early, I went to mine early too. When you don't have a newspaper or radio to give you weather bulletins, watch the birds and animals. They can tell when a storm is coming. I called the nuthatch "Barometer," and when he holed up, I holed up, lit my light, and sat by my fire whittling or learning new tunes on my reed whistle. I was now really into the teeth of winter, and quite fascinated by its activity. There is no such thing as a "still winter night." Not only are many animals running around in the breaking cold, but the trees cry out and limbs snap and fall, and the wind gets caught in a ravine and screams until it dies.

yank (yangk) *v.* to imitate the sound made by the nuthatch

barometer (bah RAH muh tur) *n.* an instrument for forecasting changes in the weather; anything that indicates a change

whittle (witl) *v.* to cut or pare thin shavings from wood with a knife

teeth of winter the coldest, harshest time of winter

EXPLORING YOUR READING

Look Back

1. How does Sam's relationship with the weather change during the story?

Think It Over

2. Sam's relationship with his environment is different from most people's. In places, he talks about wind and trees as if they were alive. Think about your relationship with nature. How is it like Sam's? How is it different?

Go Beyond

3. What things does Sam do without that you take for granted?

Ideas for Writing: Essay

4. How might you decide what to wear to school in the morning without hearing a weather forecast? Write an essay that explains to your classmates how to watch for weather signs.

Background

About the Author

Jean Craighead George was raised in a home where nature came inside to live with the people. She and her two brothers studied "with opossums in our laps." Ms. George has been writing, always about nature and its lessons for people, since she was eight years old and has completed over 40 books for young readers.

About the Selection

My Side of the Mountain, by Jean Craighead George (New York: E.P. Dutton, 1959), includes charming sketches drawn by Sam Gribley during his adventure.

Cultures of the World

To help you plan instruction, the chart below shows how teaching resources correspond to chapter content. Use the resources to vary instruction, add activities, or plan block schedules. Where appropriate, resources have **suggested time allotments** for students. Time allotments are approximate.

Managing Time and Instruction

		Geography: Tools and Concepts Teaching Resources Binder		World Explorer Program Resources Binder	
		Resource	**mins.**	**Resource**	**mins.**
1	**SECTION 1** **What Is Culture?**	**Chapter and Section Support** Reproducible Lesson Plan, p. 48 Ⓢ Guided Reading and Review, p. 49 Ⓢ Section Quiz, p. 50	 20 25	**Outline Maps** The World: Political, p. 5 **Nystrom Desk Atlas** Ⓣ **Primary Sources and Literature Readings** **Writing Process Handbook** Organizing Material in a Logical Sequence, p. 24	20 40 25
	SKILLS ACTIVITY **Locating Information**	**Social Studies and Geography Skills,** Using CD-ROM Encyclopedias, p. 98	30		
2	**SECTION 2** **Social Groups, Language, and Religion**	**Chapter and Section Support** Reproducible Lesson Plan, p. 51 Ⓢ Guided Reading and Review, p. 52 Ⓢ Section Quiz, p. 53	 20 25		
3	**SECTION 3** **Economic and Political Systems**	**Chapter and Section Support** Reproducible Lesson Plan, p. 54 Ⓢ Guided Reading and Review, p. 55 Ⓢ Section Quiz, p. 56 Critical Thinking Activity, p. 64 **Social Studies and Geography Skills,** Drawing Conclusions, p. 52	 20 25 30 30	**Outline Maps** South Asia: Political, p. 38	20
4	**SECTION 4** **Cultural Change**	**Chapter and Section Support** Reproducible Lesson Plan, p. 57 Ⓢ Guided Reading and Review, p. 58 Ⓢ Section Quiz, p. 59 Ⓢ Vocabulary, p. 61 Reteaching, p. 62 Enrichment, p. 63 Ⓢ Chapter Summary, p. 60 **Tests** Forms A and B Chapter Tests, pp. 20–25	 20 25 20 25 25 15 40	**Outline Maps** The United States: Political, p. 16	20
	LITERATURE *Rough Country* by Dana Gioia			Ⓣ **Primary Sources and Literature Readings**	40

Block Scheduling Folder
PROGRAM TEACHING RESOURCES

Activities and Projects

Block Scheduling Program Support

Interdisciplinary Links

Resource Pro™ CD-ROM

Media and Technology

Assessment Opportunities

From Guiding Questions to Assessment A series of Guiding Questions serves as an organizing framework for this book. The Guiding Question that relates to this chapter is below. Section Reviews and Section Quizzes provide opportunities for assessing students' insights into these Guiding Questions. Additional assessments are listed below.

Media and Technology

Resource	mins.
◀▶ 🖉 Ⓢ **World Video Explorer**	20
🖵 **Color Transparencies 1, 2, 4, 6, 9, 75, 95**	20
🖉 **Planet Earth CD-ROM**	20
🖵 **Color Transparency 1**	20
🖉 **Planet Earth CD-ROM**	20
🖵 **Color Transparencies 25, 26, 39, 40**	20
🖵 **Color Transparency 98**	20
🎧 Ⓢ **Guided Reading Audiotapes**	20
🖵 **Color Transparency 174** (Graphic organizer table template)	20
🖉 **The Writer's Solution CD-ROM**	30
🖫 **Computer Test Bank**	30

T **Teaming Opportunity**
This resource is especially well-suited for teaching teams.

Ⓢ **Spanish**
This resource is also in Spanish support.

🖉 **CD-ROM**

🖉 **Laserdisc**

🖵 **Transparency**

🖫 **Software**

◀▶ **Videotape**

🎧 **Audiotape**

GUIDING QUESTION

- *What does culture mean?*

ASSESSMENTS

Section 1

Students should be able to write a poem that describes elements of culture.

▶ **RUBRIC** See the Assessment booklet for a rubric on assessing a student poem.

Section 2

Students should be able to make a web that shows what elements make cultures distinct from one another.

▶ **RUBRIC** See the Assessment booklet for a rubric on assessing graphic organizers.

Section 3

Students should be able to write a glossary of the key terms in the section.

▶ **RUBRIC** See the Assessment booklet for a rubric on assessing a glossary.

Section 4

Students should be able to write an explanation about the causes of cultural change.

▶ **RUBRIC** See the Assessment booklet for a rubric on assessing cause-and-effect statements.

Activities and Projects

ACTIVITIES
To Develop a Global Perspective

Mental Mapping	Links to Current Events	Hands-On Activities

Countries and Cultures Point out that cultures do not necessarily change at political borders. For example, the culture in San Antonio, Texas may be more similar to that of northern Mexico than to the one in Minnesota, though both are in the United States.

Explain that many things contribute to culture. History, religion, and technology influence culture. Geography has a very big influence on culture. Where people live affects the food they eat, the clothes they wear, the work they do, and the kinds of buildings they create.

Ask students to make maps of an imaginary land in which there are three different cultural groups. Each group lives in an area that is geographically distinct. Have students note the kinds of work people do and the kinds of clothes they wear.

Cross-Cultural Understanding There are books and businesses that devote themselves to training government officials, businesspeople, and others in how to get along in an unfamiliar culture. People who go to a country with a very different culture must learn new ways of greeting people and new expectations for polite behavior in stores, offices, and people's homes.

Invite someone who knows another culture well to visit the class and talk about differences in customs and behavior. What advice would this person offer to people planning to visit another culture?

Cultural Signals Ask students what kinds of clues help them identify a neighborhood or city as culturally distinct. They may mention types of food and goods sold in stores, music playing in public places, clothing, and so forth.

Divide the class into three or four groups and distribute art supplies. Have each group invent a "culture" for their neighborhood of the classroom. For example, one culture might eat many types of cheese, enjoy wooden percussion instruments, and wear clothes trimmed with beads.

Have each group create some props to put up in their neighborhood. Then have representatives from each neighborhood tell the class about their culture and their neighborhood.

PROJECTS
To Develop a Global Perspective

Salad Bowl or Melting Pot? You may wish to point out to students that at some times in U.S. history, Americans have viewed their nation as a melting pot in which immigrants were expected to give up many aspects of their original culture to "fit in" to American culture. Today, many people view the United States more as a tossed salad in which many cultures mix to create a national culture yet retain their own identity. Ask students to brainstorm some ways that cultural diversity strengthens a group. Then ask them to brainstorm a list of challenges a culturally diverse society must face. Have students make lists of the results and post them on the chalkboard. *Average*

City Cultures Have students research the cultural neighborhoods of the city they know best. Has the cultural identity of these neighborhoods changed over time? For example, in some large cities, neighborhoods that were once German and Irish were taken over by Eastern European Jews and Italians, then later by Puerto Ricans and African Americans, and later still by South and East Asians. Have students create a time line of changes in the neighborhoods of a city they know. *Challenging*

Economic and Political Landmarks Have students identify five buildings and other places that are linked to the economic system and five buildings that are linked to the political system of their community. For example, banks, stores, factories, wharves, and farms are all part of the community's economy. City hall, the court house, schools, police stations, government office buildings, libraries, and public transportation stations are all part of the community's government. Have students locate some of these places on a map of their community. Encourage students to list these buildings and tell how people would use each one. *English Language Learners*

F.Y.I.

This page can help you extend your own and students' understanding of the concepts in this chapter. You may want to browse through some of the suggestions in the **Bibliography**. **Interdisciplinary Links** can connect social studies understandings to areas elsewhere in the curriculum through the use of other Prentice Hall products. **National Geography Standards** reflected specifically in this chapter are listed for your convenience. Some hints about appropriate **Internet Access** are also provided. **School to Careers** provides insights into the practical uses of some of the concepts in this chapter as they might pertain to various careers.

BIBLIOGRAPHY

FOR THE TEACHER

Faith and Belief: Five Major World Religions. Knowledge, Unlimited, 1992. Videocassette.

Fry, Plantagenet Somerset. *The Dorling Kindersley History of the World.* Dorling Kindersley, 1994.

Philip, Neil. *The Illustrated Book of World Myths: Tales and Legends of the World.* Dorling Kindersley, 1995.

FOR THE STUDENT

Easy
Lewin, Ted. *Sacred River.* Clarion, 1995.

Average
Mason, Anthony. *The Children's Atlas of Civilizations.* Millbrook, 1994.

Reynolds, Jan. *Himalaya: Vanishing Cultures.* Harcourt Brace Jovanovich, 1991.

Reynolds, Jan. *Sahara: Vanishing Cultures.* Harcourt Brace Jovanovich, 1991.

Challenging
Mozeson, I. E. and Lois Stavsky. *Jerusalem Mosaic: Young Voices from the Holy City.* Four Winds/Simon & Schuster, 1994.

LITERATURE CONNECTION

Castaneda, Omar S. *Among the Volcanoes.* Lodestar, 1991.

Hicyilmaz, Gaye. *Against the Storm.* Joy Street, 1992.

Prochazkova, Iva. *The Season of Secret Wishes.* Lothrop, 1989.

INTERDISCIPLINARY LINKS

Subject	Theme: Culture
MATH	Middle School Math: Tools for Success Course 1, Lesson 10-8, **Making Predictions** Course 2, Lesson 1-8, **Representative Samples and Surveys**
SCIENCE	Prentice Hall Science *Dynamic Earth,* Gazette, **Sara Bisel Uncovers the Past With Ancient Bones**
LANGUAGE ARTS	Choices in Literature *Joining Hands,* **Friends All of Us** *The Adventure of Me,* **The All-American Slurp** Prentice Hall Literature *Copper,* **Thunder Butte**

NATIONAL GEOGRAPHY STANDARDS

Students explore the 18 National Geography Standards throughout *Geography: Tools and Concepts.* Chapter 4, however, concentrates on investigating the following standards: 1, 3, 5, 6, 7, 9, 10, 11, 12, 13, 15, 16, 17, 18. For a complete list of the standards, see the *Teacher's Flexible Planning Guide.*

SCHOOL TO CAREERS

In Chapter 4, Cultures of the World, students learn the definition and elements of culture. Additionally, they address the skill of locating information. Understanding culture can help students prepare for careers in many fields such as history, international trade, diplomacy, and so on. Skill in locating information is particularly useful for researchers, writers, employment counselors, teachers, and others. The curriculum presented in this book, as in all eight titles of Prentice Hall's *World Explorer* program, is designed to prepare students not only for careers but also for good citizenship—of the world as well as of this country.

INTERNET ACCESS

Many social studies teachers and students use Internet browsers, or search engines, to investigate particular topics. For the best results, use narrow rather than broad topics. Try these for Chapter 4: agriculture, language, ethics, government. Finding age-appropriate sites is an important consideration when using the Internet. For links to age-appropriate sites in world studies and geography, visit the Prentice Hall Home Page at: **http://www.phschool.com**

Chapter 4

Cultures of the World

Connecting to the Guiding Questions

As students complete this chapter, they will focus on the meaning and scope of culture as shown in social groups, languages, religions, and economic and political systems. By studying the process of social change, they will recognize how cultural ideas spread. Content in this chapter thus corresponds to this Guiding Question:

● What is a culture?

Using the Picture Activities

Discuss each of the pictures. Direct students' attention to the visual clues that will help them recognize the environment.

• Answers should include environmental and cultural clues that this is an Arctic setting.

• Answers should include at least one similarity and one difference.

Heterogeneous Groups

The following Teacher's Edition strategies are suitable for heterogeneous groups.

Critical Thinking
Expressing Ideas
Clearly   p. 78

Cooperative Learning
Cultural Festival   p. 84

Interdisciplinary
Connections
Music   p. 95

SECTION 1
What Is Culture?

SECTION 2
Social Groups, Language, and Religion

SECTION 3
Economic and Political Systems

SECTION 4
Cultural Change

PICTURE ACTIVITIES

Have you ever jumped for joy? The Inuits of Alaska toss one another for joy. People gather in a circle, grab the sides of an animal skin blanket, and use it to toss one another sky-high. The people here are celebrating a whaling festival. The Inuits also toss one another to celebrate the arrival of spring or a religious holiday or a successful hunt.

Look for clues
What can you find out about where the people in this picture live? List the clues you find. Explain what they tell you about the picture.

Write a letter
Write a letter to someone in this photograph. Describe your thoughts about the tossing ceremony. Tell them about an activity you enjoy. Explain how these two activities are similar and different.

Resource Directory

Media and Technology

 What Is Culture?, from the World Video Explorer, enhances students' understanding of culture through an examination of the culture of Scotland.

Chapter 7

What Is Culture?

BEFORE YOU READ

Reach Into Your Background
You and the people you know have certain ways of doing things. You have a way of celebrating birthdays. You have a way of greeting your friends. You have a way of eating a meal. You have a way of speaking. You have ways of gesturing. Many of the ways you do things are unique to you alone. Others you share with people around you.

Questions to Explore
1. What is culture?
2. How do cultures develop?

Key Terms
culture
cultural trait
technology
cultural landscape
agriculture

"**A**ll right, students," your teacher says, "time to clean the room. Kaitlyn—I'd like you to sweep today. Guy and Keisha, please use these feather dusters to clean our shelves and windowsills. Eric and Bobby, you can do the lunch dishes today. Serena and Zack, please empty the wastebaskets and take out the trash."

Would you be surprised if this happened in your classroom? Would you pitch in—or complain? In Japan, students would pitch in to help keep their classrooms clean. Hard work and neatness are important lessons. Although Japanese schools are similar to American ones, there are differences. Japanese students generally spend more time studying than many American students. In Japan, most children go to school five days a week and often on Saturdays for half a day. Many students do many hours of homework every afternoon and evening and over vacations.

Japanese students, like many American students, also enjoy sports, music, drama, and science. They join teams and clubs. They paint and take photographs. They play baseball, soccer, and tennis. They do karate and judo. They play musical instruments.

▼ These students in Japan are listening closely as their classmate speaks. How is your own classroom like this one? How does it differ?

Section 1

Lesson Objectives

1 Define culture and describe its elements.

2 Explain how cultures are affected by their landscape and how they, in turn, affect their landscape.

3 Trace the early development of human culture.

Lesson Plan

1 Engage
Warm-Up Activity

Write the following four headings on the chalkboard: *sports, foods, clothing,* and *entertainment.* Ask students to list, under each heading, things that are important parts of American life. Ask for specific items. Summarize by saying that these different parts of our way of life are only part of American culture.

Activating Prior Knowledge

Have students read Reach Into Your Background in the Before You Read box. Invite students to discuss any customs or traditions they are familiar with that may be specific to another culture.

Teaching Resources

📁 **Reproducible Lesson Plan** in the Chapter and Section Resources booklet, p. 48, provides a summary of the section lesson.

📁 **Guided Reading and Review** in the Chapter and Section Resources booklet, p. 49, provides a structure for mastering key concepts and reviewing key terms in the section. Available in Spanish in the Spanish Chapter and Section Resources booklet, p. 30.

Program Resources

📁 Material in the **Primary Sources and Literature Readings** booklet extends content with a selection related to the concepts in this chapter.

📁 **Outline Maps** The World: Political, p. 5

2 Explore

Point out to students that geographers study how people affect their environment as well as how the environment affects people. Discuss how tools, fire, agriculture, and writing each contributed to the development of culture.

3 Teach

Have students work in small groups to create a cause-and-effect graphic showing how the environment affects people living in their community.

Cause ⟶	Effect
Climate ⟶	
Landforms ⟶	
Vegetation ⟶	
Natural resources ⟶	

Direct students to list results or effects of each cause in a connecting box. Use the completed graphics to discuss how the local environment has shaped life in your community.

Activity

Critical Thinking

Expressing Ideas Clearly
Suitable as an individual activity. Invite students to think about their own cultural beliefs and values. Encourage them to consider what they have learned about right and wrong (beliefs) and about what is most important in life (values) from their family, religion, or other groups such as the Scouts. Suggest that students create a list of three beliefs or values and an example of each. Volunteers may share their lists if they wish.

READ ACTIVELY

Predict What do you think the word *culture* means?

▼ How people live is part of their culture. Different cultures sometimes interact with their environment in similar ways. In mountainous Japan, farmers build terraces on the hillsides to increase the amount of land available for farming. Terrace farming is also used in other cultures, including those in South America and South Asia.

Culture: A Total Way of Life

What if you met students from Japan? You would probably ask many questions. "How do you feel about cleaning your classroom?" you might ask. When you heard about how much homework they do, you might also ask "How do you find time to have fun?" Later, you might wonder about other things. What do Japanese students eat for lunch? What kinds of music do they like? What makes them laugh?

Answers to these questions will tell you something about the culture of Japan. **Culture** is the way of life of a group of people who share similar beliefs and customs. The language Japanese students speak and the way they dress are both a part of their culture. So are the subjects Japanese students study and what they do after school.

Elements of Culture Culture includes the work people do, their behaviors, their beliefs, and their ways of doing things. Parents pass these things on to their children, generation after generation. A particular group's individual skills, customs, and ways of doing things are called **cultural traits.** Over time, cultural traits may change, but cultures change very slowly.

Some elements of a culture are easy to see. They include material things, such as houses and other structures, television sets, food, or clothing. Sports, entertainment, and literature are also visible elements of culture. The things you cannot see or touch are also part of culture. They include spiritual beliefs, ideals, government, and ideas about right and wrong. Language is also a very important part of culture.

Resource Directory

Program Resources

Nystrom Desk Atlas

Media and Technology

 Color Transparencies 1, 2, 4, 6, 9, 75, 95

Culture and Costume

Some aspects of culture, like the clothes people wear, may not seem important. When you visit another country, however, these differences can make you feel like an outsider. This photograph shows children who are watching an international track meet held in Los Angeles. The children are from the Los Angeles area. To make athletes from other countries feel welcome, they dressed in many different national costumes.

People and Their Land Geographers study culture, especially activities that relate to the environment. These things are part of the theme of human-environment interaction. Geographers want to know how landforms, climate, vegetation, and resources affect culture. For example, fish and seaweed are popular foods in Japan, a nation of islands. These islands are mountainous, with little farmland. Therefore, the Japanese get food from the sea.

Geographers are also interested in the effect people have on their environment. Often the effect is tied to a culture's **technology,** or tools, and the skills people need to use them. People use technology to take advantage of natural resources and change the environment. Technology can mean tools like computers and the Internet. But technology also means stone tools and the ability to make them. Geographers use levels of technology to see how advanced a culture is.

A group's **cultural landscape** includes any changes to its environment. It also includes the technology used to make the changes. They vary from culture to culture. For example, Bali, in Indonesia, has many mountains. Therefore, people carved terraces in them to create flat farmland. Other regions, such as central India, have much level land. Farmers there would not develop a technology to create terraces.

Think about your culture. What do people eat? What are the houses like? What kind of work do people do? Can you identify some beliefs and values of your culture? In your mind, describe your culture. You may find it is harder to look at your own culture than at someone else's.

HEROES

Working Together
Sometimes the old ways are best. Two Bolivians, Bonifacia Quispe and Oswaldo Rivera, discovered the ancient Aymara Indians cut terraces into the sides of mountains to create flat farmland. Terraces are easier to irrigate and fertilize than slopes. In 1986, Quispe and Rivera taught the method to today's Aymara farmers. These farmers then grew 28 times more food.

4 Assess

See the answers to the Section Review. You may also use students' completed graphics as an assessment.

Acceptable graphics contain at least two effects per cause.

Commendable graphics show a greater number of effects.

Outstanding graphics include a greater variety of effects.

Background

Across Time

Controlling the Environment Early civilizations grew as people learned to control their environment. In the Indus Valley, in what is now Pakistan and western India, people learned to irrigate with river water and to control floods about 4,500 years ago. This led to the growth of the cities of Harappa and Mohenjo-Daro, which were highly civilized, with public buildings, an organized system of producing and storing grains and other foods, and homes with interior baths and drains to carry sewage away from the houses.

The Development of Culture

Cultures develop over a long time. Geographers say early cultures went through four stages: the invention of tools, the discovery of fire, the growth of **agriculture** or farming, and the use of writing.

Technology and Weather Forecasting

Technology is a very important part of culture because it changes the way we do things. For thousands of years, people have looked up at the sky to try and forecast the weather. Today, meteorologists—scientists who study the weather—still look up at the sky. However, they use very advanced technology, including various kinds of satellites, to do their job. Our ancestors could do little more than guess about the weather. Modern meteorologists, however, can make highly accurate forecasts about the weather some weeks into the future. Below is a diagram of a weather tracking satellite system.

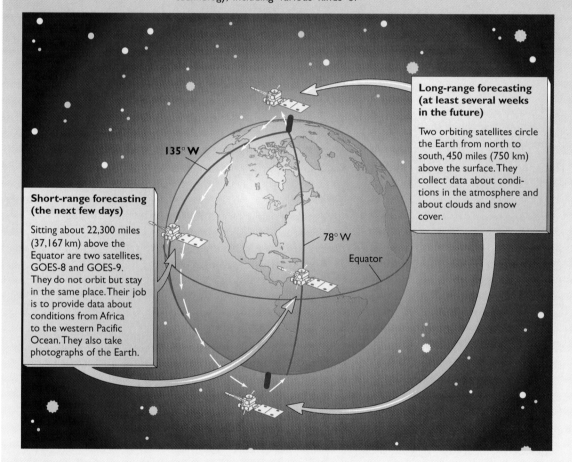

Long-range forecasting (at least several weeks in the future)

Two orbiting satellites circle the Earth from north to south, 450 miles (750 km) above the surface. They collect data about conditions in the atmosphere and about clouds and snow cover.

Short-range forecasting (the next few days)

Sitting about 22,300 miles (37,167 km) above the Equator are two satellites, GOES-8 and GOES-9. They do not orbit but stay in the same place. Their job is to provide data about conditions from Africa to the western Pacific Ocean. They also take photographs of the Earth.

135° W

78° W

Equator

Early Technology For most of human history, people were hunters and gatherers. Traveling from place to place, they collected wild plants, hunted game, and fished. Wood and stone tools and weapons helped them hunt, prepare food, and do other work. Later they learned to make and use fire, so some people began living in colder climates.

The Start of Agriculture Then, people discovered how to grow crops and tame wild animals to use as food or to help them with work. Now people no longer had to spend all their time following herds or moving from campsite to campsite in search of wild plants. Over time, societies relied on farming for most of their food. Historians call this great change the Agricultural Revolution.

By 3,000 years ago, the Agricultural Revolution had changed much of the world. Agriculture provided a steady food supply. Birthrates rose; death rates fell; population increased. Agriculture also led to the creation of cities and complex societies. Some people produced food, and others developed special skills. For example, people became potters, tailors, or metal workers. People began to develop laws and government. To record information, they developed writing. Now, people could store knowledge and pass it on to others. When a culture creates a writing system, it is called a civilization.

Early civilizations also created unique forms of art and music. They organized their beliefs into religions, with priests, temples, and ceremonies. Their roads and canals became features of the landscape. People learned to control and change their environment. Because of technological inventions such as irrigation and terracing, people could grow more and better crops in more areas. People spread over more and more regions. As they moved, they made changes to the Earth's landscape.

The Domestication of Grain Early people gathered the seeds of the wild grains for food. However, about 10,000 years ago, people in Southwest Asia decided to try to plant wild wheat to tide them over. The first crop was poor. But farmers saved seeds from the best plants and tried again the next year. Over time, this led to today's domesticated wheat.

SECTION 1 REVIEW

1. **Define** (a) culture, (b) cultural trait, (c) technology, (d) cultural landscape, (e) agriculture.

2. If someone asked you to describe your culture, what would you tell them?

3. Describe four important developments in human culture. Tell why they are important.

Critical Thinking
4. **Recognizing Cause and Effect** Agriculture encouraged people to settle in one area. Some people kept on farming. Others became specialists in other skills. How could living in a group result in some people becoming specialists?

Activity
5. **Writing to Learn** Find a photograph of a familiar scene in your town or city. List at least ten features of your culture shown by the photograph.

SKILLS MINI LESSON

Recognizing Cause and Effect
To **introduce** the skill, point out to students that events cause—and are caused by— other events. Help students **practice** the skill by having them identify the causes and effects in these groups of events. Invite students to explain their choices.

- World population increased. (effect)
- Food supply became steady. (effect)
- Agriculture improved. (cause)

- Information could be recorded. (effect)
- Writing was developed. (cause)
- Knowledge could be passed to others. (effect)

Encourage students to **apply** the skill by writing three statements based on information in the text. Suggest that they trade statements with a partner and identify statements as being either causes or effects.

Section 2

Social Groups, Language, and Religion

BEFORE YOU READ

Reach Into Your Background
Even if you can't speak a word of Chinese, Italian, French, or Spanish, you can probably get Chinese, Italian, French, or Spanish food. Here is a list of four restaurants: Hoy Hing, Bella Vista, Café de Paris, Casa Mexico. Where would you go for enchiladas? For egg rolls? You know where to go because you connect food and language. Both are parts of culture. What else is part of culture?

Questions to Explore
1. Why is social organization important to cultures?
2. What elements make cultures distinct from one another?

Key Terms
social structure   ethics
nuclear family
extended family

▼ The end of Ramadan means a joyous celebration for these Egyptian Muslims.

It is still dark when the muezzin (moo EZ in) calls the people of Cairo to prayer. Roosters crow. As you wake, you remember that today is the first day of Ramadan (ram uh DAHN). During this religious season, Muslims, followers of the religion of Islam, eat and drink nothing from sunrise to sunset. This year, Ramadan will be special. Young children do not fast during Ramadan, but now you are 12. Now you are old enough to join the fast.

You are excited and a little nervous. You want to fast. It is a way to praise Allah, and it shows you are an adult. Still, you wonder if you can go all day without eating or drinking. You join your family for the *suhoor* (SOO HOOR), the meal eaten before daybreak. Your parents and grandparents smile at you proudly. In the evening, you will join them for the *Iftar* (if TAHR), or the meal eaten after dark. That meal will taste especially good. And a month from now, when you celebrate the end of Ramadan, you will be prouder than ever. Every year you receive gifts, but this year they will be very special. You will give the prayers of thanksgiving, knowing you have joined with Muslims all over the world to celebrate Ramadan.

How Society Is Organized

Although the children of Cairo join with Muslims all over the world to celebrate Ramadan, they do so within their own households. Every culture has a **social structure.** This is a way of organizing people into

In the United States, a mother, father, and their two sons enjoy a stroll in the park (top left). In Malaysia, children join their parents, aunts, uncles, and grandparents to make music (top right). In the mountains of Tibet, a mother leads her child on a yak (bottom). As these pictures show, a family can be as small as two people or as large as a roomful of people.

smaller groups. Each smaller group has particular tasks. Some groups work together to get food. Others protect the community. Still others raise children. Social structure helps people work together to meet the basic needs of individuals, families, and communities.

The family is the basic, most important social unit of any culture. Families teach the customs and traditions of the culture. Through their families, children learn how to dress, to be polite, to eat, and to play.

Kinds of Families   All cultures do not define family in the same way. In some cultures, the basic unit is a **nuclear family,** or a mother, father, and their children. This pattern is common in industrial nations such as the United States, Great Britain, and Germany. Adults often work outside the home. They usually have money to buy what they need. They depend on the work of machines like vacuum cleaners and automobiles.

READ ACTIVELY

Ask Questions What questions would you like to ask about different kinds of families?

2 Explore

Have students read the section. Then ask the class to list the most important elements of cultures. Students should list families, other social organizations, language, and religion. With the class, create a chart that explains why a culture needs these elements to survive.

3 Teach

Invite students to tell what they know about each of the following terms: *nuclear family, extended family,* and *social class.* Have them work in pairs to create their own definitions for the words. Suggest that as students read the section, they edit and revise their definitions and include examples of each term.

4 Assess

See the answers to the Section Review. You may also use students' completed definitions as an assessment.

Acceptable definitions reflect information and examples given in the text.

Commendable definitions present definitions in students' own words.

Outstanding definitions present definitions in students' own words and give examples reflecting students' own experiences.

SKILLS MINI LESSON

Identifying Central Issues

To **introduce** the skill, remind students that to understand anything they read, they need to identify the main idea, or the central issue. To help students **practice** the skill, direct their attention to the paragraphs under the heading *Kinds of Families.* Suggest that students look for clues to the central issue, perhaps the title or a single sentence. (All cultures do not define *family* in the same way.) Encourage them to look for an idea that all the sentences support. Then have them state what they think is the main idea in their own words. (Sample: Different cultures define family differently.) Encourage students to **apply** the skill as they read the section on language.

Cultural Festival Have students identify the cultural groups united by language, religion, customs, and places of origin that live in your region or are represented in your school. Suggest that students form groups, each researching a single culture. In a group, one student can research food; another, clothing; and a third, music and dance. The fourth student can orchestrate the presentation. *Kinesthetic*

Other cultures have extended families. An **extended family** includes several generations. Along with parents and their children, there may be grandparents, aunts, uncles, cousins, and other relatives. In extended families, older people are very respected. They pass on traditions. Extended families are less common than they used to be. As rural people move to cities, nuclear families are becoming more common.

Cultures also differ when deciding who is in charge in families. Many cultures have patriarchal (PAY tree ar kal) families. That means men make most family decisions. But some African and Native American cultures have matriarchal (MAY tree ar kal) families. In these, women have more authority than in patriarchies. Today, family organizations are becoming more complicated. Men and women have started to share family power. This is partly because more and more women are working outside the home.

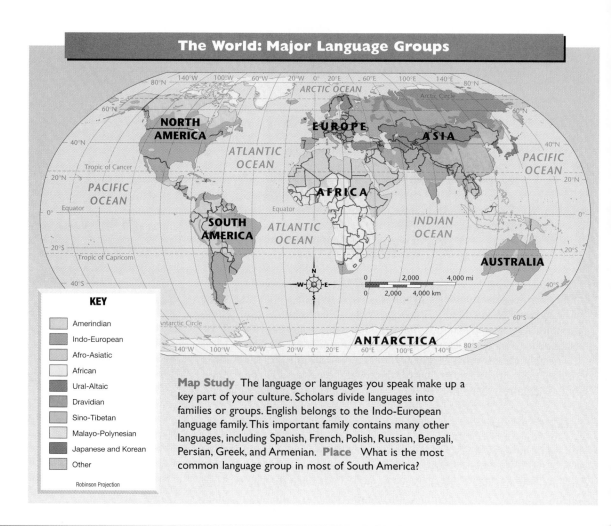

The World: Major Language Groups

KEY

- Amerindian
- Indo-European
- Afro-Asiatic
- African
- Ural-Altaic
- Dravidian
- Sino-Tibetan
- Malayo-Polynesian
- Japanese and Korean
- Other

Robinson Projection

Map Study The language or languages you speak make up a key part of your culture. Scholars divide languages into families or groups. English belongs to the Indo-European language family. This important family contains many other languages, including Spanish, French, Polish, Russian, Bengali, Persian, Greek, and Armenian. **Place** What is the most common language group in most of South America?

Resource Directory

Media and Technology

Planet Earth CD-ROM includes Thematic Maps: World Languages and World Religions which enhance students' understanding of human culture.

Answers to . . .

MAP STUDY

Indo-European

Social Classes Cultures also have another kind of social organization—social classes. These rank people in a culture. A person's status or position may come from such things as wealth, land, ancestors, or education. In some cultures in the past, it was often hard—or impossible—for people to move from one social class to another. Today, people in many societies can improve their status. They can get a good education, make more money, or even marry someone of a higher class.

Language

Culture is a total way of life. Whoever you are, wherever you live, you are part of the culture of your society. You learn your culture from your family or from others. You also learn a great deal through language. Think of how hard it would be if you had no way to say, "Meet me by the gate after school," or "I'll have a tuna sandwich." How could you learn if you could not ask questions?

All cultures have language. In fact, every culture is based on language. It lets people communicate everything they need to share in their culture. Without language, people could not pass on what they know or believe to their children.

A culture's language reflects the things that its people think are important. For example, English has the word *snow* and several adjectives for the white stuff that falls in some places in winter. But the Inuits of North America have over 13 words for snow. Why? Where the Inuits live, snow covers the ground for a good part of the year. Snow is a more important part of their environment than it is to people of other cultures. The Inuits, therefore, have created words to meet their needs. All cultures have their own unique terms.

In some countries, people speak different languages. For example, the official language of Egypt is Arabic. It is spoken by most Egyptians. But some Egyptians speak Italian, Greek, or Armenian. Canada has two official languages, French and English, and Native Americans there speak a number of languages. People who speak these languages are culturally different in some ways from other people in their country. They may celebrate different festivals, wear different clothes, or have different customs for such things as dating or education.

Ways of Believing

Language is basic to cultures. Other basics are values and religion. At the beginning of this section, you read about Ramadan, a religious celebration of Muslims, followers of the religion of Islam. Ramadan is a very important part of Islam. And Islam is a major part of Egyptian culture. Other religions are important in other cultures.

Religion helps people understand the world. Religion can provide comfort and hope for people facing difficult times. And religion helps answer questions about the meaning and purpose of life. It helps define the values that people believe are important. Religions guide people in **ethics,** or standards of accepted behavior.

Ancient Alphabets The Phoenicians were ancient traders along the Mediterranean Sea. Their alphabet had 22 letters, and they wrote from right to left. The Greeks saw this writing system and based their own alphabet on it—with one difference. The Greeks, like us, wrote from left to right. We owe our alphabet, in part, to these two ancient cultures.

Predict Why are religions an important part of cultures?

SKILLS MINI LESSON

Organizing Information
To **introduce** the skill, point out to students that as they do research, they will often need to take notes. Identify for students these steps in taking notes and organizing information.
- Use key words and phrases to record the main idea and to record details.
- Double-check your notes.

Have students **practice** the skill by taking notes on this section of the text. Record students' main ideas and details in the following manner:

Main Idea	
Σ	detail
Σ	detail
Σ	detail

Suggest that students **apply** the skill by researching the languages, religions, and customs of people who live in their area or of cultures represented in their school.

1. Definitions for all key terms appear in the Glossary. Page numbers following each key term indicate first use of the term. (a) social structure, p. 82 (b) nuclear family, p. 83 (c) extended family, p. 84 (d) ethics, p. 85

2. the family

3. social organization, language, and religion

4. In a patriarchy, men make most of the family decisions. In a matriarchy, women have more authority than in a patriarchy.

5. Religion, basic to culture, can provide comfort, hope and meaning, and purpose of life. Religions guide people in moral behavior.

6. Students should show an awareness that each language fits a particular way of life. Therefore, no language is better than others.

7. Students' diagrams should show an awareness of their own particular culture and ethnicity and of those of others.

Answers to . . .

MAP STUDY

Islam dominates the largest area of Southwest Asia. Hinduism prevails in India. In South America, most people are Roman Catholics.

The World: Major Religions

KEY

Christianity
- Roman Catholic
- Protestant
- Eastern Churches
- Other

Islam
- Sunni
- Shiite

Other Major Groups
- Hinduism
- Buddhism
- Judaism
- Traditional

Robinson Projection

Map Study Southwest Asia witnessed the founding of three great world religions: Judaism, Christianity, and Islam. **Place** Which of these religions is a major religion in the region today? What is India's major religion? What is the major religion in South America?

Religious beliefs vary. Some religions such as Islam, Judaism, and Christianity believe in one god. Other religions worship more than one god. But all religions have prayers and rituals. Every religion celebrates important places and times. Most religions expect people to treat one another well and behave properly.

SECTION 2 REVIEW

1. Define (a) social structure, (b) nuclear family, (c) extended family, (d) ethics.

2. What is the basic unit of a culture's social structure?

3. What are three important features of a culture?

4. Explain the difference between a matriarchy and a patriarchy.

5. What is the role of religion in a culture?

Critical Thinking

6. Recognizing Bias How do you know that one language is not better than another?

Activity

7. Writing to Learn Make notes about your own culture. Draw three circles labeled "social structure," "language," and "religion." In each circle, make notes about your own culture's social structure, language, and religion. Include information about others in your family or neighborhood whose culture influences you.

Resource Directory

Teaching Resources

Section Quiz in the Chapter and Section Resources booklet, p. 53, covers the main ideas and key terms in the section. Available in Spanish in the Spanish Chapter and Section Resources booklet, p. 33.

Economic and Political Systems

Reach Into Your Background

Many schools are polling places where people vote. You may have seen adults going into the gym or another part of your school to use a voting machine or mark a ballot.

Signs nearby often urge people to vote for a candidate or a certain way on an issue. Perhaps your student body holds elections, too. They are part of the political process in many places in the United States.

Questions to Explore

1. What is an economic system?

2. How do governments differ in their structure?

Key Terms

economy	government
producer	direct
goods	democracy
services	monarchy
consumer	constitution
capitalism	representative
socialism	democracy
communism	dictator

Muhammad Yunnus is a professor of economics in the country of Bangladesh. Bangladesh (bahng gluh DESH) is a very poor nation in South Asia. Yunnus wanted to understand how the people in his country really lived. His goal was to help them. He knew Bangladeshis ate only one or two meals a day. Though many had not gone to school, they were intelligent. Yunnus knew they were hard-working and could be trusted.

In the early 1970s, Yunnus met Sufiya Khatun. She made bamboo stools. But she earned only two cents a day because she had so few stools to sell. If she had more money for supplies, she could make more. But Sufiya had no way to borrow money to buy supplies. At first, Yunnus thought he would simply give her the small sum she needed. Then he wondered if others in the village were also like Sufiya. He found 42 people that needed to borrow about $26 each for their businesses.

Yunnus was shocked. So little money meant the difference between success and failure. But banks would not

▼ Most of Muhammad Yunnus's customers are women seeking to open small businesses. This woman used her loan to start a weaving shop.

Lesson Objectives

1 Summarize the purpose of economic and political systems in cultures.

2 Compare and contrast the main types of economic and political systems.

Lesson Plan

1 Engage

Warm-Up Activity

Discuss with students their answers to the following questions: What do they do when they want a glass of milk? How does milk get from the cow to their glass? Who owns the cows? Who owns the trucks or railroads that move the milk from one place to another? Elicit from students that some people choose to run farms that produce milk that they then sell directly to consumers. Similarly, help students recognize that many of the transportation systems are privately owned as well.

Activating Prior Knowledge

Have students read Reach Into Your Background in the Before You Read box. Have students discuss what they know about voting and whether or not they think the same kind of voting occurs in other nations.

Teaching Resources

📁 **Reproducible Lesson Plan** in the Chapter and Section Resources booklet, p. 54, provides a summary of the section lesson.

📁 **Guided Reading and Review** in the Chapter and Section Resources booklet, p. 55, provides a structure for mastering key concepts and reviewing key terms in the section. Available in Spanish in the Spanish Chapter and Section Resources booklet, p. 34.

Program Resources

📁 **Outline Maps** South Asia: Political, p. 38

Media and Technology

📺 **Color Transparencies** 25, 26, 39, 40, 156

2 Explore

Have students read the section. Then ask them to make a chart that identifies the roles of producers, consumers, and government in the economic systems of capitalism, socialism, and communism. Next, have students make an organizational chart comparing the hierarchies of power in a monarchy, a democracy, and a dictatorship.

3 Teach

Organize students into six groups and assign each group one of the economic or political systems discussed in this section. Direct each group to prepare for a "press conference" about their topic. Class members can act as newspaper, magazine, or television reporters, asking group members about the principles, benefits, and disadvantages of their form of government or economic system. This activity should take about an hour.

READ ACTIVELY

Connect Think about each member of your family and what he or she does. Is each a consumer, a producer, or both? Explain why.

not bother with such small loans. In 1976, Yunnus decided to do something about this situation. He started up a bank to loan small amounts of money only to poor people. Every borrower must join a group of five people. Every group member is responsible for the loans of every other member, so members must all trust and help each other. To build trust, they meet once a week to talk over their problems.

Yunnus's bank is called the Grameen Bank, which means "village bank." Today, the Grameen Bank has more than 1,000 offices and has loaned money to 2 million customers. Its interest rates are fairly high, but 98 percent of its loans are paid back. People in other countries are starting banks like Grameen. There are even some in the United States.

Economic Systems

Banks like the Grameen help people become productive members of their nation's economy. An **economy** is a system for producing, distributing, and consuming goods and services. Owners and workers are **producers.** They make products, such as bamboo baskets or automobiles. Those products are called **goods.** Some products are really **services** that producers perform for other people. They may style hair, provide hotel rooms, or heal diseases. **Consumers** are people who buy and use the goods and services.

There are two categories of businesses. Basic businesses are essential for a nation to function. They include things like transportation, television, banks, and mining. Non-basic industries are "nice but not necessary." They may make products such as compact disks or sports equipment. Services can also be basic or non-basic businesses. Hospitals are basic businesses. Singing telegram companies are non-basic businesses.

◀▼ Neighbors in the New York town of Ithaca have a very interesting system of exchange. Instead of paying dollars, they trade "Ithaca Hours" for goods like fresh bread, as well as for services like baby-sitting. Each hour is worth $10—the average hourly wage in Ithaca. "Prices" depend on the amount of labor involved in producing the good or service.

Resource Directory

Teaching Resources

📁 **Drawing Conclusions** in the Social Studies and Geography skills booklet, p. 52, provides additional skill practice.

Media and Technology

💿 **Planet Earth** CD-ROM includes Thematic Maps: Wealth, GNP which enhances students' comprehension of world economics.

Capitalism Replaces Communism

This photograph was taken in Berlin shortly after Communist East Germany united with capitalist West Germany. These East German children had never seen so many different school supplies before. The supplies came from the West, where the free market forces businesses to compete for customers.

Cultures choose the way they want to organize their economies. Today, most cultures choose from three basic systems: *capitalism, socialism,* and *communism.*

In **capitalism,** most basic and non-basic businesses are privately owned. Workers produce the goods or services. When a company sells its products, it earns profits, or money. The owners decide how much to pay workers and how to use profits.

The consumer is important in capitalism. Companies make products, but consumers might refuse to buy them. Successful companies supply goods or services that consumers need, want, and can afford. Capitalist countries include the United States, South Africa, and Japan. Capitalism is also called a free-market economy.

In **socialism,** the government owns most basic industries. It runs them for the good of society, not for profit. The government decides how much to pay workers and how much to charge for goods. It uses profits to pay for services such as health and education. Non-basic industries and services follow the capitalist model. They are privately owned, and consumers decide which products to buy. A few countries follow socialism or have socialistic programs. These countries include Spain, Portugal, and Italy.

READ ACTIVELY

Predict What do you think the three basic types of economic systems are?

LINKS ACROSS THE WORLD

Quebec In Quebec, a province in Canada, many people are descendants of French settlers. So, they speak both French and English. Some residents want Quebec to become a separate nation. This has led to much political debate. Canada is a democracy, so residents of Quebec could vote on the issue. For now, Quebec has decided to remain part of Canada, but the argument continues.

READ ACTIVELY

Ask Questions What would you like to find out about different kinds of government?

In **communism,** the government owns all basic and non-basic industries. It provides all goods and services that people need. It also decides what is produced, how much workers will be paid, and how much everything will cost. Today, only a few of the world's nations practice communism. They include Cuba, China, and North Korea.

Hardly any nation has a "pure" economic system. For example, the United States has a capitalistic economy. However, state, local, and federal governments provide educational services, build and repair roads, and regulate product safety. In communist countries, you will find some private businesses such as small farms and special stores.

Political Systems

Small groups of people can work together to solve problems that affect them all. But that is impossible in complex cultures. Still, they also have to resolve conflicts between individuals and social groups. People also need protection from other countries and cultural groups. Communities need laws, leaders, and organizations that make decisions. **Government** is the system that sets up and enforces a society's laws and institutions. Some governments are controlled by a few people. Others are controlled by many.

STUDENT ART

Lacquer Painting

Olga Loceva
Age 14
Russia
Under communism, traditional Russian arts and crafts, such as lacquer painting of boxes and vases as shown here, were discouraged. Since the collapse of the Soviet Union, many Russians have begun to practice these arts once again. What traditions do you value? How would you feel if the government banned those traditions?

Direct Democracy The earliest governments were probably simple. People lived in small groups and practiced **direct democracy.** That means everyone participated in running the day-to-day affairs of the group. Chiefs or elders decided what was right or what to do. Decisions were based upon the culture's customs and beliefs. Today, government plays much the same role for complex cultures.

Monarchy Until about 100 years ago, one of the most common forms of government was a **monarchy.** In this system, a king or queen rules the government. The ruler inherits the throne by birth. Monarchies still exist today. Sweden, Denmark, Great Britain, Spain, and Swaziland are examples. But the rulers of these countries do not have the power their ancestors did. Instead, they are constitutional monarchs. Their countries have **constitutions,** or sets of laws that define and often limit the government's power. In a constitutional monarchy, the king or queen is often only a symbol of the country.

▲ In Great Britain's constitutional monarchy, the monarch has little authority. The real power is wielded by Parliament, an elected body like our Congress.

Representative Democracy A constitutional monarchy usually is a **representative democracy.** That means citizens elect representatives to run the country's affairs. Democracy comes from the Greek word *demos,* which means "common people." In a democracy, the people hold power to govern and rule indirectly. They elect representatives, who create laws. If the people do not like what a representative does, they can refuse to re-elect that person. They can also work to change laws they do not like. This system ensures that power is shared. The United States, Canada, and Israel are examples of representative democracies.

Dictatorship "If I ruled the world. . . . " Have you ever said or heard those words? It's fun to think about. You could give away free ice cream. You could give 12-year-olds the right to vote. Maybe you could end war and poverty.

◀ Josef Stalin was one of the world's cruelest dictators. He ruled the former Soviet Union from 1929 until 1953. He controlled every aspect of Soviet life and jailed or executed anybody who opposed him.

Of course, no one person rules the world. There are some countries, though, where one person and a small group rules. A person who has almost total power over an entire country is called a **dictator.**

Dictators decide what will happen in their countries. They make the laws. They decide if there will be elections. When dictators take over, they often make promises that sound good. They may promise to end crime or to make a country strong. Sometimes they keep their promises. More often, they do not. Either way, people lose the right to make their own decisions.

SECTION 3 REVIEW

1. Define (a) economy, (b) producer, (c) goods, (d) services, (e) consumer, (f) capitalism, (g) socialism, (h) communism, (i) government, (j) direct democracy, (k) monarchy, (l) constitution, (m) representative democracy, (n) dictator.

2. Describe the three main types of economic systems.

3. Which form of government gives power to make decisions to the greatest number of people—a monarchy, a democracy, or a dictatorship?

Critical Thinking

4. Drawing Conclusions You hear on the news an announcement from the newly elected leader of a foreign country. The announcement states that the country's representatives will not meet. It also says that no elections will be held until further notice. What kind of a government does this country have? How do you know?

Activity

5. Writing to Learn You are working on a project to increase voting in your community. A statewide election is approaching. On behalf of your project, write a letter to a newspaper. In it, describe two reasons why people who are eligible to vote should do so.

Cultural Change

BEFORE YOU READ

Reach Into Your Background

If you like to listen to rap, rock, folk, or jazz music, you like music from many different cultures. The rhythms you like might have come from Ireland, Jamaica, or Peru. You probably like some artists from different countries, too. Name some music you like that you think is a cultural blend.

Questions to Explore

1. What causes cultures to change?

2. Why has the rate of cultural change been increasing?

Key Terms
cultural diffusion
acculturation

Most people think that blue jeans are typical American clothes. But many cultures contributed to them. Blue jeans were created in the United States in the 1800s, by Levi Strauss, a German salesman who went to California. He made the jeans with cloth from France, called *serge de Nîmes*. The name was shortened to denim. Strauss dyed the denim with indigo, a plant from India and China. The indigo colored the denim dark blue.

In the 1980s, the Japanese and the French developed stonewashing. It made brand-new denim jeans look worn. Then, an Italian company created acid-washed jeans. Today, jeans are still popular in America. They are also very popular in Britain, the former Soviet Union, India, and parts of Africa. And the name *jeans*? It's French, for Italian sailors who wore sturdy cotton pants. What is more American than jeans?

Always Something New

Just as jeans have changed over time, so, too, has American culture. Cultures change all the time. Because culture is a total way of life, a change in one part changes other parts. Changes in the natural environment, technology, and new ideas affect culture.

▼ Blue jeans are a popular form of casual wear across the world. These blue-jeans clad dancers are from Barcelona, Spain.

Teaching Resources

 Reproducible Lesson Plan in the Chapter and Section Resources booklet, p. 57, provides a summary of the section lesson.

Guided Reading and Review in the Chapter and Section Resources booklet, p. 58, provides a structure for mastering key concepts and reviewing key terms in the section. Available in Spanish in the Spanish Chapter and Section Resources booklet, p. 36.

Program Resources

Outline Maps The United States: Political, p. 16

Media and Technology

Color Transparency 98

Lesson Objectives

1 Summarize reasons why cultures change.

2 Explain why cultures are changing rapidly today.

3 Evaluate the benefits and problems of rapid cultural change.

Lesson Plan

1 Engage

Warm-Up Activity

Encourage students to list things Americans have today that we did not have 50 years ago. Compile a list on the chalkboard. Ask students to identify which items people in other parts of the world also have.

Activating Prior Knowledge

Have students read Reach Into Your Background in the Before You Read box. List students' suggestions concerning types of music that show a cultural blend.

---

2 Explore

Have students read the section. Work with the class to create a chart titled *Cultural Change* with these headings: *Natural Environment, Technological Changes,* and *New Ideas.* Ask the class for examples of how each has changed cultures. Discuss cultural diffusion and acculturation and ask for examples. Ask students why cultural change can sometimes be negative.

3 Teach

After students have read the chapter, suggest that they form two competing quiz show teams. Each team prepares answers for the opposing team using key terms and main ideas presented in the section. Teams, in turn, respond to the answers by providing the question appropriate to the answer. If a "contestant" cannot respond, or responds incorrectly, the team loses a turn. Correct answers get one point each.

4 Assess

See the answers to the Section Review. You may also use the quiz show answers and responses as an assessment of student understanding of the section and chapter material.

◄ Explorers brought crops native to the Americas, such as corn, squash, potatoes, and tomatoes back to Europe. This greatly changed the diet—and life—of Europeans.

Predict What are some changes that technology has made in our culture in modern times?

A Change in the Environment If the weather changes long enough, the climate will change. That affects the kinds of food people can grow. It affects the kinds of clothes they wear. Changes in climate affect ways of making a living. But other changes can affect a culture, too.

A New Idea New ideas also change a culture. People used to take nature for granted. They thought anyone could use resources without damaging the overall supply. Since the 1950s, people in the United States and all over the world have become concerned about the environment. They recycle and work to protect endangered species and preserve forests. People also realized that we can use up or pollute many natural resources. The desire to save nature is a cultural change.

Technology Equals Change Cultural change has been going on for a long time. New technological discoveries and inventions may have had the most effect on cultures. The discovery of fire helped early people to survive colder climates. When people invented wood and stone tools and weapons, ways of living also changed. Hunters could kill animals such as the mammoth and the giant bear. These animals had been too large to hunt without weapons.

Think of how technology has changed the culture of the United States. Radio and television brought entertainment and news into homes. Such things as TV dinners and instant information are now part of our culture. Computers change how and where people work. Computers even help people live longer. Doctors use computers to treat patients. Radio, television, and computers add new words to our language. *Broadcast, channel surfing,* and *hacker* are three. What other new words can you think of?

Heard It Through the Grapevine People are on the move all over the world. People come to the United States from other countries. Americans travel to other countries. In the process, they all bring new things such as clothing and tools with them. They also bring ideas about such things as ways to fix food, teach children, or worship and govern. Sometimes a culture adopts these new ideas. The movement of customs and ideas is **cultural diffusion.**

The blue jeans story is a good example of cultural diffusion. Jeans were invented in the United States but now are popular around the world. People in other countries changed jeans. People in the United States adopted the changes. The process of accepting, borrowing, and exchanging ideas is called **acculturation.**

You can see cultural diffusion and acculturation if you study the history of baseball. It began as an American sport, but today it is played all over the world. That is an example of cultural diffusion. The Japanese love baseball. However, they changed the game to fit their culture. This change is an example of acculturation. Americans value competition. They focus on winning. But in Japan, a game can end in a tie. The

Tuning In to Cyberspace
Many record companies are now on the Internet. They talk about things like a band's latest musical release and upcoming tours. Some let people hear a band's music before buying it. Some bands have even tried live concerts over the Internet. This could be a big cultural change—listening to live performances at home instead of at a concert!

Working in a Canning Factory, 1912

Immigrants to the United States, like these young workers in a New York canning-factory, came from many different ethnic backgrounds. The mixing of their various cultures produced a new, American culture.

Activity

Interdisciplinary Connections

Music Suggest that the class work in small groups. Each should choose a country or locality that has a distinctive style of music. Direct student groups to find a representative musical selection to present to the class along with some background information on music of that culture. Encourage discussions of how musical styles have influenced each other (cultural diffusion) and how music from foreign cultures has been adapted by the borrowing culture. (An example might be African rhythms and European melody and harmony in American jazz and rock-and-roll.) Tapes can be placed in a classroom listening center for individual use. *Auditory*

Japanese do not mind a tie game for several reasons. For instance, in Japan, how well you play is more important than winning. Also, people try hard not to embarrass someone.

Technology and the Speed of Change

What's the fastest way to get from your house to Japan? A jet plane? A phone call? A television broadcast? The Internet? A fax? All these answers can be right. It depends on whether you want to transport your body, your voice, a picture, an interactive game, or a sheet of paper.

For thousands of years, cultures changed slowly. People moved by foot or wagon or sailing ship, so ideas and technology also moved slowly. Recently, technology has increased the speed of change. People no longer have to wait for a newcomer to bring changes. Faxes and computers transport information almost instantly. Magazines and television shows bring ideas and information from all over the world to every home. This rapid exchange of ideas speeds up cultural change.

A Global Village A village is a small place where people all know each other. It doesn't take long to get from one place to another. Today, many people call the Earth a "global village." That is because modern transportation and communications tell everyone about far-away people, businesses, and governments almost instantly.

Technology has brought many benefits. Computers let scientists share information about how to clean up oil spills. Telephones let us instantly talk to relatives thousands of miles away. In the Australian Outback, students your age use closed-circuit television and two-way radios to go to school in their own homes.

The Exchange Between East and West

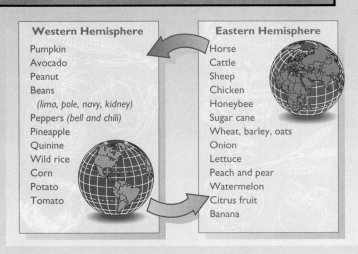

Chart Study Unlike in today's global village, the peoples of North and South America lived in almost complete isolation from Europe and Africa until 1492. When Europeans first settled in the Americas, they brought horses, wheat, and other important products. In return, they brought back to Europe and Africa crops such as potatoes and corn. What familiar food combinations would have been impossible before this exchange?

Western Hemisphere
Pumpkin
Avocado
Peanut
Beans
 (lima, pole, navy, kidney)
Peppers (bell and chili)
Pineapple
Quinine
Wild rice
Corn
Potato
Tomato

Eastern Hemisphere
Horse
Cattle
Sheep
Chicken
Honeybee
Sugar cane
Wheat, barley, oats
Onion
Lettuce
Peach and pear
Watermelon
Citrus fruit
Banana

Keeping Traditions Alive

In recent years, people across the world have made greater efforts to preserve their traditions. In this picture, for example, young people from 20 Native American nations perform a dance at a gathering near Lake Casitas, California. **Critical Thinking** Why do you think it has become more important in recent years for people to preserve their traditions?

Information Overload? Change can help, but it can also hurt. If things change too fast, people can become confused, and culture is threatened. Valuable traditions can disappear. Once important sources of knowledge are lost, they can never be regained. In many parts of the world, people are working to save their own cultures before it is too late. They do not want to lose what is good in their culture. They understand it is important to remember where they came from if they are to understand where they are going.

SECTION 4
REVIEW

1. **Define** (a) cultural diffusion, (b) acculturation.

2. List three things that can cause a culture to change.

3. Explain the meaning of the term "global village."

Critical Thinking
4. **Distinguishing Fact From Opinion** A friend who has a computer tells you she has an e-mail pal in Singapore. "You learn more by having a pen pal on the Internet than by having one through regular mail," she says. You point out that you get drawings and photos in the mail from your pen pal in Turkey. Which of you has stated a fact? Which has stated an opinion? How do you know?

Activity
5. **Writing to Learn** Interview an older person about what changes she or he has seen in the culture over the years. Write two paragraphs summarizing what they say.

Chapter Summary in the Chapter and Section Resources booklet, p. 60, provides a summary of chapter content. Available in Spanish in the Spanish Chapter and Section Resources booklet, p. 38.

Cooperative Learning Activity in the Activities and Projects booklet, pp. 32–35, provides two student handouts, one page of teacher's directions, and a scoring rubric for a cooperative learning activity on making a relief map.

Media and Technology

 Guided Reading Audiotapes (English and Spanish)

Answers to ...

KEEPING TRADITIONS ALIVE

Answers will vary. Most students will suggest that people fear that as the rate of cultural change increases, valued traditional ways may be forgotten.

SKILLS ACTIVITY

Locating Information

Rhonda was puzzled. "Did you hear that?" she whispered to Denise. "He just told me to shrink the panic! What does he mean?" Rhonda and Denise were staying in the home of a family in Argentina, a country in South America. They had traveled there as exchange students. The family had a mother, a father, a young girl, and a teenage boy. Rhonda had just told the teenage boy that she felt nervous about finding her way around.

That's when he turned to her and said, "Achicar el panico! I'll help you." Rhonda knew "achicar el panico" translated as "shrink the panic" in English. But what did it mean? The boy smiled at her puzzled look. "In Argentina, that's how we say 'chill out!'" he said. Rhonda smiled back.

"I get it," she said. "I guess I also need help learning the slang you use here!"

You know that people in different cultures live lives that are very different from yours. But do you know just how different? Even little things like slang can have completely different meanings. Before you travel to another country, it helps to learn as much about its culture as possible. The trick, believe it or not, is to build a pyramid!

Get Ready

This pyramid is not a real pyramid, of course, but a "pyramid of knowledge." There

Pyramid of Information About a Culture

Specific Information
travel books, articles by visitors, interviews with visitors or members of the culture

Somewhat Specific Information
books about the culture, magazine articles about the culture

General Information
encyclopedias, almanacs, atlases

are thousands of sources of information about the peoples and cultures of the world. By organizing your search into the form of a pyramid, you can easily learn what you need to know. You will build your pyramid in a library.

Try It Out

Follow the steps below to build a pyramid of knowledge. As you work, refer to the diagram.

A. Choose a culture to learn about. You might choose a culture in a country in Europe, Latin America, Africa, or Asia.

B. Build a base of general information. Pyramids are built from the bottom up. The base of your pyramid of knowledge about a culture is general information. This includes such things as the correct name of a cultural group, its geographic location, the language the people speak, the population, and so on. Find this information by consulting the sources listed in the diagram of the pyramid.

C. Build the middle of the pyramid with more detailed information. The middle of the pyramid is made up of more detailed information about how people live in the culture. What are schools like? What customs are important? What are some common foods? What types of jobs do people have?

D. Build the top with specific information. Complete the pyramid by building the very top. It is made up of specific information about how individuals in the culture interact. Find out, for example, what proper greetings are and what certain gestures mean. Learn how to say basic phrases such as "How do you do?" and "Good-bye" in the language of the culture. Add specific information about anything else that interests you.

You can see you have learned a great deal about the culture in a short time. It takes a lifetime to develop a deep understanding of any culture. But by building a pyramid and continually adding to it, you can add to what you know.

Apply the Skill

Building a "pyramid of knowledge" is as simple as 1-2-3:

1. **Build the base.**
2. **Build the middle.**
3. **Build the top.**

As the pyramid grows, so does your knowledge. Practice applying this skill the next time you have any assignment requiring research. Find general information first, then more detailed information, and then very specific information. Work your way from the bottom to the top.

2 Explore

After reading the text under Get Ready, discuss the pyramid on the chalkboard. Ask students how they think information sources might be organized on such a diagram (progressing from most general at the bottom to most specific at the top). Invite volunteers to place some of the students' suggested data sources in the pyramid. Then tell students to read the rest of the skills activity.

3 Teach

Organize students into research teams of three to complete the Try It Out exercise. As students **practice** their skills, help them always to focus on information that can be located in available sources. For example, students should be encouraged to select significant world cultures *or* to search for specialized information sources such as museum libraries. Encourage students to share and brainstorm problems and ideas within and across the groups.

For additional reinforcement, ask students to identify a specific example of an information source at each pyramid level.

4 Assess

Students will **apply** their skill on a later assignment. You can **assess,** however, with the pyramids students built in Try It Out. Post each group's pyramid and let the class ask questions of the group members. Evaluate the pyramids and the answers group members provide. Ask each group to identify the sources in which they located their information. Verify that students have logically progressed through the sources taught in the skill pyramid.

CHAPTER 4 Review and Activities

Reviewing Main Ideas

1. Students' answers should include the idea that the culture that develops in a particular environment matches the natural resources available and fits the needs people must satisfy in order to survive in that environment.

2. Students' answers will vary, but should include three of these: use of tools, discovery of fire, agriculture or the agricultural revolution, and the invention of writing.

3. Technology such as terraced land tells about a culture's farming skills and work. Technology such as stone tools also tell about a culture's work. If tools are used to carve images or small statues, they may reveal information about a culture's values.

4. It provided a steady food supply. This allowed birthrates to rise, death rates to fall, and complex societies to farm.

5. Students' answers will vary, but should include three of these: social organization, language, religion, economic system, and political system.

6. Capitalism: basic and nonbasic businesses are privately owned, profits go to businesses, and consumers determine production; **Socialism:** government owns basic businesses, nonbasic businesses are privately owned; **Communism:** government owns all businesses, profits are shared by all, and government determines production

7. Governments were established to resolve conflicts and offer protection.

8. Culture has changed more rapidly in modern times because of the speed of modern communication and travel and the resulting movement of people from one culture to another all over the world.

Reviewing Key Terms

Each sentence should reveal the meaning of the key term through the context.

Reviewing Main Ideas

1. What is the relationship between the environment people live in and their culture?

2. Describe three developments that have affected human culture.

3. Explain how the technology used in a culture reveals things about the culture's daily life, work, and values.

4. Why was the Agricultural Revolution so important in human history? What changes did it bring about?

5. Explain three important ways in which cultures can differ from one another.

6. Compare the three economic systems described in this chapter: capitalism, socialism, and communism.

7. Explain why people formed governments.

8. Why has culture changed more rapidly in modern times than in the past?

Reviewing Key Terms

Use each key term below in a sentence that shows the meaning of the term.

1. culture
2. technology
3. cultural landscape
4. social structure
5. nuclear family
6. extended family
7. economy
8. producer
9. goods
10. services
11. capitalism
12. socialism
13. government
14. constitution
15. representative democracy
16. dictator
17. cultural diffusion
18. acculturation

Critical Thinking

1. Identifying Central Issues Why is no culture exactly like any other culture?

2. Expressing Problems Clearly Why do you think people in one culture sometimes do not understand people in another?

Graphic Organizer

Think about how having less fresh water would affect society. Copy this flowchart. Then choose from these categories: social organization, language, economic system, or government. Fill in the boxes, explaining how a water shortage might affect each category.

Graphic Organizer

Students' answers should accurately show how having less water might affect a social organization, a language, a religion, an economic system, and a government. Sample answer shown.

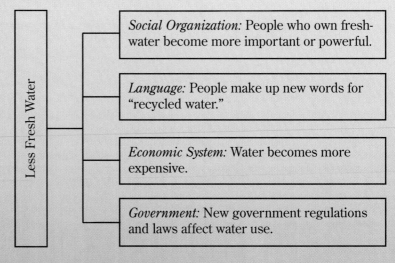

Less Fresh Water

Social Organization: People who own fresh-water become more important or powerful.

Language: People make up new words for "recycled water."

Economic System: Water becomes more expensive.

Government: New government regulations and laws affect water use.

Vocabulary Activity

Many terms in this chapter compare and contrast similar ideas or activities. For instance, in capitalism, businesses are run by private individuals, but in communism, businesses are run by government. On a separate sheet of paper, explain how these terms compare and contrast similar ideas or activities.

1. goods and services

2. direct democracy and representative democracy

3. nuclear family and extended family

Writing Activity

Writing a Public Service Message
Your town or city is going to have a culture fair. The fair will introduce people to new cultures. It will also introduce people to different cultures within the United States. Write a public service message for a local radio station. A public service message includes the time, place, and purpose of a cultural event. Your notice should tell people why and how they should get involved with the culture fair.

Internet Activity

Use a search engine to find the **Human-Languages Page.** Click on **Languages and Literature.** Use the dictionaries and common phrases sections to learn how to say and write a greeting in five languages. Write your greetings, and an English translation, on a sheet of construction paper. Hang your greetings on a class "World Greetings" bulletin board.

Skills Review

Turn to the Skills Activity.
Review the steps for locating information. Then complete the following: (a) How can building a pyramid of knowledge help you to locate information? (b) Explain the difference between general information and specific information.

How Am I Doing?

Answer these questions to help you check your progress.

1. Do I understand how environment affects culture and that culture affects environment?
2. Can I list the major elements of culture and the forms that they take?
3. Can I describe the ways that cultures change?
4. What information from this chapter can I use in my unit project?

Internet Activity

If students are having difficulty finding this site, you may wish to have them use the following URL, which was accurate at the time this textbook was published:

> **http://www.willamette. edu/~tjones/ Language-Page.html**

You might also guide students to a search engine. Four of the most useful are Infoseek, AltaVista, Lycos, and Yahoo. For additional suggestions on using the Internet, refer to the Prentice Hall Social Studies' Educator's Handbook "Using the Internet," in the *Prentice*

Hall World Explorer Program Resources.

For additional links to world history and culture topics, visit the Prentice Hall Home Page at:
> **http://www.phschool.com**

How Am I Doing?

Point out to students that this checklist is just a quick reminder for them of what they learned in the chapter. If their answer to any of the questions is *no* or if they are unsure, they may need to review the topic.

Vocabulary Activity

Students' explanations should be consistent with comparisons and contrasts presented in the text.

Critical Thinking

1. Students' answers should include the idea that each culture is unique because it developed to meet the specific needs of people in a specific environment.

2. Students' answers should show an awareness that people are so used to their own ways of doing things that other people's ways seem a bit strange to them.

Skills Review

Students' answers will vary. However, every student should do the following: After choosing a country, write at the base of the pyramid general information about the chosen culture; in the middle, more detailed information; and at the top, specifics about how individuals in the culture interact.

Writing Activity

Students' messages should include good reasons why people would enjoy learning about other cultures.

Resource Directory

Teaching Resources

 Chapter Tests Forms A and B are in the Tests booklet, pp. 20–25.

Program Resources

Writing Process Handbook includes Organizing Material in a Logical Sequence, pp. 23–24, to help students with the Writing Activity.

Media and Technology

Color Transparencies
Color Transparency 174 (Graphic organizer table template)

Prentice Hall Writer's Solution Writing Lab CD-ROM

Computer Test Bank

Resource Pro™ CD-ROM

Lesson Objectives

1. Explain a poem about a special place in nature.

2. Link a literary work to the geography theme of *place*.

Lesson Plan

1 Engage

Building Vocabulary

Point out that notes in the margin can help students understand certain words and can give helpful hints as students read.

Vocabulary words defined in the margin include *glacial, bottomlands,* and *tendril*.

Activating Prior Knowledge

Ask students to explain the geography theme of *place*. Blend their suggestions into a class definition and record this on the chalkboard. Then read the text under Before You Read. Encourage students to describe a special place in their lives. Link their descriptions to the *place* theme defined on the chalkboard.

2 Develop Student Reading

Explain that poetry readers should not pause at the ends of lines lacking punctuation. Invite a volunteer to read the poem aloud as the class follows along. Identify the margin question and definitions as helpful resources.

Rough Country

BY DANA GIOIA

Reach Into Your Background

Think about the area where you live. It has many characteristics that make it unique. Perhaps there is a flood plain, hills, flat land, or an earthquake fault. Perhaps there are special stores or restaurants in your neighborhood. Perhaps the people who live there speak several languages. Or, perhaps, when you first think about it, you cannot see anything about your neighborhood that is different from anywhere else.

Most people are so used to their surroundings that they do not pay any attention to them. But Dana Gioia goes into great detail to explain why "Rough Country" is a very special place. As you read the poem, notice how Gioia emphasizes the unique nature of "Rough Country."

Questions to Explore

1. What characteristics make the country described in the poem "rough"?

2. What is so special about this spot in the country?

Rough Country

Give me a landscape made of obstacles,
of steep hills and jutting glacial rock,
where the low-running streams are quick to flood
the grassy fields and bottomlands.
                A place
no engineers can master—where the roads
must twist like tendrils up the mountainside
on narrow cliffs where boulders block the way.

Where tall black trunks of lightning-scalded pine
push through the tangled woods to make a roost
for hawks and swarming crows.
                And sharp inclines
where twisting through the thorn-thick underbrush,
scratched and exhausted, one turns suddenly
to find an unexpected waterfall,

glacial (GLAY shul) *adj.* from a glacier; here, rocks left behind by a glacier
bottomlands *n.* low land through which a river flows; flood plain
tendril (TEN drihl) *n.* thread-like part of a climbing plant that supports the plant

Resource Directory

Program Resources

Material in the **Primary Sources and Literature Readings** booklet provides additional literature selections related to the concepts under study.

not half a mile from the nearest road,
a spot so hard to reach that no one comes—

a hiding place, a shrine for dragonflies
and nesting jays, a sign that there is still
one piece of property that won't be owned.

READ ACTIVELY

Visualize What does this place look like in your mind's eye?

◀▼ Where do you call home? Some people live in the Canadian Rockies, and others live in Washington farmlands. What unique features might you find if you lived in those places?

▲ What might you find if you lived in Chicago, Illinois?

EXPLORING YOUR READING

Look Back
1. What human activities would be difficult or impossible in this place?

Think It Over
2. In the fourth stanza of "Rough Country," the poet describes a hike that suddenly opens onto a waterfall. What makes the waterfall seem especially beautiful to the poet?

Go Beyond
3. In "Rough Country," the poet describes "one piece of property that won't be owned." Antarctica is another place that no one "owns." No country can claim any part of it. Why might people think a place was so important that no one should own it?

Ideas for Writing: Poem
4. Think about the place where you live. Make a list of its characteristics, and draw a picture of it. Then, write a poem about your place. Finally, compare your poem with "Rough Country."

3 Assess

Evaluate students' responses in a class discussion of Exploring Your Reading.

1. Possible answers: Any activity requiring flat ground, electricity, buildings, or moving goods.
2. It is unexpected and private.
3. Possible answer: The place is so unique that all humans should share access to its data and resources while also sharing the responsibility of protecting it.
4. Acceptable poems will identify and describe a specific place. Outstanding poems will use vivid language.

Background

About the Author

Dana Gioia, poet and onetime vice president of General Foods, was born in Los Angeles in 1950. Although Gioia's Harvard education focused on comparative literature, he opted instead to collect a business degree from Stanford. Throughout his studies and his duties for marketing Kool-Aid®, Gioia set aside time for poetry. He writes for general readers in the hopes of bringing poetry to a wider audience.

About the Selection

"Rough Country" appears in *Wherever Home Begins: 100 Contemporary Poems,* selected by Paul B. Janeczko (New York: Orchard Books, 1995). All the poems in the collection address the theme of *place* and its importance to us as humans.

Earth's Natural Resources

To help you plan instruction, the chart below shows how teaching resources correspond to chapter content. Use the resources to vary instruction, add activities, or plan block schedules. Where appropriate, resources have **suggested time allotments** for students. Time allotments are approximate.

Managing Time and Instruction

	Geography: Tools and Concepts Teaching Resources Binder		World Explorer Program Resources Binder	
	Resource	**mins.**	**Resource**	**mins.**
SECTION 1 **What Are Natural Resources?**	**Chapter and Section Support** Reproducible Lesson Plan, p. 66 Ⓢ Guided Reading and Review, p. 67 Ⓢ Section Quiz, p. 68 **Social Studies and Geography Skills,** Reading a Natural Resources Map, p. 34	20 25 30	**Outline Maps** The World: Political, p. 3 **Nystrom Desk Atlas** Ⓣ Primary Sources and Literature Readings **Writing Process Handbook** Writing Effective Paragraphs, pp. 27–28 **Environmental and Global Issues** Topic: Water, pp. 43–48	20 40 25 30
SKILLS ACTIVITY **Writing for a Purpose**	**Social Studies and Geography Skills,** Writing to Persuade, p. 89	30		
2 SECTION 2 **How People Use the Land**	**Chapter and Section Support** Reproducible Lesson Plan, p. 69 Ⓢ Guided Reading and Review, p. 70 Ⓢ Section Quiz, p. 71	20 25	**Outline Maps** East Asia: Physical, p. 40 The World: Political, p. 5 **Environmental and Global Issues** Topic: Energy and Resources, pp. 2–7	20 20 30
3 SECTION 3 **People's Effect on the Environment**	**Chapter and Section Support** Reproducible Lesson Plan, p. 72 Ⓢ Guided Reading and Review, p. 73 Ⓢ Section Quiz, p. 74 Ⓢ Vocabulary, p. 76 Critical Thinking Activity, p. 79 Reteaching, p. 77 Enrichment, p. 78 Ⓢ Chapter Summary, p. 75 **Tests** Forms A and B Chapter Tests, pp. 26–31 Forms A and B Final Exams, pp. 32–37	20 25 20 30 25 25 15 40 40	**Environmental and Global Issues** Topic: Environmental Destruction, pp. 14–19 Topic: Waste Disposal and Recycling, pp. 31–36 Ⓣ Interdisciplinary Explorations *Where River Meets Sea: Estuaries at Risk* *Fate of the Rain Forest*	30 30 40 40

Block Scheduling Folder
PROGRAM TEACHING RESOURCES

Activities and Projects

Block Scheduling Program Support

Interdisciplinary Links

Resource Pro™ CD-ROM

Media and Technology

Assessment Opportunities

From Guiding Questions to Assessment A series of Guiding Questions serves as an organizing framework for this book. The Guiding Question that relates to this chapter is below. Section Reviews and Section Quizzes provide opportunities for assessing students' insights into these Guiding Questions. Additional assessments are listed below.

Media and Technology

Resource	mins.
(◄►) 🖸 Ⓢ **World Video Explorer**	20
🖸 **Planet Earth CD-ROM**	20
🖵 **Color Transparencies 6, 9, 10, 11, 13, 14,**	
41, 44, 45, 46, 111, 112	20
🖵 **Color Transparencies 9, 10, 11, 15, 17**	20
🖸 **Planet Earth CD-ROM**	20
🖵 **Color Transparencies 13, 14, 15, 16,**	
113, 114	20
🎧 Ⓢ **Guided Reading Audiotapes**	20
🖵 **Color Transparency 174**	
(Graphic organizer table template)	20
🖸 **The Writer's Solution CD-ROM**	30
🖫 **Computer Test Bank**	30

Ⓣ **Teaming Opportunity**
This resource is especially well-suited for teaching teams.

Ⓢ **Spanish**
This resource is also in Spanish support.

🖸 **CD-ROM**
🖸 **Laserdisc**
🖵 **Transparency**
🖫 **Software**
(◄►) **Videotape**
🎧 **Audiotape**

GUIDING QUESTION

- *How do people use the world's resources?*

ASSESSMENTS

Section 1

Students should be able to give an oral presentation describing different kinds of natural resources.

▶ **RUBRIC** See the Assessment booklet for a rubric on assessing an oral presentation.

Section 2

Students should be able to create a chart that names and defines the stages of economic development.

▶ **RUBRIC** See the Assessment booklet for a rubric on assessing charts.

Section 3

Students should be able to write a letter to the editor describing people's effect on the environment.

▶ **RUBRIC** See the Assessment booklet for a rubric on assessing a letter to the editor.

Activities and Projects

Mental Mapping

Changing the Land Ask students to discuss some of the ways people use land and water. Be sure they mention land uses such as building houses; farming and mining; factories; parks; trees for lumber; power plants and roads; and parking lots. Point out that people may use water for fishing, transportation, and making electricity.

Discuss the ways that these uses change the land. Farming may involve removing trees or natural grassland and bringing in water and new types of plants, for example.

Have students draw maps of a community showing some or all of these uses of land and water. Ask them to think about ways to show these different kinds of uses on a map. Tell them to create a key that will help people using the map understand it.

Links to Current Events

Recognizing Sources of Conflict Explain that people often have conflicting ideas about the use of resources. People disagree about how to use water, land, minerals, and other natural resources. Ask students to offer some examples of points of view about the use of natural resources. Examples may include whether land should be used for farming or parking lots, but may also include disagreements about what kinds of chemicals farmers can use on their crops.

Have students look through newspapers, news magazines, and other periodicals for examples of different opinions about natural resources. Ask students to clip or photocopy one article about a conflict. Have them summarize the main points of the conflict and list the organizations involved.

Hands-On Activities

Natural Resource Show and Tell Ask students to name some natural resources that they use or that are part of things they use. They may mention foods, metal, electric power, oil, cotton, and other materials.

Have each student find, either at home or in the classroom, an object that is made of a natural resource.

Give students a chance to display their objects, and name the natural resource. Ask students whether they think the object could have been produced using local natural resources or whether it came from another part of the country or the world.

Natural Resources Symbols
Tell students that maps that show natural resources often use symbols, or small pictures, to represent different resources. For example, a single fish might stand for a fishing area. Have students find out what the natural resources of their state are. Invite them to create symbols for these natural resources. Capable students may want to add the symbols to a map of the state. *English Language Learners*

Land-Use Policies States, counties, and communities have different rules and laws for ways people and businesses can use land and water. For example, people probably cannot build a factory near houses. People cannot keep cows in their backyards in most suburban neighborhoods. Have students find out the local laws and rules that govern what people and businesses can and cannot do. Ask them to summarize what they find out on a chart or poster. *Challenging*

Effects on the Environment
Take a field walk with students in the area immediately surrounding your school. As they walk, ask students to note the ways that people have changed the environment. When you return to the classroom, ask students to draw "before" and "after" pictures of the area. Students may choose the time of their "before" picture; it may be before any human beings at all, before the arrival of Europeans, or simply right before the school was built. *Basic*

Natural Resources Brochure
Natural resources often become a source of work and business in a region. Some businesses locate in a certain area because it has natural resources important to that business. For example, good transportation routes and plenty of lumber might make a community appealing to a furniture manufacturer. Businesses bring jobs and money to a community. Ask students to write a brochure describing the natural resources of a community that might make a business want to move there. *Average*

This page can help you extend your own and students' understanding of the concepts in this chapter. You may want to browse through some of the suggestions in the **Bibliography. Interdisciplinary Links** can connect social studies understandings to areas elsewhere in the curriculum through the use of other Prentice Hall products. **National Geography Standards** reflected specifically in this chapter are listed for your convenience. Some hints about appropriate **Internet Access** are also provided. **School to Careers** provides insights into the practical uses of some of the concepts in this chapter as they might pertain to various careers.

BIBLIOGRAPHY

FOR THE TEACHER

Fisher, Maxine P. *Women in the Third World.* Franklin Watts, 1989.

Keene, Ann T. *Earthkeepers: Observers and Protectors of Nature.* Oxford, 1993.

Minds-On Science: For the Sake of the Nation. Smithsonian Institution/ Tom Snyder Productions, 1995. Videodisc.

FOR THE STUDENT

Easy

Cone, Molly. *Come Back, Salmon: How a Group of Dedicated Kids Adopted Pigeon Creek and Brought It Back to Life.* Sierra Club, 1992.

Average

McVey, Vicki. *Sierra Club Kid's Guide to Planet Care and Repair.* Sierra Club, 1993.

Challenging

Klass, David. *California Blue.* Scholastic, 1994.

Rybolt, Thomas R. *Environmental Experiments About Life.* Enslow, 1993.

LITERATURE CONNECTION

George, Jean Craighead. *Everglades.* HarperCollins, 1995.

Yolen, Jane. *Letting Swift River Go.* Little Brown, 1991.

INTERDISCIPLINARY LINKS

Subject	Theme: Preservation
MATH	Course 1, Chapter 5, **Investigation: Mountains of Garbage** Course 2, Lesson 4-7, **Make a Table**
SCIENCE	Prentice Hall Science *Earth's Natural Resources*, Lesson 2-1, **Land and Soil Resources**, Lesson 2-2 **Water Resources** *Dynamic Earth*, Gazette, **Wasting Time: The Nuclear Clock Ticks Down**
LANGUAGE ARTS	Choices in Literature *The Me You See*, **A Ribbon for Baldy** Prentice Hall Literature *Copper*, **Letter to the U.S. Government** *Copper*, **The Hatchling Turtles**

NATIONAL GEOGRAPHY STANDARDS

Students explore the 18 National Geography Standards throughout *Geography: Tools and Concepts.* Chapter 5, however, concentrates on investigating the following standards: 1, 3, 4, 5, 6, 8, 9, 10, 11, 12, 13, 14, 15, 16, 17, 18. For a complete list of the standards, see the *Teacher's Flexible Planning Guide.*

SCHOOL TO CAREERS

In Chapter 5, Earth's Natural Resources, students learn about the environment and human impact on it. Additionally, they address the skill of writing for a purpose. Understanding natural resources can help students prepare for careers in many fields such as politics, farming, park management, and so on. Writing for a purpose is a skill particularly useful for writers, editors, journalists, politicians, and others. The curriculum presented in this book, as in all eight titles of Prentice Hall's *World Explorer* program, is designed to prepare students not only for careers but also for good citizenship—of the world as well as of this country.

INTERNET ACCESS

Many social studies teachers and students use Internet browsers, or search engines, to investigate particular topics. For the best results, use narrow rather than broad topics. Try these for Chapter 5: natural resources, fossil fuels, global warming, deforestation. Finding age-appropriate sites is an important consideration when using the Internet. For links to age-appropriate sites in world studies and geography, visit the Prentice Hall Home Page at: **http://www.phschool.com**

Connecting to the Guiding Questions

As students complete this chapter, they will focus on the ways people use the Earth's renewable and nonrenewable resources. Further, students will be introduced to central issues concerning the ways in which human activity affects the environment. Content in this chapter thus corresponds to this Guiding Question:

- How do people use the world's resources?

Using Picture Activities

Discuss with students what they see in the picture that they would characterize as "natural" and what items show the influence of humans.

- Lists should include advantages such as electricity, industry, jobs, and flood control; disadvantages such as the destruction of natural landscape and the relocation of settlements.

- Students' lists should include forests and water resources.

Heterogeneous Groups

The following Teacher's Edition strategies are suitable for heterogeneous groups.

Interdisciplinary Connections

CHAPTER 5

Earth's Natural Resources

SECTION 1
What Are Natural Resources?

SECTION 2
How People Use the Land

SECTION 3
People's Effect on the Environment

PICTURE ACTIVITIES

Think of the power of a water-fall as it tumbles from high places to low ones. Today, dams like this one on the Brazil-Paraguay border create water-falls. In the process, they harness river power to create electricity for homes and businesses. This helps economies grow. A dam across a river also has a huge effect on the environment. The dam holds back the water of the river. It floods acres of land and creates a lake. Sometimes such lakes flood forests, farmland, and even towns and villages.

Examine both sides of an issue
Think about how this dam changes the natural landscape and how it helps people. Make a list of the advantages and disadvantages of such a project.

Study the picture
Each country has natural resources. From this picture, what resources do you think Brazil has? As you read this chapter, think about how a country's wealth relates to its land and climates.

Resource Directory

Media and Technology

Fossil Fuels, from the World Video Explorer, enhances students' understanding of the effects of burning fossil fuels and of energy alternatives.

Endangered Soil, from the World Video Explorer, enhances students' understanding of soil as a natural resource.

What Are Natural Resources?

Reach Into Your Background
How much do you throw away each day? How much do you recycle? What do you own that is made of recycled material? Jot down your answers.

Questions to Explore
1. What are natural resources?
2. What is the difference between renewable and nonrenewable natural resources?

Key Terms
natural resource
raw material
recyclable resource
renewable resource
nonrenewable resource
fossil fuel

What can we do with the garbage we create? People are searching for answers. Some are unique. In 1995, architect Kate Warner built a house in Martha's Vineyard, Massachusetts. She used materials most people call trash. The builders mixed concrete with ash left over from furnaces that burn trash. Then they used the mixture to make the foundation of the house. To make the frame of the house, they used wood left over from old buildings, not fresh lumber. Warner wanted glass tiles in the bathroom. So she had glassmakers create them out of old car windshields. "We ask people to recycle, but then we don't know what to do with the stuff," Warner says. "By making use of waste materials, the manufacturers of these new building materials are creating exciting new markets and completing a loop." In this loop, materials are used over and over again. Garbage becomes a natural resource.

▼ Factories make new steel for bicycles and buildings by combining iron and other natural resources with recycled or "scrap" steel.

Natural Resources

Kate Warner is one of many people who want to use the Earth's natural resources wisely. These people believe this is the only way for humans to survive. A **natural resource** is any useful material found in the environment. Usually when people talk about natural resources, they mean such things as soil, water, minerals, and vegetation. A natural resource, then, is anything from the Earth that helps meet people's needs for food, clothing, and shelter.

2 Explore

Direct students to read the section. Encourage them to look for answers to questions such as these: Why do people need natural resources? How are some natural resources changed before they are used? What happens if a renewable resource is not replaced? Why is it a good idea to use recycled materials? Why have people started looking for new energy resources?

3 Teach

Have students identify the basic materials they see around them in the classroom and create a chart with the following column headings:
• Item
• Wood, Metal, or Plastic?
• Renewable or Nonrenewable Resource?
• Recyclable?
• Energy Resources Used to Produce?

Ask students to indicate whether each item is from a renewable or nonrenewable resource and whether it can be recycled or not. Then have them describe the energy resources that were used to produce each item. Use completed charts as a basis for discussion about how resources are used in your society. This activity should take about 30 minutes.

Answers to ...
MAP STUDY

Most natural resources must be changed before they can be sold for profit. Not all countries have well developed industries to perform such tasks.

The World: Natural Resources

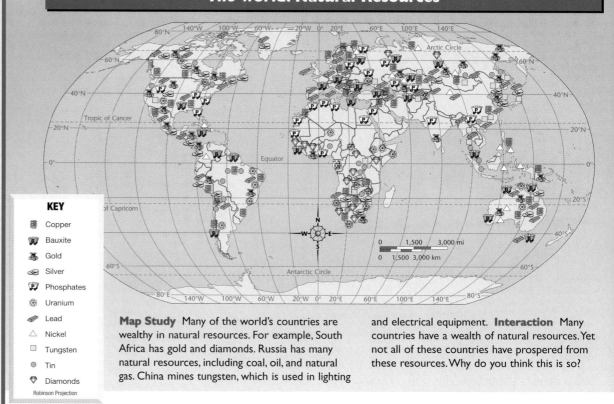

KEY
- Copper
- Bauxite
- Gold
- Silver
- Phosphates
- Uranium
- Lead
- Nickel
- Tungsten
- Tin
- Diamonds

Robinson Projection

Map Study Many of the world's countries are wealthy in natural resources. For example, South Africa has gold and diamonds. Russia has many natural resources, including coal, oil, and natural gas. China mines tungsten, which is used in lighting and electrical equipment. **Interaction** Many countries have a wealth of natural resources. Yet not all of these countries have prospered from these resources. Why do you think this is so?

All people need food, clothing, and shelter to survive. People drink water. People eat the food that the soil produces. So do the animals that provide eggs, cheese, and meat. People get such things as fish and salt from the ocean. Homes are made from wood, clay, and steel. Every day you benefit from the natural resources in the environment.

People can use some resources just the way they come from nature. Fresh water is one. But most resources must be changed before people use them. For example, people cannot just go out and cut down a tree to make a house. Even if they want to build a log cabin, they must cut the tree into pieces first. For a modern home, the wood must have the bark shaved away. Then the wood is cut into boards of various sizes. Resources that must be altered, or changed, before they can be used are called **raw materials.** Trees are the raw material for paper and wood.

Three Kinds of Resources The environment is full of natural resources. But all resources are not alike. Geographers divide them into three groups. The first group of resources cycle naturally through the environment. They do so because of the way the Earth works. In the water cycle, water evaporates into the air and falls as rain, snow, hail, or sleet. This happens over and over again. Therefore, the Earth has the

---

Resource Directory

Teaching Resources

📁 **Reading a Natural Resources Map** in the Social Studies and Geography Skills booklet, p. 34, provides additional skill practice.

Program Resources

Nystrom Desk Atlas
📁 **Environmental and Global Issues** Topic: Water, pp. 43–48

same amount of water, although there may be too much of it in some places and not enough in others. For this reason, geographers call water a **recyclable resource.** Some other materials that cycle through natural processes as recyclable resources are nitrogen and carbon.

A second group of resources includes trees and other living things on the Earth. These things are different from recyclable resources. It is possible for people to gather plants or hunt animals until they no longer exist. But it does not have to happen. For example, a timber company may cut down all the trees in an area. But the company may then plant new trees to replace the ones they cut. Every day the people of the world eat many chickens and ears of corn. But farmers and chicken ranchers make sure there are always more corn plants and baby chicks to replace the ones people eat. If a resource can be replaced, it is called a **renewable resource.** If people are careful, they can have a steady supply of renewable resources.

The third group of resources is called **nonrenewable resources.** When they are used up, they cannot be replaced. Most nonliving things, such as minerals, coal, natural gas, and petroleum—or oil—are nonrenewable resources. So are metals. City recycling programs are often eager to recycle aluminum cans and plastic bottles. That is because these cans and bottles are made of nonrenewable resources.

Ancient Energy: Fossil Fuel   Often people take some things for granted. Lights turn on when a switch is flicked. The house is warm in winter or cool in summer. The car runs. All of these things require

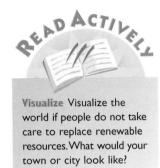

READ ACTIVELY

Visualize Visualize the world if people do not take care to replace renewable resources. What would your town or city look like?

Rain Forests: A Nonrenewable Resource

Rain forests once covered millions of acres in Asia. Today, the rain forests of Asia are rapidly disappearing. Using heavy equipment to harvest the most valuable woods, loggers often damage huge areas of forest. In this photograph of the Malaysian rain forest, notice the sawmills that process the valuable tropical lumber and the roads that carry the wood out of the area. Once this rain forest is cut down, it will be very difficult to replace.

Media and Technology

Planet Earth CD-ROM includes
Countries: Economy which allows students to explore a country's resources.
Color Transparencies 6, 9, 10, 11, 13, 14, 41, 44, 45, 46, 111, 112

Ask students to work in groups of four. Have them determine what materials were used to produce the clothing they wear. Ask them to trace the process from raw materials, such as cotton plants, to finished garments. Suggest that one student can look for information on textile manufacturing in resource books. A second student can describe the energy resources used in the process, identifying them as recyclable, renewable, or nonrenewable. Two students can work together to develop text and pictures for a poster or bulletin board display that describes their findings.

Kinesthetic

fossil fuels, which include coal, natural gas, and petroleum. Fossil fuels were created over millions of years from the remains of prehistoric plants and animals. These fuels are no longer being created. As a result, fossil fuels are nonrenewable resources. If people continue using coal, natural gas, and petroleum at today's rate, the Earth will run out of fossil fuels in 100 to 200 years.

A Special Resource: Energy

Imagine that you are in your room, reading your geography book. What items around you require energy? Some are obvious. A clock, a radio, or a lamp all use energy directly, in a form called electricity. Others are not so obvious because they use energy indirectly. Consider a water glass on a dresser or athletic shoes on the floor. These things were manufactured in a factory, and that process uses energy.

What about things made of plastic—a toy, a comb, or a pen? If you have a rug, it may be made of a synthetic material that looks like wool but is really a kind of plastic. These things are manufactured, so they use energy indirectly. But they also use energy directly. The reason is that plastics are made from petroleum, and petroleum is an energy source.

Getting everything to your room required energy, too. Your family bought them at a store, so you used energy to travel back and forth. The store bought them from a manufacturer, which required more energy. It takes a great deal of energy to put a small plastic glass in your room. So it is easy to see why people value energy sources so highly.

Energy "Have's" and "Have Not's" Everyone in the world needs energy. But energy resources are not evenly spread around the world. Certain areas are rich in some energy resources. Others have very few.

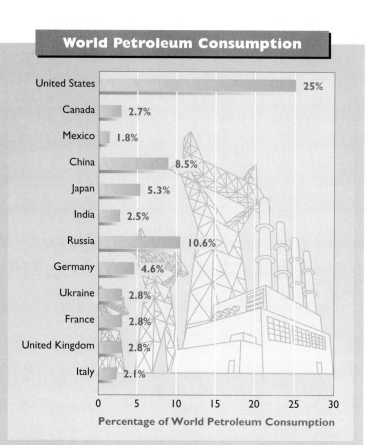

World Petroleum Consumption

Country	Percentage
United States	25%
Canada	2.7%
Mexico	1.8%
China	8.5%
Japan	5.3%
India	2.5%
Russia	10.6%
Germany	4.6%
Ukraine	2.8%
France	2.8%
United Kingdom	2.8%
Italy	2.1%

Percentage of World Petroleum Consumption

Chart Study Products made from petroleum are used to provide heat for buildings and power for automobiles, airplanes, and factories. People use so much petroleum that experts think that world supplies will be almost exhausted by about the mid-2000s. **Critical Thinking** What countries consume the most petroleum? Think of some ways that these countries could reduce their consumption of petroleum.

Answers to ...

CHART STUDY

The United States, Russia, and China; They could use more renewable forms of energy, such as hydroelectric and solar power.

108   CHAPTER 5

World Petroleum Production

Chart Study Petroleum is a nonrenewable resource, one that cannot be replaced once it is used. As a result, it is very valuable. Countries that have deposits can sell petroleum for a profit. **Critical Thinking** Compare this chart with the one on the previous page. Notice that the United States uses about twice as much petroleum as it produces. How does Russia's production compare with its consumption?

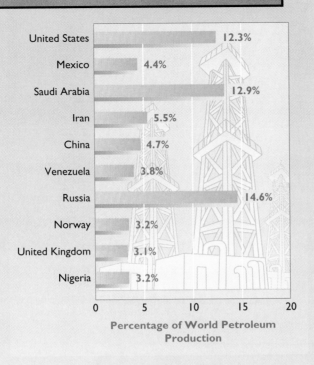

Country	Percentage
United States	12.3%
Mexico	4.4%
Saudi Arabia	12.9%
Iran	5.5%
China	4.7%
Venezuela	3.8%
Russia	14.6%
Norway	3.2%
United Kingdom	3.1%
Nigeria	3.2%

Percentage of World Petroleum Production

Countries like Saudi Arabia and Mexico have huge amounts of oil. Others, like the United States and China, have coal and natural gas. Countries with many rivers, such as the countries of Northwestern Europe, can use water energy to create electricity. Others, such as Japan, have very few energy sources. These countries must buy their energy from other countries.

Growing Needs and the Search for New Supplies In 1973, members of the Organization of Petroleum Exporting Countries (OPEC) decided to sell less of their oil. In the United States, this caused a shortage of gasoline, which is made from oil. When there is a shortage of something, it is more expensive. The price of gas more than doubled. Drivers sat in long lines at gas stations. Companies that used fuel oil to make electricity sent notices to families and businesses. The notices asked people to use as little electricity as possible. How could OPEC members have such an effect on the United States?

The answer is that just because a country uses large amounts of energy does not mean that country has its own large energy resources. The biggest users of energy are industrial countries like the United States and the nations of Western Europe. Japan, which has few petroleum resources of its own, uses over twice as much energy as all of

READ ACTIVELY

Connect What things can you and your family do to use fewer fossils fuels in your everyday life?

Oil From Under the Ocean

In the chilly waters of the North Sea, European companies drill deep wells to tap the area's large oil deposits. Increased production of North Sea oil may reduce the world's demand for oil from Southwest Asia. **Critical Thinking** How might technological improvements such as more modern drilling rigs cut the cost of oil?

Africa. If a country does not have enough energy resources of its own, it must buy them from other countries. In the 1970s, the United States used so much energy that it had to buy oil from OPEC members. When they limited the supply of oil, they could charge much more for their product. The United States had to pay whatever the producing country asked. The oil shortages of the 1970s made people see they needed to find more sources of energy, including petroleum.

SECTION 1 REVIEW

1. Define (a) natural resource, (b) raw material, (c) recyclable resource, (d) renewable resource, (e) nonrenewable resource, (f) fossil fuel.

2. (a) Name two renewable resources. (b) What are two nonrenewable resources?

3. Name some ways that people use fossil fuels.

4. What is the difference between indirect energy use and direct energy use?

Critical Thinking

5. Expressing Problems Clearly Explain why people must be careful about how they use nonrenewable resources.

Activity

6. Writing to Learn Early pioneers in North America used forests and grasslands as they pleased. Write a paragraph explaining why it might have been less important then to replace those resources.

Resource Directory

Teaching Resources

Section Quiz in the Chapter and Section Resources booklet, p. 68, covers the main ideas and key terms in the section. Available in Spanish in the Spanish Chapter and Section Resources booklet, p. 42.

How People Use the Land

BEFORE YOU READ

Reach Into Your Background
How many manufactured, or factory-made, items do you use in a day? What natural resources were used to make them? Make a list of these resources.

Questions to Explore
1. What are the stages of economic development?
2. How do different cultures use land?

Key Terms
manufacturing
developed nation
developing nation
commercial farming
subsistence farming
plantation
foreign aid

"**A**ll this water started flowing, but we were told it was restricted for use only by the oil company and we were not allowed to use it," said Li Lixing, a Chinese farmer. "We had to go at night and secretly take some for our crops." Li Lixing lives in a village by the banks of the Huang He. People have farmed here for hundreds of years. In Li's region, the government wants to help the economy by supporting businesses like the oil company. Farmers, therefore, face problems.

Many countries face problems of limited resources, increasing population, and growing demand. Studying how countries use their natural resources shows three basic patterns of economic activity.

Stages of Resource Development

Water from the Huang He is essential for Chinese farmers like Li. But industry needs resources, too. Which group is more important? In some cultures, industry comes first. In others, farmers do. Geographers study how people in different cultures use land and develop their resources. This tells geographers much about a culture. Geographers also compare land use and resource development all over the world.

First-Level Activities Geographers study three stages of economic activity. In the first, people use land and resources directly to make products. They may hunt, cut wood, mine, and fish. They also may herd animals and farm. This is the first stage of activities. People are beginning to develop their land. About half the world's population works in first-level activities. In countries like the United States, however, fewer people do this kind of work every year.

Teaching Resources

📁 **Reproducible Lesson Plan** in the Chapter and Section Resources booklet, p. 69, provides a summary of the section lesson.

📁 **Guided Reading and Review** in the Chapter and Section Resources booklet, p. 70, provides a structure for mastering key concepts and reviewing key terms in the section. Available in Spanish in the Spanish Chapter and Section Resources booklet, p. 43.

Program Resources

📁 **Outline Maps** East Asia: Physical, p. 40; The World: Political, p. 5

Media and Technology

💻 **Color Transparencies** 9, 10, 11, 15, 17

Lesson Objectives

1. Identify stages of economic development and describe some of the problems faced at each stage.

2. Compare and contrast ways different cultures use land and other resources.

3. Describe patterns of economic activity on a global scale, including the relationship between developed and developing countries.

Lesson Plan

1 Engage
Warm-Up Activity
Help students recognize that one of the most important natural resources is human labor. As an example, ask students to describe a favorite meal. Ask them who worked to make the food, including everyone along the way, from the farmer, the worker in the manufacturing plant, the packer, the trucker, the grocery store clerks, and the cooks. Encourage them to include the person who wrote the advertising copy or the gas station attendant who filled the tanks of the truck or the clerk who sold the seeds. Then ask them to summarize the human resources used to make their meal.

Activating Prior Knowledge
Have students read Reach Into Your Background in the Before You Read box. Most students' lists will include resources such as metal, plastics from petroleum products, plants, and animals.

2 Explore

As they read the section, have students consider the following questions. Who works directly with natural resources? Who works with changing raw materials into goods? Why do both service and manufacturing industries rely on natural resources? Why are there conflicts between small farmers and big industries? Why are large commercial farms successful in some regions? Why don't developing countries use modern technology?

Activity

Critical Thinking

Drawing Conclusions
Have students compare the information about first-level economic activities with the information on the World Economic Activity map. Ask students what information they can find to support the following conclusion: Sub-sistence farming is a first-level economic activity.

Harvesting Corn

Farmers in the midwest United States are part of the first level of economic activity. Before you eat this corn, it may be frozen, canned, or processed. It may be made into corn meal, cornflakes, corn tortillas, grits, or even corn muffins. Then it must be delivered to a store where you can buy it.

Connect Think about members of your family and friends who work. Do they do first-, second-, or third-level activities?

Second-Level Activities Suppose a farmer takes his corn crop to a mill and has the miller grind the corn into corn meal. This is an example of the second step in developing a resource. People turn raw materials into things they use. When a product is processed, it is changed from a raw material into a finished product. That process is called **manufacturing.** The farmer can pay the miller for his service and take the corn meal back home. Or the miller can sell the corn meal to someone else for further processing. Manufacturing may turn the farmer's corn crop into cornflakes for your breakfast.

Third-Level Activities In the third stage, a person delivers boxes of corn flakes to a local grocery store so you can buy one. In this stage, products are distributed to people who want them. People who distribute products do not make them. They produce a service by making sure products are delivered to people who want and need them.

Industrial nations require service industries. Transportation systems carry products from manufacturer to consumer. Communication for people and businesses comes from telephones, computers, and satellites. Other services—doctors' offices, shopping malls, and fast-food stores—are part of everyday living.

Resource Directory

Program Resources

Environmental and Global Issues
Topic: Energy and Resources, pp. 2–7

Economic Patterns: Developed and Developing Countries

Today, most manufacturing takes place in factories. Two hundred years ago, that was not so. People produced goods in their homes or small shops. Then came a great change. People invented machines to make goods. They built factories to house the machines. They found new sources of power to run the machines. This change in the way people made goods was called the Industrial Revolution.

The Industrial Revolution created a new pattern of economic activity. It separated countries into two groups—those with many industries and those with few. Countries that have many industries are called developed nations. Countries with few industries are called developing nations. People live differently in developed and developing nations.

Industrial Societies: Providing Goods and Services

Only about one quarter of the people in the world live in developed nations. These nations include the United States, Canada, Japan, Singapore, Australia, and most European countries. People in these nations use goods made in factories. Their industries consume great amounts of raw materials. They also use power-driven machinery. Businesses spend money on technology, transportation, and communications. Factories produce goods for the country's citizens and extra goods to sell to other countries.

▼ In a Detroit factory, a worker carefully assembles the same part on each automobile that comes down the power-driven assembly line.

3 Teach

Ask students to choose a familiar manufactured product—a CD or a video game, for example—and figure out the raw materials, manufacturing processes, and service tasks that moved that product from natural resources to their daily use. Have students create a diagram that shows all of the human and natural resources involved in producing the product. Use the diagrams as a basis for discussion of the relationship between economic activity and resource use. This activity should take about 40 minutes.

4 Assess

See the answers to the Section Review. You may also use students' completed diagrams as an assessment.

Acceptable diagrams include the basic raw materials and natural resources from which the product has been made, and the human resources central to the production.

Commendable diagrams include energy resources used in the process.

Outstanding diagrams indicate the global connections implied by the manufacture of the product.

SKILLS MINI LESSON

Using Regional Maps
To **introduce** the skill, point out to students that a regional map uses different colors to present information about the regions shown in the map. Indicate that, because economic activity can vary from one region to another, a regional map is a useful way to show types of economic activity that occur throughout the world. Help students **practice** the skill by working with them as they locate areas of subsistence farming. Ask: *Is subsistence farming common throughout the world? Is it practiced in large areas of the world?* (mostly, yes) Suggest that students **apply** the skill by finding areas that are home to manufacturing and trade, and areas that support little or no economic activity.

Interdisciplinary Connections

Language Arts Have students choose a developing nation project to research, for example, building a dam for hydroelectric power or cutting timber for export sales. Have students summarize the benefits of the project (providing power or bringing in money) as well as the costs (including the effects on the environment and the existing population). Suggest that students form groups for and against the project and have them debate the proposed project. Encourage them to support their opinions with facts.

English Language Learners

The World: Economic Activity

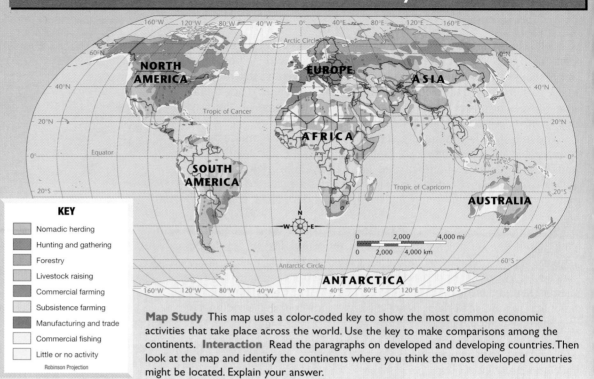

KEY

- Nomadic herding
- Hunting and gathering
- Forestry
- Livestock raising
- Commercial farming
- Subsistence farming
- Manufacturing and trade
- Commercial fishing
- Little or no activity

Robinson Projection

Map Study This map uses a color-coded key to show the most common economic activities that take place across the world. Use the key to make comparisons among the continents. **Interaction** Read the paragraphs on developed and developing countries. Then look at the map and identify the continents where you think the most developed countries might be located. Explain your answer.

In developed countries, most people live in towns and cities. They work in business and industry. Machines do most of the work. Most people have enough food and water. Most citizens can get a good education and adequate health care.

Developed nations rely on **commercial farming** to produce enough food for their people. Commercial farms are very large. Companies run most of them, not single families. These farms rely on modern technology, so they often need far fewer workers than small traditional farms. Commercial farms are very successful. In the United States, a few million farmers raise enough food to feed more than 250 million people. There is plenty left over to sell to other countries.

People in developed nations depend on each other. Farmers rely on industries for goods and services. City people depend on farmers for food. Anything, like wars and natural disasters, that stops the movement of goods and services can make life hard for everyone.

Developed nations can have some serious problems. Unemployment is a challenge. Not everyone can find a job. Manufacturing can also threaten the environment with air, land, and water pollution. Heavy production uses up natural resources, so shortages develop. Developed nations are working to solve these problems.

READ ACTIVELY

Predict What are the problems of developed nations?

Answers to ...

MAP STUDY

subsistence farming; livestock raising; in North America and Europe, because the developed countries are industrialized, and there are more manufacturing and trade centers on those two continents than others.

114 **CHAPTER 5**

Developing Nations   It is important to remember that every culture is not like that of the United States. Most of the people of the world live in developing countries. Many of these countries are in Africa, Asia, and Latin America.

Developing countries often do not have great wealth. Many people work at **subsistence farming**. That means farmers raise enough food and animals to feed their own families. The farms require much labor, but they do not yield many crops. Often, the only commercial farms are **plantations**. These farms employ many workers but are owned by only a few people. Plantations usually raise a single crop for export, such as bananas, coffee, sugar cane, or tea.

In some developing countries, certain groups herd animals that provide families with milk, meat, cheese, and skins. In the deserts of Africa and Asia, vegetation and water are scarce. Herders in these regions are nomads. They travel from place to place to find food and water for their animals. In some developing nations, some people live as hunter-gatherers. Such groups are found in the Kalahari Desert in Africa and the Amazon region of South America.

Challenges in Developing Nations   Developing countries often face great challenges. These include disease, food shortages, unsafe water, poor education and health services, and changing governments. Farmers often rely on one or two crops. That puts farmers at risk if the crops fail. Thousands move to cities, but jobs there are often scarce.

Some challenges are connected to rapid population growth. It strains resources. For example, in the late 1990s, the supply of fresh water was becoming a problem. As populations grow, they need more water. Larger populations also need more food. This means that farms need more water. Industries also require large amounts of fresh water.

Developing countries are working to improve their people's lives. One way is to use their natural resources or sell them to other countries. Some countries have grown richer by selling natural resources, such as oil and other minerals, to others.

LINKS ACROSS THE WORLD

A Nation of Herders The Tuareg of the Sahara in northern Africa herd camels, goats, sheep, and cattle. They travel along the edge of the great desert. Here there are seasonal rains so there is pasture for the herds. Men and women are equals in Tuareg culture. Both can own their own herds of animals and other property.

Construction in Vietnam

Vietnam's economy is run by a communist government. But the government now allows some forms of free enterprise. As a result, the economy is improving. Hanoi, the capital of Vietnam, is a trade center. It is located on the Red River, which provides access to the Pacific Ocean. Most workers in Vietnam are farmers. In Hanoi, however, workers can find jobs in factories that process food or produce bicycles and farm machinery. Or, like these workers, they can help to construct new buildings as Hanoi expands.

1. Key term definitions appear in the Glossary. Page numbers here indicate first use of the term in the text. (a) manufacturing, p. 112 (b) developed nation, p. 113 (c) developing nation, p. 113 (d) commercial farming, p. 114 (e) substance farming, p. 115 (f) plantation, p. 115 (g) foreign aid, p. 116

2. Answers will vary. Students' responses should indicate that developed nations have many industries and rely on commercial farming; developing nations have few industries and rely on subsistence farming.

3. In subsistence farming, individuals or families use land and natural resources to raise enough food for their own use. Commercial farming uses land, technology, and natural resources to produce huge quantities of food.

4. Countries can use resources directly by hunting, farming, mining, cutting wood, and fishing, or they can manufacture goods from their resources.

5. Developed nations face unemployment; air, land, and water pollution; and shortages of natural resources. Developing nations face disease, food shortages, unsafe water, poor education and health services, over-reliance by farmers on one or two crops, and not enough jobs.

6. Student answers will vary, but will likely include disease, scarce food, unsafe water, poor education and health services, changing governments, and increasing populations.

7. Students should interview a service worker from the school. Encourage students to include a description of the work and working environment in their article.

▶ This woman works in the city of Bangalore, India. In recent years, many Indian businesses have improved their services by using computers.

Developing countries sometimes receive help from developed nations. The help could be in the form of foreign aid, or gifts and loans from one government to another or from the United Nations. This aid is often used for special projects, such as building roads to move food and other goods from one area to another. Sometimes conflicts arise when the two governments do not agree on the best way to use foreign aid funds.

Sometimes help comes from businesses in developed countries. They may build factories in developing nations. This provides jobs and money for people. Sometimes building communication systems helps spread new ideas for farming and industries.

SECTION 2 REVIEW

1. Define (a) manufacturing, (b) developed nation, (c) developing nation, (d) commercial farming, (e) subsistence farming, (f) plantation, (g) foreign aid.

2. What are the characteristics of a developed nation? Of a developing nation?

3. How is subsistence farming different from commercial farming?

4. How can countries use their natural resources?

5. What challenges face developed nations? Developing nations?

Critical Thinking

6. Identifying Central Issues How are developing nations working to improve their people's lives?

Activity

7. Writing to Learn People who work at your school have jobs in a service industry. Interview a teacher, a server in the cafeteria, or a receptionist in the office. Find out what that person's duties are and what that person likes about his or her job. Write a brief profile for your school newspaper.

Resource Directory

Teaching Resources

Section Quiz in the Chapter and Section Resources booklet, p. 71, covers the main ideas and key terms in the section. Available in Spanish in the Spanish Chapter and Section Resources booklet, p. 44.

People's Effect on the Environment

BEFORE YOU READ

Reach Into Your Background

Many of the environmental problems we face are the result of actions people took in the past. Now people pay more attention to environmental issues. Make a list of things you and your community are doing to improve the environment.

Questions to Explore

1. How do people's actions affect the environment?
2. What are people doing to improve the environment?

Key Terms

ecosystem
deforestation
habitat
acid rain
ozone layer
global warming
recycle

Try to picture the United States as one huge desert. Africa's Sahara is even bigger than that. What's more, the Sahara is spreading. Wangari Maathai of Kenya, in East Africa, works to stop it. She heads Africa's Green Belt Movement. It urges people in a dozen African countries to plant trees. Tree roots hold valuable topsoil in place, stopping the spread of the desert. When their leaves fall to the ground, trees add nutrients to the soil. This will make rich soil good for other plants. Since 1977, this organization has planted more than 10 million trees.

Danger to Land, Water, and Air

Wangari Maathai is saving forests in Africa. Other people around the world are also working to preserve the environment. If we learn to identify environmental problems, we too can protect our world.

The Sahara is a desert. The Amazon River valley is a rain forest. The Great Plains is an area of grasslands. Each of these regions is an **ecosystem,** a place where living elements depend on one another—and on nonliving elements—for their survival. Living elements are plants and animals. Nonliving elements are water, soil, rocks, and air. Desert birds cannot live in a rain forest. Grassland plants cannot survive in a desert. Living things are tied to their ecosystems.

▼ Coral reefs, like this one, take millions of years to construct. They can be completely destroyed in a matter of decades by such things as water pollution.

Teaching Resources

📁 **Reproducible Lesson Plan** in the Chapter and Section Resources booklet, p. 72, provides a summary of the section lesson.

📁 **Guided Reading and Review** in the Chapter and Section Resources booklet, p. 73, provides a structure for mastering key concepts and reviewing key terms in the section. Available in Spanish in the Spanish Chapter and Section Resources booklet, p. 45.

Media and Technology

📺 **Color Transparencies** 13, 14, 15, 16, 113, 114

💿 **Planet Earth** CD-ROM includes Natural Landscapes which allows students to focus on a particular vegetation region and discover how people there use the land.

Section ③

Lesson Objectives

❶ Summarize some of the ways in which people's actions affect the environment.

❷ Describe actions taken to protect endangered species and ecosystems.

❸ Identify energy sources that can be used in place of fossil fuels.

Lesson Plan

1 Engage

Warm-Up Activity

Have students describe a park they are familiar with. Ask them to describe the grasses, plants, bushes, and trees they find there. Are there many kinds of plants? Do they think that all of the plants in the park were planted by people? Are there any animals, insects or birds in the park? If so, what do they eat? What things in the park were put there by humans? What would happen to the trees and wildlife if the park were to be used as an airport?

Activating Prior Knowledge

Have students read Reach Into Your Background in the Before You Read box. If students aren't aware of local environmental issues, you might suggest that they look for information in the local newspaper. Encourage students to think about actions they can take to improve the environment such as recycling, putting litter in its place, helping to plant trees, and so on.

2 Explore

As students read the section, suggest that they look for answers to these questions: Why is it important to plant trees? Why is deforestation a problem? How does industry contribute to environmental problems? How does commercial farming contribute? Why does it matter what we do with our sewage and garbage? Why are ultraviolet rays from the sun more of a problem now than they were 100 years ago? How does burning fossil fuels contribute to pollution?

3 Teach

Have students make a chart similar to the following.

	Problems	Possible Solutions
Air		
Water		
Plants		
Animals		

Suggest that students fill in each column with information from the text. Opinions can be included when supported by fact. Use the completed charts as a basis for discussion on environmental problems. This activity should take about 40 minutes.

4 Assess

See the answers to the Section Review. You may also use students' completed charts as an assessment.

Acceptable charts include at least one entry under each category.

Commendable charts include opinions supported by facts.

Outstanding charts show an understanding of the complexities of the issues and the potential for solutions.

LINKS ACROSS THE WORLD

Death of a Sea The border between Kazakstan and Uzbekistan in western Asia runs through the Aral Sea. Until about 1960, this shallow sea was the fourth largest inland lake or sea in the world. Two rivers fed into the Aral. Then people started diverting the water for irrigation projects. By 1987, the Aral Sea had less than half as much water as before. Its fish were dead. Fishing villages now sat far from the water's edge. Some experts believe it may take 30 years to repair the damage done to the Aral Sea.

If one part of an ecosystem changes, other parts are also affected. For example, ecosystems that have standing water like puddles have mosquitoes. They lay their eggs on the surface of water. A rainy summer produces more standing water. This means that more mosquito eggs will hatch. A dry summer means less water and fewer mosquitoes.

Some changes can destroy an ecosystem. Probably the greatest loss of ecosystems is happening in South America. Rain forests cover more than one third of the continent. They are home for more species, or kinds, of plants and animals than anywhere else in the world. But South Americans need land for farms, so they are cutting down the forests. This process is called **deforestation.** When the forests are gone, many plant and animal species become extinct, or die out.

Protecting Endangered Species How can we prevent species of animals and plants from dying out? One way is through laws. In 1973, Congress passed the Endangered Species Act. It gave the government power to protect not only species that might become extinct but also the places that they live, or their **habitats.** Today, the act protects almost 1,000 kinds of living things in the United States that are threatened, or endangered.

Extinction has many causes. People may build houses or businesses on land that is the habitat of particular animals or plants. The air, soil, or water may be too polluted for a species of plant or animal to survive. Sometimes, a species is hunted until it disappears. Usually, more than one thing threatens a species. The goal of the Endangered Species Act is to stop extinction. But people disagree about the law. Some think humans should be allowed to use natural resources as they need them. Others think people should stop doing things that hurt other species.

Factories and Acid Rain Often, endangered animal species are just one sign of an ecosystem with problems. Visitors to the New York's Adirondack Mountains see an ecosystem in trouble. Its vast forests are centuries old. But today, the needles of the spruce trees are brown, and birch trees have no leaves at all. There are few fish in the rivers. Frogs, certain kinds of birds, and many insects are hard to find. What happened?

According to scientists, **acid rain** is to blame. Acid rain is rain that carries

Saving the Gray Whale

Temporarily trapped in Alaska's ice, this gray whale may survive to make its yearly journey down the Pacific Coast to Mexico. Whaling nearly destroyed the world's population of gray whales. Protection as an endangered species, however, brought their numbers back up.

Resource Directory

Teaching Resources

📁 **Critical Thinking Activity** in the Chapter and Section Resources booklet, p. 79, helps students apply the skill of identifying central issues.

Program Resources

📁 **Environmental and Global Issues** Topics: Environmental Destruction, pp. 14–19; Waste Disposal and Recycling, pp. 31–36
Interdisciplinary Explorations *Where River Meets Sea: Estuaries at Risk; Fate of the Rain Forest*

The Greenhouse Effect

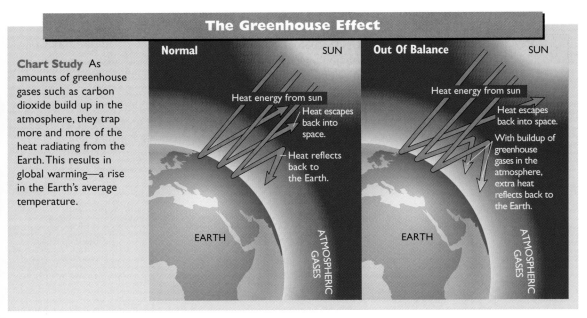

Chart Study As amounts of greenhouse gases such as carbon dioxide build up in the atmosphere, they trap more and more of the heat radiating from the Earth. This results in global warming—a rise in the Earth's average temperature.

Normal — SUN
Heat energy from sun
Heat escapes back into space.
Heat reflects back to the Earth.
EARTH
ATMOSPHERIC GASES

Out Of Balance — SUN
Heat energy from sun
Heat escapes back into space.
With buildup of greenhouse gases in the atmosphere, extra heat reflects back to the Earth.
EARTH
ATMOSPHERIC GASES

dangerous chemicals. The fossil fuels used by industries and automobiles release chemicals into the air. The chemicals combine with water vapor in the air, making the rain as acid as vinegar.

Canada and the United States now have laws to reduce acid rain. Coal-burning electricity plants must cut pollution in half by the year 2000. Factories are installing new devices called filters and scrubbers to clean up the fumes they release. Car makers have added devices to reduce the dangerous chemicals in car exhaust.

Rivers and Sewage Pollution People have always dumped waste products into rivers, lakes, and oceans. These wastes can harm or destroy living things in the water. They also endanger people. Water creatures take in substances from the water. Little fish eat the creatures, big fish eat the little fish, and animals and people eat the fish. The substances pass from one living thing to another. Some of these substances are poisons.

Fertilizers and pesticides from farms also pollute water. (Pesticides are chemicals that kill insects.) Rainwater washes the substances into lakes and rivers. There, the fertilizers cause water plants to grow too fast, and they use up oxygen needed by fish and other water life.

The Ozone Layer and Ultraviolet Rays In the 1970s, scientists realized that chemicals called chlorofluorocarbons (CFCs) were destroying the atmosphere's ozone layer. This is a layer of gas in the upper part of our atmosphere. The ozone layer blocks most of the harmful ultraviolet rays from the sun. These rays cause skin cancer in humans. They also damage other forms of life.

SKILLS MINI LESSON

Distinguishing Facts From Opinions
As you **introduce** the skill, point out to students that distinguishing fact from opinion is a skill they will need nearly every day of their lives. Tell students that:
- Facts can be proved true.
- Opinions cannot be proved true.
- Opinions are often indicated by words and phrases such as "I think," "ought to," and "beautiful" or "ugly."

To help students **practice** the skill, provide current articles on an environmental subject, for example, cleaning up a dump or leasing mineral rights on public land. After students read the article for understanding, direct students to read the sentences one-by-one, asking 1) Is this a fact that *can* be proved true? 2) Is this an opinion that *cannot* be proved true? 3) Are there words in the sentence that give it away as an opinion? Hold a class discussion on whether the articles they read were mostly fact or mostly opinion.

Exploring Technology

Using the caption, walk students through the diagram and confirm their understanding. If necessary, explain that a solar collector works very much like the conventional hot water heating systems many people have in their homes—water is warmed by a heat source. The difference is that the heat source warming the water is the sun's rays instead of an artificial source such as an oil–fired furnace.

Have students survey their families as well as nearby business owners. What kinds of energy are used to heat these homes and businesses? Together, make a bar graph showing the results. Discuss which heat sources are most and least common in your area. Using what they know about the geography of their community, invite students to hypothesize about the results. For example, if your area has a very rainy climate and a local hydroelectric plant, solar energy may be unsuitable, and electric heat may be inexpensive.

Then tell students that solar energy is used for more than heating homes and businesses. For example, solar batteries on space vehicles collect energy for astronauts' use. Challenge students to name other ways solar energy can be harnessed to improve peoples' lives. Have students focus on the role such inventions would play in peoples' lives rather than on the scientific detail.

READ ACTIVELY

Connect What are some things you and your friends could do to protect the environment?

Until recently, aerosol spray cans, refrigerators, and air conditioners used CFCs. In 1985, a United Nations conference discussed the ozone layer. Many nations agreed to get rid of ozone-destroying chemicals by 2000. And scientists are searching for safe chemicals to replace CFCs.

Global Warming   The summer of 1995 in New England was unusually hot and dry. Temperatures stayed above 90 degrees for weeks. Heat and drought caused water shortages and killed crops. Some scientists feared this was the start of global warming, a slow increase in the Earth's temperature. Global warming may be caused by

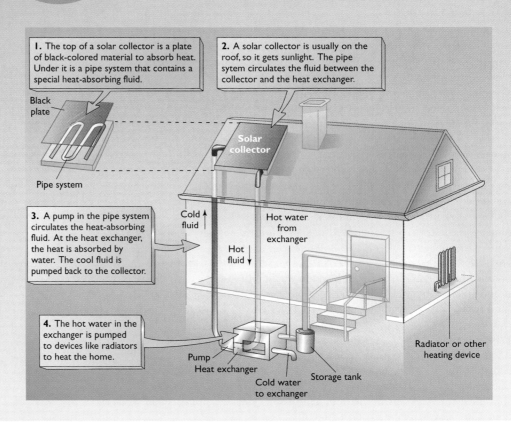

EXPLORING TECHNOLOGY

A Sun-Powered House

If you have spent a few hours outside on a hot summer day, then you are well aware of the heating power of the sun. Scientists knew all about it, too. They also knew that if they could find a way to store that power, they would have a cheap, abundant source of energy. The diagram below shows how they solved the problem of storing the heat of the sun.

1. The top of a solar collector is a plate of black-colored material to absorb heat. Under it is a pipe system that contains a special heat-absorbing fluid.

Black plate

Pipe system

2. A solar collector is usually on the roof, so it gets sunlight. The pipe sytem circulates the fluid between the collector and the heat exchanger.

Solar collector

3. A pump in the pipe system circulates the heat-absorbing fluid. At the heat exchanger, the heat is absorbed by water. The cool fluid is pumped back to the collector.

Cold fluid

Hot fluid

Hot water from exchanger

4. The hot water in the exchanger is pumped to devices like radiators to heat the home.

Pump
Heat exchanger
Cold water to exchanger
Storage tank

Radiator or other heating device

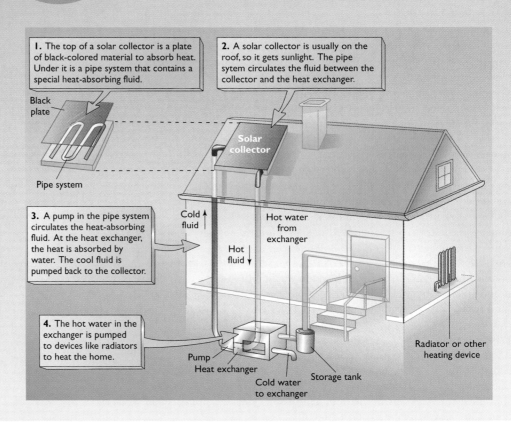

Resource Directory

Teaching Resources

📁 **Section Quiz** in the Chapter and Section Resources booklet, p. 74, covers the main ideas and key terms in the section. Available in Spanish in the Spanish Chapter and Section Resources booklet, p. 46.

📁 **Vocabulary** in the Chapter and Section Resources booklet, p. 76, provides a review of key terms in the chapter. Available in Spanish in the Spanish Chapter and Section Resources booklet, p. 48.

📁 **Reteaching** in the Chapter and Section Resources booklet, p. 77, provides a structure for students who may need additional help in mastering chapter content.

📁 **Enrichment** in the Chapter and Section Resources booklet, p. 78, extends chapter content and enriches students' understanding.

📁 **Spanish Glossary** in the Spanish Chapter and Section Resources, pp. 49–53, provides key terms translated from English to Spanish as well as definitions in Spanish.

gases like carbon dioxide that are released into the air. They are called greenhouse gases. Industrial countries produce about 75 percent of these gases. They are released when fossil fuels burn. These fuels produce most of the world's electricity. They also run the world's 550 million cars, buses, and trucks. Developing countries produce these gases when they burn forests to clear land and use wood for heating and cooking.

Normally, heat on the Earth escapes back into space. Some scientists theorize that greenhouse gases trap the heat and reflect it back to Earth. The result is a rise in the Earth's average temperature.

The Challenge of Energy

Because pollution is often tied to using fossil fuels, scientists are exploring other ways to get inexpensive energy. Their research concentrates on nuclear power, water, wind, and the sun. Individuals can protect the environment, too. For example, the United States produces more waste than any other nation in the world. To change that, people now **recycle**, or re-use, old materials to make new products. Today, most American cities have recycling programs.

◀ It looks as if a fire burned these trees near the peak of Mount Mitchell in North Carolina. In fact, acid rain killed them.

SECTION 3 REVIEW

1. **Define** (a) ecosystem, (b) deforestation, (c) habitat, (d) acid rain, (e) ozone layer, (f) global warming, (g) recycle.

2. How do fossil fuels create pollution?

3. Why is global warming a problem?

4. What alternatives to fossil fuels are scientists researching?

Critical Thinking

5. **Expressing Problems Clearly** Explain why some species are endangered. Why do people disagree about reserving land for them?

Activity

6. **Writing to Learn** Write a persuasive paragraph explaining why fresh water should be protected. Include facts to support your reasons.

1 Define the skill of writing to persuade.

2 Explain the four basic steps in persuasive writing.

3 Practice writing persuasively in context.

Lesson Plan

1 Engage

Warm-Up Activity

Ask students to tell some ways in which they have worked to protect the environment. Then have a volunteer read the opening paragraphs. **Introduce** the skill by drawing students' attention to the tool of *persuasive writing* mentioned in the third paragraph.

Activating Prior Knowledge

Ask students whether they can explain the purpose of a letter to the editor. Invite students to tell whether they or a family member has ever written a letter to the editor. If possible, allow students to scan some appropriate examples from a school or local publication.

Writing for a Purpose

Have you ever testified before Congress about pollution? Or stopped a company from pumping poison into a river? Or organized a demonstration to make people more aware of the environment? You may think kids your age do not do such things. But the kids of KAP do.

KAP stands for *Kids Against Pollution.* These young people work to stop pollution. Nineteen students in Closter, New Jersey, formed KAP in 1987. Today, there are more than 13,000 KAP chapters across the United States and in other countries. KAP's motto is "Save the Earth Not Just For Us But For Future Generations."

One of KAP's main weapons is writing. It can be very powerful. KAP members use the power of persuasive writing, or writing that tries to show other people how their point of view can help solve a problem.

Get Ready

Writing to persuade means taking a stand and trying to convince others to agree with your opinion. There are four basic steps:

1 **Decide what your opinion is.** Your opinion is the position you plan to take. For example, suppose your opinion is "Our city should make a law to require people to recycle newspapers."

"SAVE THE EARTH NOT JUST FOR US BUT FOR FUTURE GENERATIONS" ™

2 **Choose your audience.** Your audience is the people to whom you will be writing. You might write to a senator or a mayor. You might write to the general public in a magazine article or letter to the editor of a newspaper.

3 **Find support for your opinion.** Your writing must give reasons for your opinion and the facts to support each reason. For example, the statement "Recycling would prevent burying six tons of paper trash in our town's landfill every month" is a fact that supports an opinion. Find as many facts as you can to support your opinion. They will help make your message stronger.

④ Write persuasively. Finally, write a letter or an essay. Present one idea at a time, and defend it with facts. Although persuasive writing emphasizes facts, it often includes an appeal to emotions. Add a sentence or two that does this. KAP's motto, for instance, is an emotional appeal. The combination of facts and emotion can make persuasive writing work.

Try It Out

Suppose you are concerned about the growing amount of litter in a local park. Follow these four steps to write a persuasive letter.

A. What is your opinion? Decide upon a plan to solve the park's problem. Should there be stronger anti-litter laws? Should people be urged to litter less, or should they be required to participate in a community cleanup? Choose one of these opinions or develop your own solution.

B. Who is your audience? If you want a local law passed, write to a member of your local government. To address your fellow citizens, write to the editor of a local newspaper.

C. Why do you hold this opinion? Identify at least two reasons for your opinion. Then support each reason with facts.

D. How will you persuade your audience to agree with your opinion? Before you write your letter, make an outline. Start your letter with a catchy opening. Then present your reasons in logical order. In the conclusion, sum up your arguments and appeal to people's emotions.

Apply the Skill

Now, apply the skill to the real world. Choose a topic, and write a persuasive letter about it to the editor of your local newspaper. Try to persuade your fellow citizens to agree with your opinion.

> To the Editor:
> The time has come to do something about the litter ruining Peace Park. First of all, the Parks Department has released a study that shows littering has increased 10 percent in two years.
> Also,

2 Explore

Read and discuss the steps outlined in Get Ready. Confirm students' understanding of each step. For example, volunteers can describe an opinion, an audience, a supporting reason or fact, and an emotional appeal. Examples need not relate to the same subject. Then have students read the remainder of the skills activity.

3 Teach

Students can **practice** their skill independently with the writing prompt outlined in Try It Out. Guide students in progressing toward clearly defined positions. Student groups can then exchange and discuss their writing efforts. Which opinions were persuasively presented? What facts and reasons were most effective? Which openings were most engaging?

For additional reinforcement, have students identify the four basic elements (opinion, audience, support, emotional appeal) in a peer's persuasive letter.

4 Assess

Before they **apply** their skill on the final activity, help students select an appropriate topic. You can **assess** the letters as follows: **acceptable** letters contain clearly stated opinions; **commendable** letters include at least two relevant supporting facts or opinions; **outstanding** letters are logically organized and include effective emotional appeals.

Reviewing Main Ideas

1. (a) Answers will vary, but may include forests, metals, soil, fish, plants, water, and fossil fuels. (b) Answers will vary. Students may say that forests are used to get wood for building; metals are used to make many manufactured products; soil is used to raise crops to provide food; fish are used for food; plants are used for food and clothing; and water and fossil fuels are used to produce energy.

2. Nonrenewable resources, such as fossil fuels, are resources that are no longer being created and cannot be replaced. Renewable resources such as trees, food crops, and animals, are resources that can be replaced as they are used.

3. Developing nations have mainly agricultural activities, and developed nations have mainly industrial activities.

4. Commercial farming is dependent on the use of modern technology, which is not available in developing nations.

5. Foreign aid can help countries build roads, factories, or communication systems.

6. because all the living elements in an ecosystem depend on one another for survival

7. Acid rain can hurt or kill the animals that people depend on or pollute water, thereby making people sick.

8. Governments can pass and enforce laws to protect endangered animals and their habitats.

9. Answers will vary. Students may mention that recycling may help conserve energy or provide materials for new products.

10. Burning fewer fossil fuels can help prevent global warming.

Reviewing Key Terms

Each sentence should reveal the meaning of the key term through the context.

CHAPTER 5 Review and Activities

Reviewing Main Ideas

1. (a) Name two natural resources. (b) Describe how they are used.
2. What is the difference between renewable resources and nonrenewable resources?
3. (a) What kind of nation has mainly agricultural activities? (b) What kind of nation has mainly industrial activities?
4. Why is commercial farming part of a developed nation instead of a developing nation?
5. How can foreign aid help a developing nation?
6. Why might one simple change in an ecosystem have many effects in the system?
7. Acid rain hurts forests and lakes. How could acid rain endanger people?
8. What can governments do to protect endangered species?
9. Why is recycling a good use of natural resources?
10. How can people work to prevent global warming?

Reviewing Key Terms

Use each key term below in a sentence that shows the meaning of the term.

1. natural resource
2. raw material
3. recyclable resource
4. renewable resource
5. nonrenewable resource
6. fossil fuel
7. manufacturing
8. developed nation
9. developing nation
10. commercial farming
11. subsistence farming
12. plantation
13. foreign aid
14. ecosystem
15. deforestation
16. habitat
17. acid rain
18. ozone layer
19. global warming
20. recycle

Critical Thinking

1. **Identifying Central Issues** Do you think people should do more to protect the environment? Use facts from the chapter to support your answer.
2. **Recognizing Cause and Effect** Think about the problems that arose during the oil shortage of 1973. It affected the supply of gasoline and heating fuel. Write a paragraph about how a gasoline shortage today would affect the lives of people in your family.

Graphic Organizer

Answers will vary. Sample chart shown.

	Sources	Damage to Environment	Possible Solutions
Water Pollution	runoff of pesticides and fertilizers, sewage and industrial waste dumping	poisoning of fish and food supplies	better control of waste treatment, less industrial waste dumping, fewer industries, stronger environmental protection laws
Land Pollution	too much use of fertilizers and pesticides, acid rain from burning fossil fuels	buildup of pesticides and fertilizers, vegetation dying	less burning of fossil fuels, less use of chemicals in farming, stronger environmental protection laws
Air Pollution	burning fossil fuels in factories, vehicles	acid rain, thinning of the ozone, increase in greenhouse gases	scrubbers on factory smokestacks, fewer vehicles by using more public transportation, shift to alternate energy sources, stronger environmental protection laws

Graphic Organizer

Copy and fill in the flowchart to show some activities that might pollute the water, the land, and the air.

Sources	Damage to Environment	Possible Solutions
Water Pollution		
Land Pollution		
Air Pollution		

Writing Activity

Writing a Letter
Become part of the global community by contacting an organization that works to protect the environment. Two groups are listed here. Describe what you have learned about threats to the environment. Explain how you use natural resources responsibly. Find out if the organization has suggestions for other actions.

Addresses

Greenpeace
1436 U Street NW
Washington, D.C. 20009

World Wildlife Fund
1250 24th Street
Washington, D.C. 20037

Internet Activity

Use a search engine to find the **U.S. Geological Survey.** Click on **Fact Sheets.** Scroll down and click on **State** to find a USGS program in your area. Click on your state and then choose a program. Write a paragraph that explains the goal of the program and the actions taken to reach the goal.

Skills Review

Turn to the Skills Activity. Review the steps for writing for a purpose. Then complete the following: (a) Why do you think that it is important to choose your audience when you are writing to persuade? (b) Do you think that you need to do research in order to write to persuade? Why or why not?

How Am I Doing?

Answer these questions to help you check your progress.

1. Can I describe natural resources and how different countries use them?
2. Do I understand how the stages of economic development are related to a nation's wealth?
3. Can I identify some threats to the environment?
4. What information from this chapter can I use in my book project?

Internet Activity

If students are having difficulty finding this site, you may wish to have them use the following URL, which was accurate at the time this textbook was published:
http://www.usgs.gov/

You may also guide students to a search engine. Four of the most useful are Infoseek, AltaVista, Lycos, and Yahoo. For additional suggestions on using the Internet, refer to the Prentice Hall Social Studies' Educator's Handbook "Using the Internet." in the *Prentice Hall World Explorer Program Resources.*

For additional links to world history and culture topics, visit the Prentice Hall Home Page at:
http://www.phschool.com

How Am I Doing?

Point out to students that this checklist is just a quick reminder for them of what they learned in the chapter. If their answer to any of the questions is *no* or if they are unsure, they may need to review the topic.

Critical Thinking

1. **Identifying Central Issues** Answers will vary. Students may cite examples of environmental destruction and the fact that so many species and ecosystems are endangered as evidence that people should do more to protect the environment.

2. Students' paragraphs will vary, but should mention higher costs for gasoline, the likelihood of reduced auto travel, and increased costs for foods and other goods transported to their home community.

Skills Review

Student answers will vary, but may include the idea that choosing the audience for a letter helps to target the emotional appeal of a persuasive letter. Students will probably agree that it is important to conduct research in order to support their opinions.

Writing Activity

Student letters will vary, but should mention threats to the environment from the chapter such as deforestation, acid rain, river pollution, global warming, and so on. Indications of personal environmental responsibility should also be evident.

Resource Directory

Teaching Resources

Chapter Tests Forms A and B are in the Tests booklet, pp. 26–31.

Final Exams Forms A and B are in the Tests booklet, pp. 32–37

Program Resources

Writing Process Handbook includes Writing Effective Paragraphs, pp. 27–28, to help students with the Writing Activity.

Media and Technology

Color Transparencies
Color Transparency 174
(Graphic organizer table template)

Prentice Hall Writer's Solution Writing Lab CD-ROM

Computer Test Bank

Resource Pro™ CD-ROM

1 Exhibit knowledge of physical and human geography in posters, maps, displays, games, or other projects.

2 Apply understanding of world geography to creative presentations.

Lesson Plan

1 Engage

Warm-Up Activity

Invite a volunteer to read aloud the Guiding Questions that begin the page. Note that geographers often try to answer questions like these through experiments and projects. Now students will have the opportunity to learn by doing as they complete one of the projects described here.

Activating Prior Knowledge

Ask students to list some research strategies they have used on other class projects. Have volunteers also share project stumbling blocks they have experienced, for example, choosing too broad a research topic. As a class, evaluate all the strategies, developing a list of research "dos and don'ts."

GEOGRAPHY
TOOLS AND CONCEPTS
PROJECT POSSIBILITIES

The chapters in this book have some answers to these important questions.

☞ **What is the Earth's geography like?**

☞ **Where do the world's people live?**

☞ **What is a culture?**

☞ **How do people use the world's resources?**

Doing a project shows what you know about geography! The knowledge and skills you have gained will help you do a great job.

GEO LEO

Project Menu

Now it's time for you to find your own answers by doing projects on your own or with a group. Here are some ways to make your own discoveries about geography.

The Geography Game
Every place in the world has unique characteristics. Use them to create a geography game with your classmates. Choose a country. Find one fact each about its (1) physical features, (2) climate, (3) population, (4) cultures, and (5) natural resources. These facts will be clues in the game. Practice writing them out until they are short and clear. Clues should not be too easy or too hard. They must provide enough information so that someone can figure out the answer. Now

make five playing cards. On one side of each card, write a clue. On the other side, write the name of your country.

Divide into three teams. Each team needs the Atlas in the back of this book. Mix up the cards. Have your teacher or a volunteer pick a card and read the clue to team one. Members have 30 seconds to agree on an answer. If it is correct, the team earns one point. If not, the next team has a chance. Play until the cards are gone. The team with the most points wins.

126

Resource Directory

Teaching Resources

📁 **Book Projects** in the Activities and Projects booklet, pp. 8–19, provides a guide to completing the projects described on these two pages. Each project is supported by three pages of structured guidance.

From Questions to Careers
JOBS IN THE EARTH SCIENCES

People who want to preserve the Earth often have jobs in the sciences. Environmental engineers may figure out how to clean up oil spills or make better use of natural resources. Soil scientists find ways to increase the crops a farmer can grow on a piece of land, or they may work on soil conservation. Ethnobotanists study how certain cultures use plants, especially as medicines. These jobs require a college degree.

Some jobs that help preserve the Earth require less education. People who assist scientists are called technicians. Usually they need only an associate's degree, which takes two years. Technicians may work in agriculture, chemistry, energy, or weather research. All these jobs are vital to helping preserve the environment.

▼A scientist and technician are shown collecting water quality samples from a stream.

World News Today
Collect newspaper and magazine articles about natural resources, economies, and businesses in countries around the world. Display the clippings on a poster. Choose one country, and study the relationship between its economy and its natural resources. Prepare a five-minute speech to tell your class what you found.

Focus on Part of the Whole
The world and its population are extremely varied. Choose a particular region or country. If you are working with a group, have each person choose a different country on a continent. Learn everything you can about the land's physical geography, the population, and the lifestyles of the people there. Use encyclopedias, almanacs, or other books.

Set up a display based on your research. Prepare a large map that includes important physical features of the land. Add captions that explain how the land's physical geography affects people's lives.

Desktop Countries
What countries did your ancestors come from? Select one and do some research on it. Interview someone, perhaps a relative from there, or read about it. Find a recipe you can prepare to share with the class. Then make a desktop display about your country. Write the name of the country on a card and put it on your desk. Add a drawing of the country's flag or map, or display a souvenir. On place cards, write several sentences about each object. Take turns visiting everyone's "desktop countries."

2 Explore
When students have read the lesson text, elicit and discuss their questions. Invite students to suggest which posted research strategies might be most useful to each project. For example, students working on *Desktop Countries* might use e-mail to interview a distant relative or use the Internet to locate and interview someone else from their chosen country. Then talk with students about environmental careers. Invite students to share their own experiences with environmental protection—perhaps from working on a school recyling program.

3 Teach
Students may select a project, suggest an alternative project, or be assigned a project by you. With students, develop clear sequences of steps and realistic schedules. Note that some projects are suited to individual effort while others, such as *The Geography Game,* require a group. Monitor project progress at regular intervals.

4 Assess
Set aside class time for project display and presentation.

Acceptable projects include accurate data reflecting project directions.

Commendable projects build on thoughtful research and present knowledge of world geography.

Outstanding projects show detailed research, a creative approach, and clear links to the Guiding Questions.

Reference

TABLE OF CONTENTS

Atlas

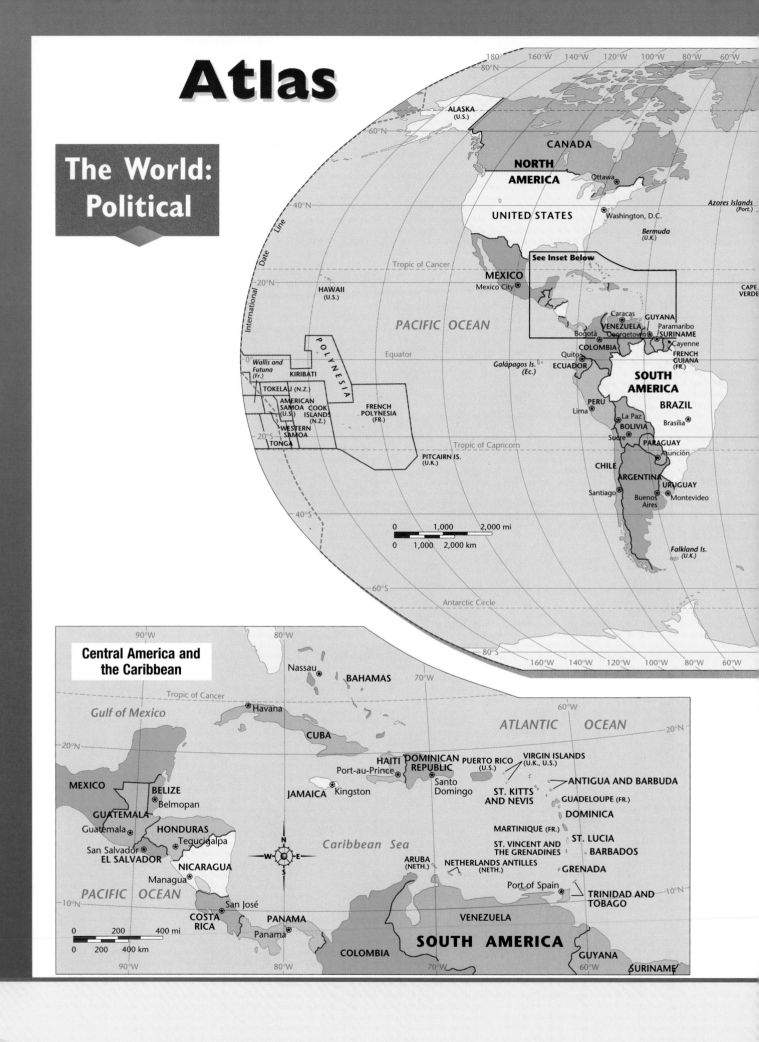

180° 160°W 140°W 120°W 100°W 80°W 60°W
80°N

ALASKA
(U.S.)

60°N

CANADA

NORTH
AMERICA

Ottawa ⊛

40°N

UNITED STATES

⊛ Washington, D.C.

Azores Islands
(Port.)

Bermuda
(U.K.)

See Inset Below

Tropic of Cancer

MEXICO

Mexico City ⊛

CAPE
VERDE

HAWAII
(U.S.)

PACIFIC OCEAN

Caracas
VENEZUELA   GUYANA
Bogotá ⊛ Georgetown ⊛ Paramaribo
                                    SURINAME
COLOMBIA   ● Cayenne
                                    FRENCH
Quito ⊛   GUIANA
ECUADOR   (FR.)

POLYNESIA

Equator

Galápagos Is.
(Ec.)

SOUTH
AMERICA

0° Wallis and
    Futuna
    (Fr.)   KIRIBATI

PERU   BRAZIL
Lima ⊛

TOKELAU (N.Z.)

La Paz   Brasília ⊛
⊛ BOLIVIA
Sucre ⊛

AMERICAN
SAMOA COOK
(U.S.) ISLANDS
       (N.Z.)   FRENCH
                 POLYNESIA
WESTERN   (FR.)
SAMOA

PARAGUAY
⊛ Asunción

20°S
TONGA

Tropic of Capricorn

CHILE
ARGENTINA   URUGUAY

PITCAIRN IS.
(U.K.)

Santiago ⊛ Buenos ● Montevideo
            Aires

40°S

0   1,000   2,000 mi
0 1,000 2,000 km

Falkland Is.
(U.K.)

60°S

Antarctic Circle

80°S

International Date Line

160°W 140°W 120°W 100°W 80°W 60°W

**Central America and
the Caribbean**

90°W   80°W

Nassau
⊛   BAHAMAS   70°W

Tropic of Cancer

Gulf of Mexico

⊛ Havana

ATLANTIC   OCEAN

60°W

20°N

20°N

CUBA

HAITI DOMINICAN PUERTO RICO VIRGIN ISLANDS
       REPUBLIC   (U.S.)   (U.K., U.S.)

MEXICO

BELIZE
⊛ Belmopan

Port-au-Prince ⊛ ⊛ Santo
                    Domingo   ANTIGUA AND BARBUDA
JAMAICA Kingston ⊛ ST. KITTS
                     AND NEVIS   GUADELOUPE (FR.)

GUATEMALA

DOMINICA

Guatemala ⊛   HONDURAS
San Salvador ⊛ Tegucigalpa ⊛
EL SALVADOR

MARTINIQUE (FR.) ST. LUCIA
Caribbean Sea
              ST. VINCENT AND
              THE GRENADINES   BARBADOS
ARUBA
NICARAGUA   (NETH.) NETHERLANDS ANTILLES
Managua ⊛   (NETH.)   GRENADA

PACIFIC OCEAN

Port of Spain ⊛
                    TRINIDAD AND
                    TOBAGO

10°N

10°N

San José ⊛
COSTA   PANAMA
RICA

VENEZUELA

0   200   400 mi
0 200 400 km

Panama ⊛

COLOMBIA SOUTH AMERICA

GUYANA

90°W   80°W   70°W   60°W   SURINAME

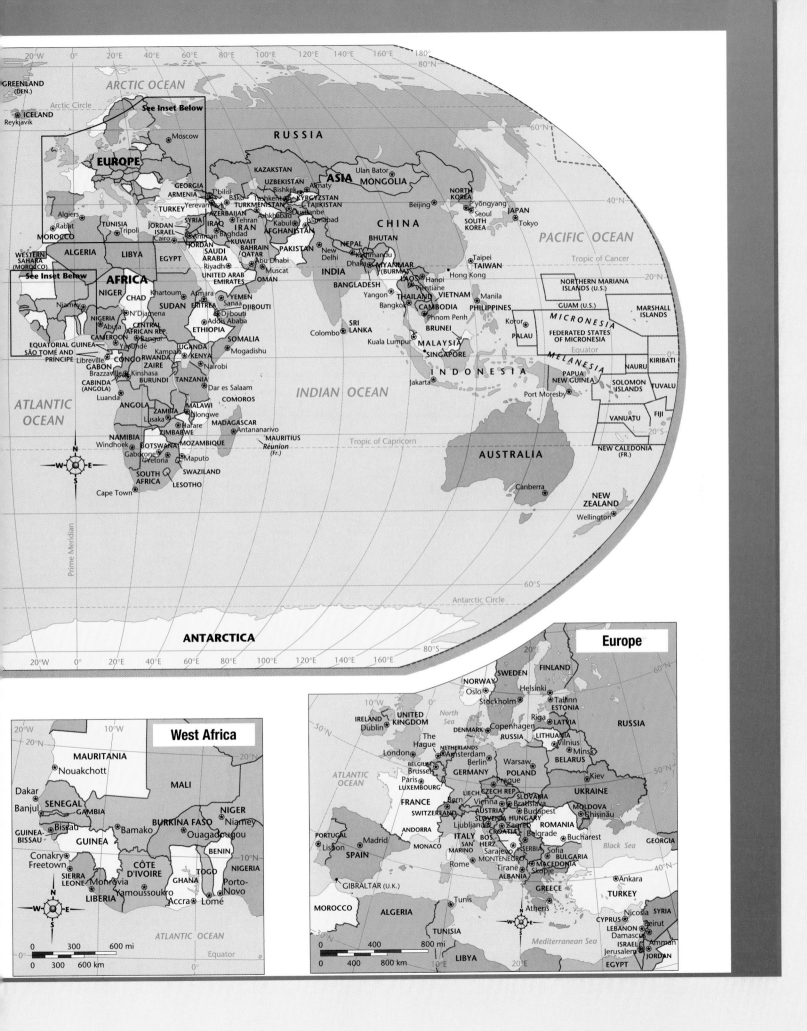

ARCTIC OCEAN

GREENLAND
(DEN.)

Arctic Circle

ICELAND
Reykjavik

See Inset Below

EUROPE

Moscow

RUSSIA

Algiers
Rabat

TUNISIA
Tripoli

MOROCCO

WESTERN
SAHARA
(MOROCCO)

See Inset Below

ALGERIA

LIBYA

EGYPT

AFRICA

NIGER

CHAD

Khartoum

SUDAN

NIGERIA
Abuja

N'Djamena

CENTRAL
AFRICAN REP.
Bangui

ETHIOPIA

EQUATORIAL GUINEA
SÃO TOMÉ AND
PRÍNCIPE

Libreville

CAMEROON
Yaoundé

CONGO

UGANDA

Kampala

GABON
Brazzaville

RWANDA
Kinshasa

ZAIRE

BURUNDI

Luanda

CABINDA
(ANGOLA)

TANZANIA

ATLANTIC
OCEAN

ANGOLA

ZAMBIA

MALAWI
Lilongwe

COMOROS

Lusaka

Harare

MADAGASCAR

NAMIBIA
Windhoek

ZIMBABWE

BOTSWANA

MOZAMBIQUE

MAURITIUS
Réunion
(Fr.)

Gaborone

Pretoria

Maputo

SWAZILAND

SOUTH
AFRICA

LESOTHO

Cape Town

GEORGIA
ARMENIA
T'bilisi
Baku
Yerevan
AZERBAIJAN

KAZAKSTAN

UZBEKISTAN
Tashkent
Bishkek

ASIA

Ulan Bator

MONGOLIA

KYRGYZSTAN

TURKEY

TURKMENISTAN
Ashkhabad

TAJIKISTAN
Dushanbe

Almaty

NORTH
KOREA

Beijing

JORDAN
ISRAEL

SYRIA
Amman
Cairo

IRAQ
Baghdad

Tehran

IRAN

Kabul

Islamabad

CHINA

P'yŏngyang
Seoul

SOUTH
KOREA

JAPAN

Tokyo

SAUDI
ARABIA
Riyadh

JORDAN

KUWAIT

BAHRAIN
QATAR

Abu Dhabi

UNITED ARAB
EMIRATES

AFGHANISTAN

PAKISTAN

New
Delhi

NEPAL
Kathmandu

BHUTAN

Dhaka

PACIFIC OCEAN

Tropic of Cancer

YEMEN
Sanaa

OMAN

Muscat

INDIA

BANGLADESH

MYANMAR
(BURMA)

Taipei

TAIWAN

Hong Kong

NORTHERN MARIANA
ISLANDS (U.S.)

ERITREA

DJIBOUTI
Djibouti

Addis Ababa

SOMALIA

KENYA

Nairobi

Dar es Salaam

Colombo

SRI
LANKA

LAOS
Hanoi

Vientiane

THAILAND

Yangon

Bangkok

CAMBODIA
Phnom Penh

BRUNEI

VIETNAM

Manila

PHILIPPINES

GUAM (U.S.)

MICRONESIA

MARSHALL
ISLANDS

Koror

PALAU

FEDERATED STATES
OF MICRONESIA

MALAYSIA

Kuala Lumpur

SINGAPORE

Equator

MELANESIA

NAURU

KIRIBATI

INDONESIA

INDIAN OCEAN

Jakarta

PAPUA
NEW GUINEA

Port Moresby

SOLOMON
ISLANDS

TUVALU

VANUATU

FIJI

20°S

NEW CALEDONIA
(Fr.)

Tropic of Capricorn

AUSTRALIA

Canberra

NEW
ZEALAND

Wellington

Prime Meridian

Antarctic Circle

ANTARCTICA

20°W   0°   20°E   40°E   60°E   80°E   100°E   120°E   140°E   160°E

West Africa

20°W   10°W

MAURITANIA

Nouakchott

20°N

MALI

Dakar

Banjul

SENEGAL

GAMBIA

GUINEA-
BISSAU
Bissau

GUINEA

Conakry
Freetown

SIERRA
LEONE

Monrovia

LIBERIA

NIGER

BURKINA FASO
Niamey

Bamako

Ouagadougou

BENIN

CÔTE
D'IVOIRE

GHANA

TOGO

Yamoussoukro

Accra

Porto-
Novo

Lomé

NIGERIA

10°N

ATLANTIC OCEAN

Equator

0°

0   300   600 mi

0   300   600 km

Europe

SWEDEN

FINLAND

NORWAY
Oslo

60°N

Stockholm

Helsinki

Tallinn

ESTONIA

10°W

IRELAND
Dublin

UNITED
KINGDOM

North
Sea

Riga

LATVIA

RUSSIA

50°N

DENMARK
Copenhagen

LITHUANIA
Vilnius

Minsk

The
Hague

London

NETHERLANDS
Amsterdam

RUSSIA

BELARUS

ATLANTIC
OCEAN

BELGIUM
Brussels

Berlin

Warsaw

Kiev

Paris

GERMANY

POLAND

UKRAINE

LUXEMBOURG

Prague

FRANCE

LIECH.

CZECH REP.

SLOVAKIA

MOLDOVA
Chişinău

Bern

Vienna

Bratislava

Budapest

SWITZERLAND

AUSTRIA

SLOVENIA

HUNGARY

ROMANIA

ANDORRA

Ljubljana

Zagreb

CROATIA

Belgrade

Bucharest

GEORGIA

PORTUGAL

Madrid

ITALY

BOS.
HERZ.

SERBIA

Black Sea

Lisbon

SPAIN

MONACO

SAN
MARINO

Rome

Sarajevo

MONTENEGRO

Sofia

BULGARIA

40°N

Tirane

MACEDONIA

Skopje

ALBANIA

GIBRALTAR (U.K.)

GREECE

Ankara

TURKEY

MOROCCO

ALGERIA

Tunis

Athens

CYPRUS

Nicosia

SYRIA

LEBANON
Beirut

Damascus

TUNISIA

Mediterranean Sea

ISRAEL
Jerusalem

Amman

JORDAN

LIBYA

EGYPT

0   400   800 mi

0   400   800 km

10°E   20°E

The World: Physical

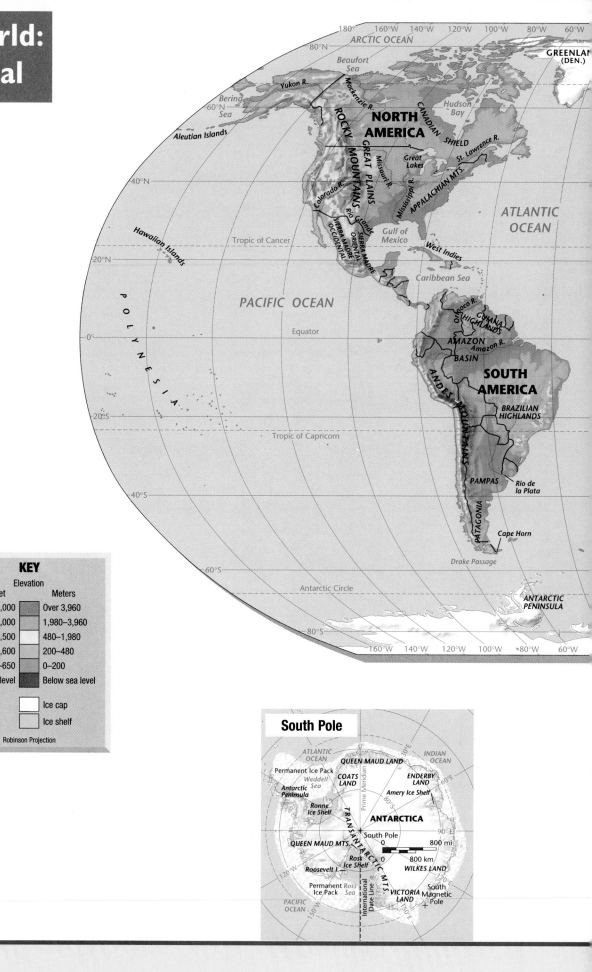

KEY

Elevation

Feet	Meters
Over 13,000	Over 3,960
6,500–13,000	1,980–3,960
1,600–6,500	480–1,980
650–1,600	200–480
0–650	0–200
Below sea level	Below sea level
	Ice cap
	Ice shelf

Robinson Projection

South Pole

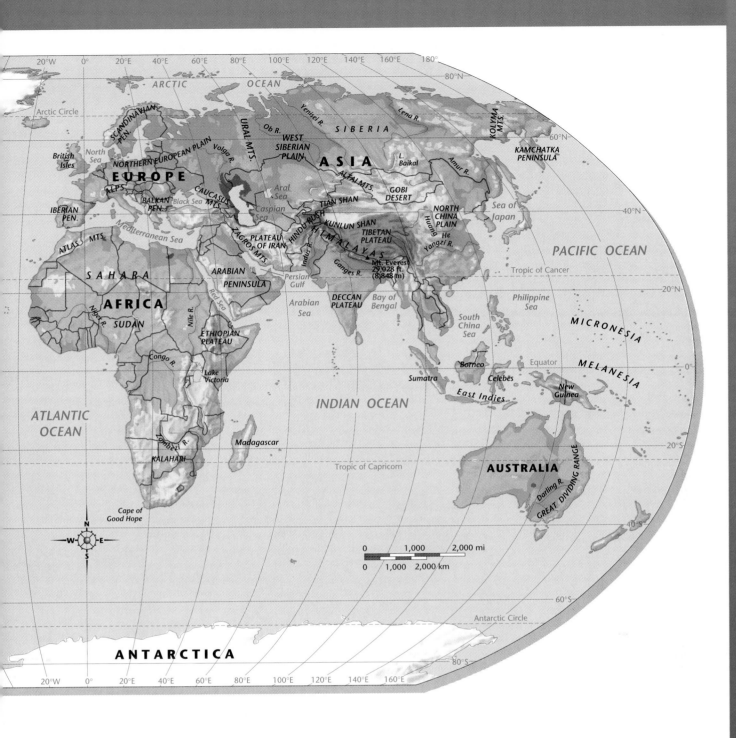

20°W 0° 20°E 40°E 60°E 80°E 100°E 120°E 140°E 160°E 180°

80°N

ARCTIC   OCEAN

Arctic Circle

SCANDINAVIAN PEN.

British Isles

North Sea

NORTHERN EUROPEAN PLAIN

URAL MTS.

Ob R.

WEST SIBERIAN PLAIN

Yenisei R.

S I B E R I A

Lena R.

KOLYMA MTS.

60°N

EUROPE

ALPS

Volga R.

A S I A

L. Baikal

KAMCHATKA PENINSULA

ALTAI MTS.

CAUCASUS MTS.

BALKAN PEN.

Black Sea

Caspian Sea

Aral Sea

TIAN SHAN

GOBI DESERT

Amur R.

Sea of Japan

40°N

IBERIAN PEN.

ATLAS MTS.

Mediterranean Sea

ZAGROS MTS.

PLATEAU OF IRAN

HINDU KUSH

KUNLUN SHAN

TIBETAN PLATEAU

H I M A L A Y A S

Indus R.

NORTH CHINA PLAIN

Huang He

Yangzi R.

PACIFIC OCEAN

SAHARA

ARABIAN PENINSULA

Persian Gulf

Mt. Everest 29,028 ft. (8,848 m)

Ganges R.

Tropic of Cancer

20°N

AFRICA

Niger R.

Red Sea

Nile R.

Arabian Sea

DECCAN PLATEAU

Bay of Bengal

Philippine Sea

SUDAN

ETHIOPIAN PLATEAU

Congo R.

MICRONESIA

0°

Lake Victoria

South China Sea

Borneo

Celebes

Equator

MELANESIA

ATLANTIC OCEAN

INDIAN OCEAN

Sumatra

East Indies

New Guinea

20°S

Zambezi R.

Madagascar

KALAHARI

Tropic of Capricorn

AUSTRALIA

Darling R.

GREAT DIVIDING RANGE

Cape of Good Hope

N
W   E
S

0   1,000   2,000 mi

0   1,000   2,000 km

40°S

60°S

Antarctic Circle

A N T A R C T I C A

80°S

20°W 0° 20°E 40°E 60°E 80°E 100°E 120°E 140°E 160°E

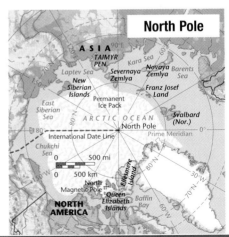

North Pole

A S I A

90°E

TAIMYR PEN.

Kara Sea

Laptev Sea

Severnaya Zemlya

Novaya Zemlya

Barents Sea

New Siberian Islands

Franz Josef Land

East Siberian Sea

Permanent Ice Pack

Svalbard (Nor.)

ARCTIC OCEAN

North Pole

International Date Line

Prime Meridian

Chukchi Sea

0   500 mi

0   500 km

North Magnetic Pole

Ellesmere Island

Queen Elizabeth Islands

Baffin Bay

NORTH AMERICA

United States: Political

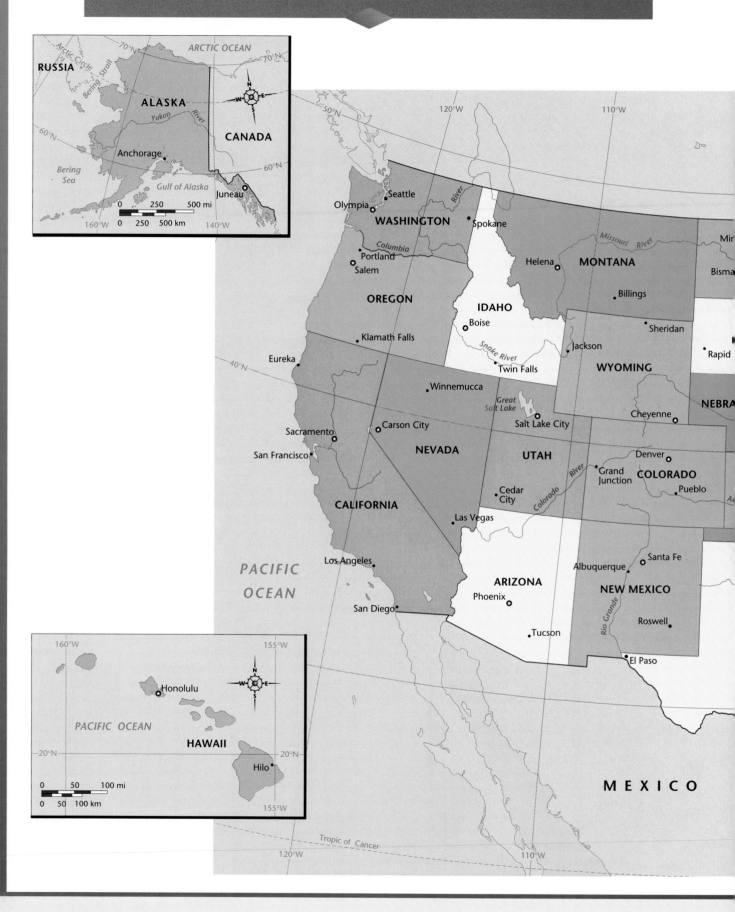

RUSSIA

ALASKA

CANADA

ARCTIC OCEAN

Arctic Circle

70°N

70°N

60°N

60°N

160°W

140°W

Yukon River

Anchorage

Bering Sea

Gulf of Alaska

Juneau

0   250   500 mi

0   250   500 km

PACIFIC OCEAN

160°W

155°W

Honolulu

PACIFIC OCEAN

HAWAII

20°N

20°N

Hilo

0   50   100 mi

0   50   100 km

155°W

50°N

120°W

110°W

River

Missouri River

Mir

Seattle

Olympia

WASHINGTON

Spokane

Columbia

Portland

Salem

OREGON

Helena

MONTANA

Bisma

Billings

IDAHO

Boise

Sheridan

Klamath Falls

Snake River

Jackson

Eureka

40°N

Twin Falls

WYOMING

Rapid

Winnemucca

Great Salt Lake

Salt Lake City

Cheyenne

NEBRA

Carson City

Sacramento

NEVADA

UTAH

Denver

COLORADO

San Francisco

Colorado River

Grand Junction

Pueblo

Cedar City

Las Vegas

CALIFORNIA

Los Angeles

Santa Fe

Albuquerque

ARIZONA

NEW MEXICO

San Diego

Phoenix

Roswell

Tucson

Rio Grande

El Paso

PACIFIC OCEAN

MEXICO

Tropic of Cancer

120°W

110°W

CANADA

Lake Superior

Duluth

Sault Ste. Marie

NORTH DAKOTA

MINNESOTA

MICHIGAN

Lake Huron

Presque Isle

MAINE

Augusta

Portland

Montpelier

VERMONT

NEW HAMPSHIRE

Concord

Boston

SOUTH DAKOTA

Minneapolis

St. Paul

WISCONSIN

Lake Michigan

Lansing

Lake Ontario

Buffalo

NEW YORK

Albany

MASSACHUSETTS

Providence

Hartford

RHODE ISLAND

Milwaukee

Madison

Detroit

Lake Erie

Cleveland

PENNSYLVANIA

Harrisburg

New Haven

CONNECTICUT

New York City

Missouri

Mississippi River

Chicago

Pittsburgh

Trenton

NEW JERSEY

Philadelphia

IOWA

Cedar Rapids

OHIO

Columbus

Baltimore

Dover

DELAWARE

Omaha

Des Moines

INDIANA

Indianapolis

Cincinnati

Washington, D.C.

Annapolis

MARYLAND

Lincoln

ILLINOIS

Springfield

WEST VIRGINIA

Richmond

Topeka

Kansas City

Louisville

Frankfort

Charleston

VIRGINIA

Norfolk

KANSAS

St. Louis

Ohio River

KENTUCKY

Jefferson City

River

MISSOURI

Tennessee River

Raleigh

Wichita

Nashville

NORTH CAROLINA

OKLAHOMA

Tulsa

ARKANSAS

Memphis

TENNESSEE

Charlotte

ATLANTIC OCEAN

Oklahoma City

Little Rock

Columbia

SOUTH CAROLINA

Mississippi River

Birmingham

Atlanta

Charleston

Pine Bluff

GEORGIA

Red River

Dallas

Shreveport

MISSISSIPPI

Jackson

ALABAMA

Columbus

Savannah

Montgomery

Jackonsville

TEXAS

Hattiesburg

Tallahassee

Austin

Baton Rouge

LOUISIANA

New Orleans

FLORIDA

San Antonio

Houston

Tampa

Lake Okeechobee

Gulf of Mexico

Miami

Rio Grande

90°W

80°W

70°W

40°N

30°N

90°W

80°W

0   150   300 mi

0   150   300 km

KEY

——— National boundary

——— State boundary

⊛ National capital

⊙ State capital

• Other city

Transverse Mercator Projection

North and South America: Political

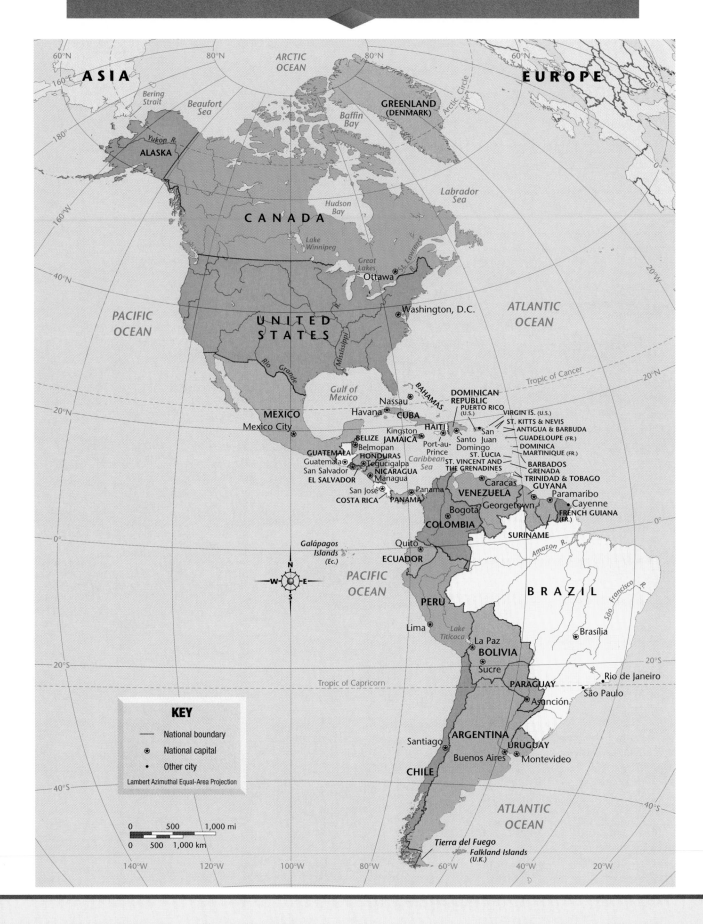

ASIA

EUROPE

ARCTIC OCEAN

60°N
80°N
80°N
60°N
160°E
20°E

Bering Strait

Beaufort Sea

GREENLAND (DENMARK)

Arctic Circle

180°
160°W

Yukon R.
ALASKA

Baffin Bay

0°

Labrador Sea

40°N

CANADA

Hudson Bay

Lake Winnipeg

Great Lakes

St. Lawrence R.

Ottawa

20°W

PACIFIC OCEAN

UNITED STATES

Mississippi

Washington, D.C.

ATLANTIC OCEAN

Rio Grande

Tropic of Cancer

20°N

Gulf of Mexico

BAHAMAS

DOMINICAN REPUBLIC

20°N

MEXICO

Nassau

PUERTO RICO (U.S.)

VIRGIN IS. (U.S.)

Mexico City

Havana

CUBA

Kingston

HAITI

San Juan

ST. KITTS & NEVIS

ANTIGUA & BARBUDA

BELIZE

JAMAICA

Port-au-Prince

Santo Domingo

GUADELOUPE (FR.)

GUATEMALA

Belmopan

HONDURAS

Caribbean Sea

ST. LUCIA

DOMINICA

MARTINIQUE (FR.)

Guatemala

Tegucigalpa

ST. VINCENT AND THE GRENADINES

BARBADOS

San Salvador

NICARAGUA

GRENADA

EL SALVADOR

Managua

Caracas

TRINIDAD & TOBAGO

San José

Panama

VENEZUELA

GUYANA

COSTA RICA

PANAMA

Bogotá

Georgetown

Paramaribo

Cayenne

FRENCH GUIANA (FR.)

COLOMBIA

SURINAME

0°

Galápagos Islands (Ec.)

Quito

Amazon R.

0°

ECUADOR

N
W E
S

BRAZIL

São Francisco R.

PACIFIC OCEAN

PERU

Lima

Lake Titicaca

Brasília

La Paz

20°S

BOLIVIA

20°S

Tropic of Capricorn

Sucre

Rio de Janeiro

PARAGUAY

Asunción

São Paulo

KEY

— National boundary

⊛ National capital

• Other city

Lambert Azimuthal Equal-Area Projection

ARGENTINA

Santiago

URUGUAY

Buenos Aires

Montevideo

CHILE

0   500   1,000 mi
0   500   1,000 km

40°S

ATLANTIC OCEAN

40°S

Tierra del Fuego

Falkland Islands (U.K.)

140°W
120°W
100°W
80°W
60°W
40°W
20°W

North and South America: Physical

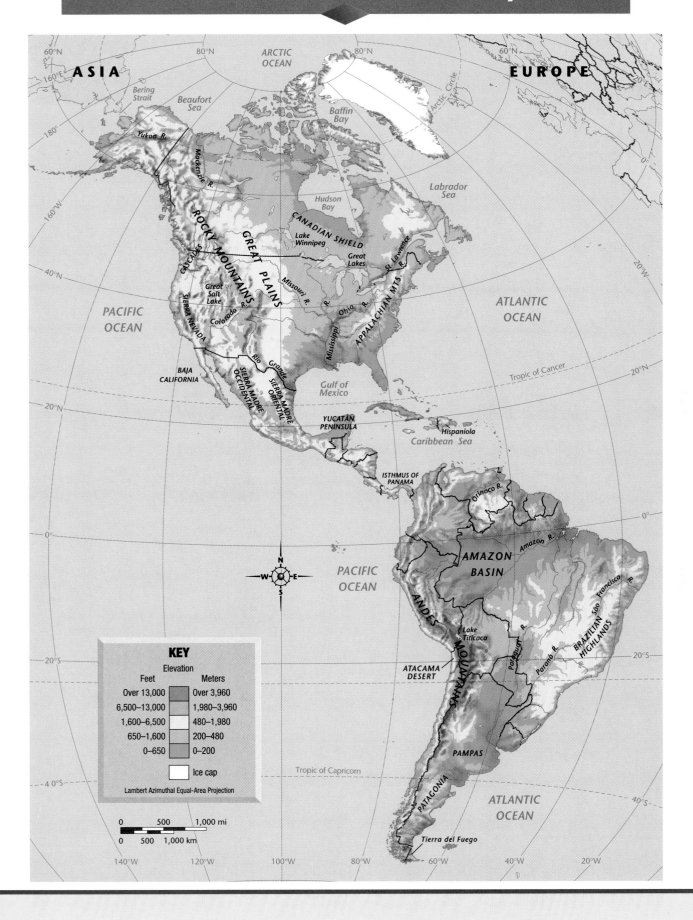

ASIA

EUROPE

ARCTIC OCEAN

Bering Strait

Beaufort Sea

Baffin Bay

Arctic Circle

Yukon R.

Mackenzie R.

Hudson Bay

Labrador Sea

ROCKY MOUNTAINS

CASCADES

GREAT PLAINS

CANADIAN SHIELD

Lake Winnipeg

Great Lakes

St. Lawrence R.

APPALACHIAN MTS.

Missouri R.

SIERRA NEVADA

Great Salt Lake

Colorado R.

Mississippi R.

Ohio R.

PACIFIC OCEAN

ATLANTIC OCEAN

BAJA CALIFORNIA

SIERRA MADRE OCCIDENTAL

SIERRA MADRE ORIENTAL

Rio Grande

Gulf of Mexico

Tropic of Cancer

YUCATÁN PENINSULA

Hispaniola

Caribbean Sea

ISTHMUS OF PANAMA

Orinoco R.

AMAZON BASIN

Amazon R.

ANDES MOUNTAINS

Lake Titicaca

São Francisco R.

BRAZILIAN HIGHLANDS

PACIFIC OCEAN

ATACAMA DESERT

Paraguay R.

Paraná R.

PAMPAS

Tropic of Capricorn

PATAGONIA

ATLANTIC OCEAN

Tierra del Fuego

KEY
Elevation

Feet		Meters
Over 13,000		Over 3,960
6,500–13,000		1,980–3,960
1,600–6,500		480–1,980
650–1,600		200–480
0–650		0–200
Ice cap		

Lambert Azimuthal Equal-Area Projection

0   500   1,000 mi

0   500 1,000 km

Europe: Political

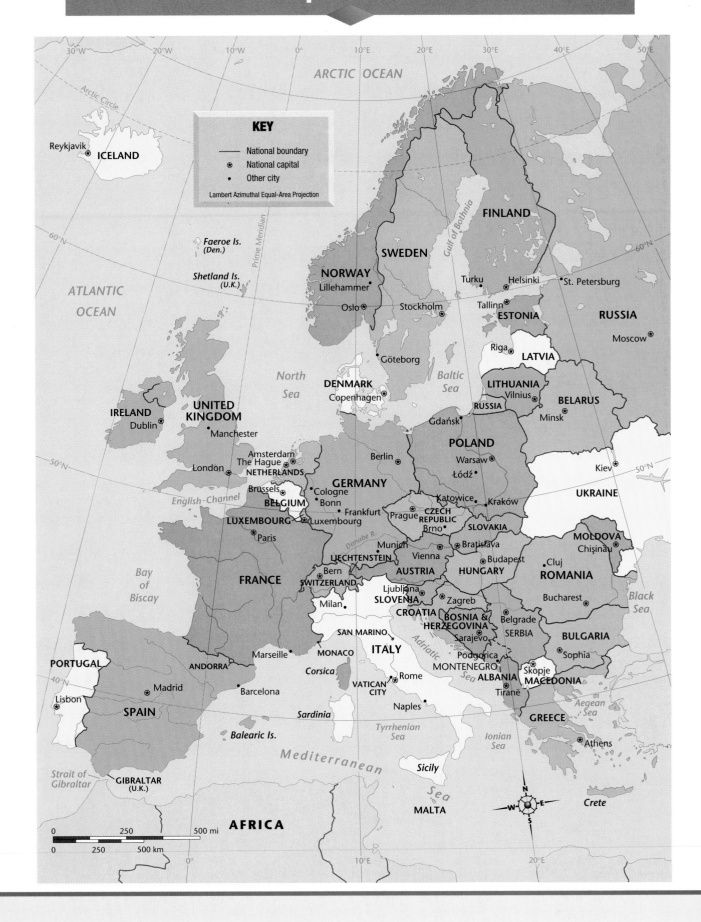

KEY

— National boundary
⊛ National capital
• Other city

Lambert Azimuthal Equal-Area Projection

ARCTIC OCEAN

Arctic Circle

Reykjavik ICELAND

ATLANTIC OCEAN

Faeroe Is. (Den.)

Shetland Is. (U.K.)

Prime Meridian

FINLAND

SWEDEN

NORWAY
Lillehammer
Oslo
Stockholm

Turku Helsinki • St. Petersburg

Tallinn ESTONIA

RUSSIA
Moscow ⊛

Göteborg

Riga LATVIA

North Sea

Baltic Sea

LITHUANIA
Vilnius

BELARUS
Minsk

DENMARK
Copenhagen

RUSSIA

Gdańsk

POLAND
Warsaw ⊛
Łódź

Kiev ⊛

IRELAND
Dublin

UNITED KINGDOM
• Manchester

London

Amsterdam
The Hague
NETHERLANDS

Brussels
BELGIUM

English Channel

Berlin

GERMANY
Cologne
Bonn
Frankfurt

LUXEMBOURG
Luxembourg

Prague
CZECH REPUBLIC
Brno

Katowice Kraków

SLOVAKIA

UKRAINE

MOLDOVA
Chişinău ⊛

Paris

Danube R.

Munich

LIECHTENSTEIN

Vienna

Bratislava

Budapest

Cluj

ROMANIA
Bucharest

FRANCE

Bay of Biscay

Bern
SWITZERLAND

AUSTRIA

HUNGARY

Ljubljana
SLOVENIA
Milan

Zagreb

CROATIA

BOSNIA & HERZEGOVINA
Sarajevo

Belgrade
SERBIA

Black Sea

BULGARIA
Sophia

PORTUGAL

ANDORRA

Marseille

SAN MARINO

MONACO

ITALY

Corsica

VATICAN CITY
Rome

Podgorica
MONTENEGRO

Skopje
MACEDONIA

ALBANIA
Tiranë

Adriatic Sea

Madrid

Barcelona

Naples

Aegean Sea

GREECE

Lisbon

SPAIN

Sardinia

Balearic Is.

Tyrrhenian Sea

Ionian Sea

Athens

Strait of Gibraltar

GIBRALTAR (U.K.)

Mediterranean Sea

Sicily

MALTA

N
W E
S

Crete

AFRICA

0   250   500 mi
0   250   500 km

Europe: Physical

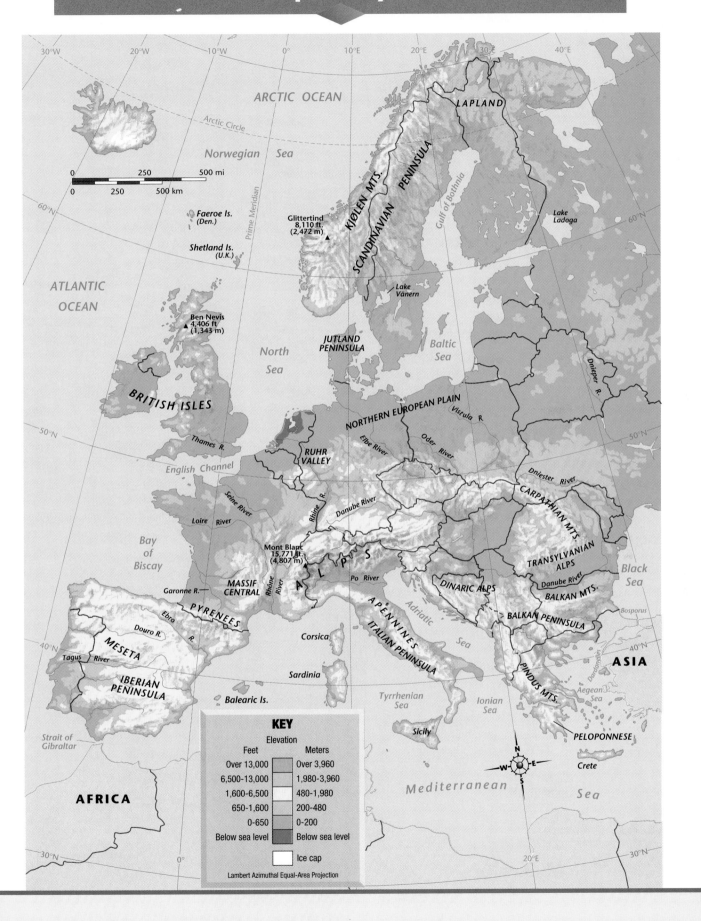

ARCTIC OCEAN

LAPLAND

Norwegian Sea

KJØLEN MTS.

SCANDINAVIAN PENINSULA

Gulf of Bothnia

Lake Ladoga

Faeroe Is. (Den.)

Glittertind 8,110 ft. (2,472 m)

Shetland Is. (U.K.)

ATLANTIC OCEAN

Ben Nevis 4,406 ft (1,343 m)

Lake Vänern

North Sea

JUTLAND PENINSULA

Baltic Sea

BRITISH ISLES

NORTHERN EUROPEAN PLAIN

Vistula R.

Dnieper R.

Thames R.

Elbe River

Oder River

RUHR VALLEY

English Channel

Seine River

Rhine R.

Danube River

Dniester River

CARPATHIAN MTS.

Loire River

Bay of Biscay

Mont Blanc 15,771 ft. (4,807 m)

A L P S

Rhône River

Po River

TRANSYLVANIAN ALPS

Danube River

MASSIF CENTRAL

Garonne R.

DINARIC ALPS

BALKAN MTS.

PYRENEES

A P E N N I N E S

ITALIAN PENINSULA

Adriatic Sea

BALKAN PENINSULA

Bosporus

Black Sea

Ebro R.

Douro R.

MESETA

Corsica

PINDUS MTS.

Dardanelles

ASIA

Tagus River

IBERIAN PENINSULA

Sardinia

Tyrrhenian Sea

Ionian Sea

Aegean Sea

Balearic Is.

PELOPONNESE

Strait of Gibraltar

Sicily

Crete

Mediterranean Sea

AFRICA

KEY

Elevation

Feet	Meters
Over 13,000	Over 3,960
6,500–13,000	1,980–3,960
1,600–6,500	480–1,980
650–1,600	200–480
0–650	0–200
Below sea level	Below sea level
	Ice cap

Lambert Azimuthal Equal-Area Projection

0   250   500 mi
0   250   500 km

Africa: Political

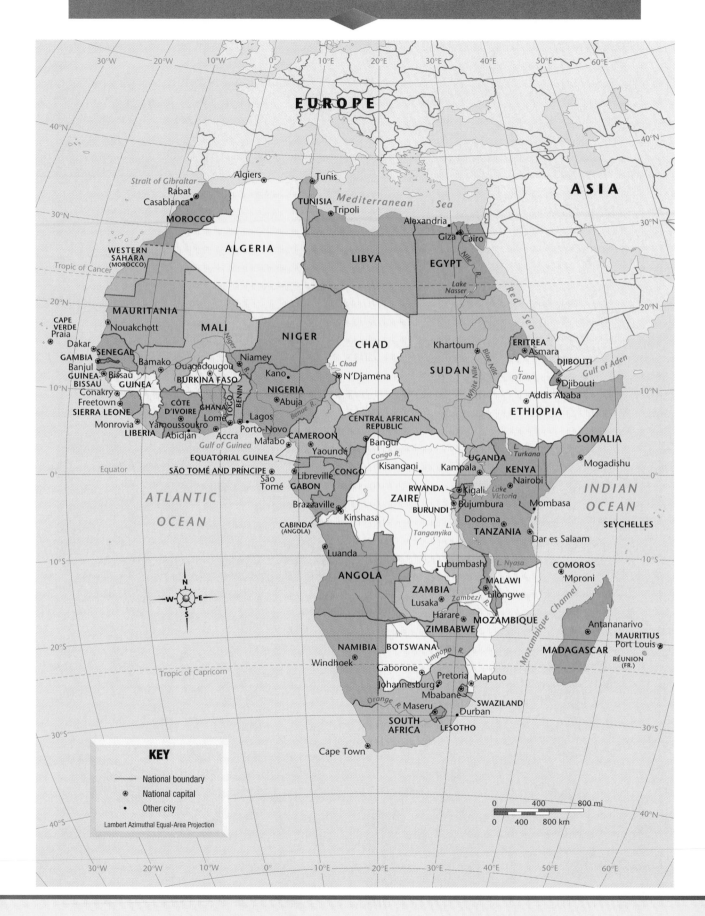

EUROPE

ASIA

Strait of Gibraltar
Algiers ⊛
Rabat ●
Casablanca ●
MOROCCO
Tunis ⊛
TUNISIA
Tripoli ●
Mediterranean Sea
Alexandria ●
Giza ● Cairo ⊛
EGYPT
Nile R.

WESTERN SAHARA (MOROCCO)
ALGERIA
LIBYA
Tropic of Cancer
Lake Nasser

MAURITANIA
CAPE VERDE
Praia ⊛
Nouakchott ⊛
Dakar ●
MALI
Bamako ●
SENEGAL
NIGER
Niamey ⊛
Ouagadougou ⊛
BURKINA FASO
Kano ●
CHAD
Khartoum ⊛
N'Djamena ⊛
L. Chad
Niger R.
SUDAN
Blue Nile
ERITREA
Asmara ⊛
DJIBOUTI
L. Tana
Gulf of Aden
Djibouti ⊛
White Nile

GAMBIA
Banjul ⊛
GUINEA-BISSAU
Bissau ⊛
GUINEA
Conakry ⊛
Freetown ⊛
SIERRA LEONE
NIGERIA
Abuja ⊛
CÔTE D'IVOIRE
GHANA
Lome ⊛
TOGO
BENIN
Lagos ●
Porto-Novo ⊛
Monrovia ⊛
Yamoussoukro ⊛
LIBERIA
Abidjan ●
Accra ⊛
Malabo ⊛
CAMEROON
Yaoundé ⊛
Benue R.
CENTRAL AFRICAN REPUBLIC
Bangui ⊛
Addis Ababa ⊛
ETHIOPIA
SOMALIA
L. Turkana
Mogadishu ⊛

Gulf of Guinea
EQUATORIAL GUINEA
SÃO TOMÉ AND PRÍNCIPE
São Tomé ●
Libreville ⊛
GABON
CONGO
Kisangani ●
Congo R.
ZAIRE
Kampala ⊛
UGANDA
RWANDA
Kigali ⊛
KENYA
Nairobi ⊛
Lake Victoria
BURUNDI
Bujumbura ⊛
Mombasa ●

Equator

ATLANTIC OCEAN

Brazzaville ⊛
Kinshasa ⊛
CABINDA (ANGOLA)
L. Tanganyika
Dodoma ⊛
TANZANIA
Dar es Salaam ●
SEYCHELLES

INDIAN OCEAN

Luanda ⊛
Lubumbashi ●
L. Nyasa
ANGOLA
ZAMBIA
Lusaka ⊛
MALAWI
Lilongwe ⊛
COMOROS
Moroni ⊛

NAMIBIA
BOTSWANA
Windhoek ⊛
Zambezi R.
Hárare ⊛
ZIMBABWE
MOZAMBIQUE
Mozambique Channel
Antananarivo ⊛
MADAGASCAR
MAURITIUS
Port Louis ⊛
RÉUNION (FR.)

Tropic of Capricorn
Gaborone ⊛
Limpopo R.
Pretoria ⊛
Maputo ⊛
Johannesburg ●
Mbabane ⊛
SWAZILAND
Orange R.
Maseru ⊛
Durban ●
SOUTH AFRICA
LESOTHO
Cape Town ⊛

KEY

— National boundary
⊛ National capital
● Other city

Lambert Azimuthal Equal-Area Projection

0   400   800 mi
0   400   800 km

Africa: Physical

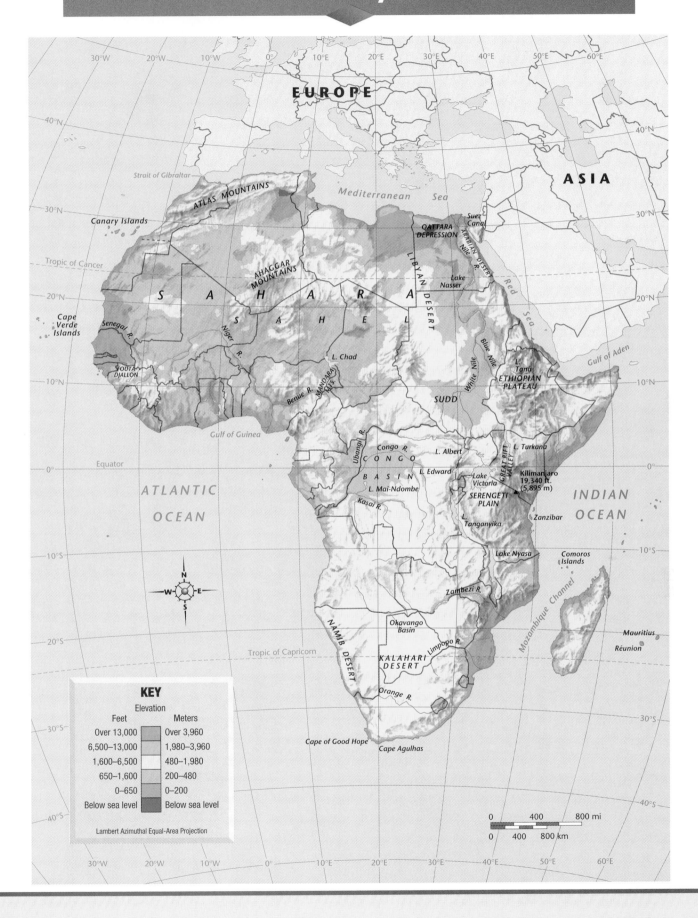

EUROPE

ASIA

Strait of Gibraltar

Mediterranean Sea

ATLAS MOUNTAINS

Canary Islands

Tropic of Cancer

QATTARA DEPRESSION

Suez Canal

Cape Verde Islands

S A H A R A

AHAGGAR MOUNTAINS

ARABIAN DESERT

LIBYAN DESERT

Nile R.

Lake Nasser

Senegal R.

S A H E L

Red Sea

Niger R.

FOUTA DJALLON

L. Chad

Benue R.

MANDARA MTS.

Blue Nile

White Nile

L. Tana

ETHIOPIAN PLATEAU

Gulf of Aden

Gulf of Guinea

SUDD

Ubangi R.

Congo R.

L. Albert

L. Turkana

C O N G O

B A S I N

L. Edward

GREAT RIFT VALLEY

Kilimanjaro 19,340 ft. (5,895 m)

Equator

L. Maï-Ndombe

Lake Victoria

Kasai R.

SERENGETI PLAIN

Zanzibar

ATLANTIC OCEAN

INDIAN OCEAN

L. Tanganyika

Lake Nyasa

Comoros Islands

Zambezi R.

Mozambique Channel

Mauritius

Réunion

NAMIB DESERT

Okavango Basin

Limpopo R.

Tropic of Capricorn

KALAHARI DESERT

Orange R.

Cape of Good Hope

Cape Agulhas

KEY

Elevation

Feet	Meters
Over 13,000	Over 3,960
6,500–13,000	1,980–3,960
1,600–6,500	480–1,980
650–1,600	200–480
0–650	0–200
Below sea level	Below sea level

Lambert Azimuthal Equal-Area Projection

0   400   800 mi

0   400   800 km

N
W   E
S

Asia: Political

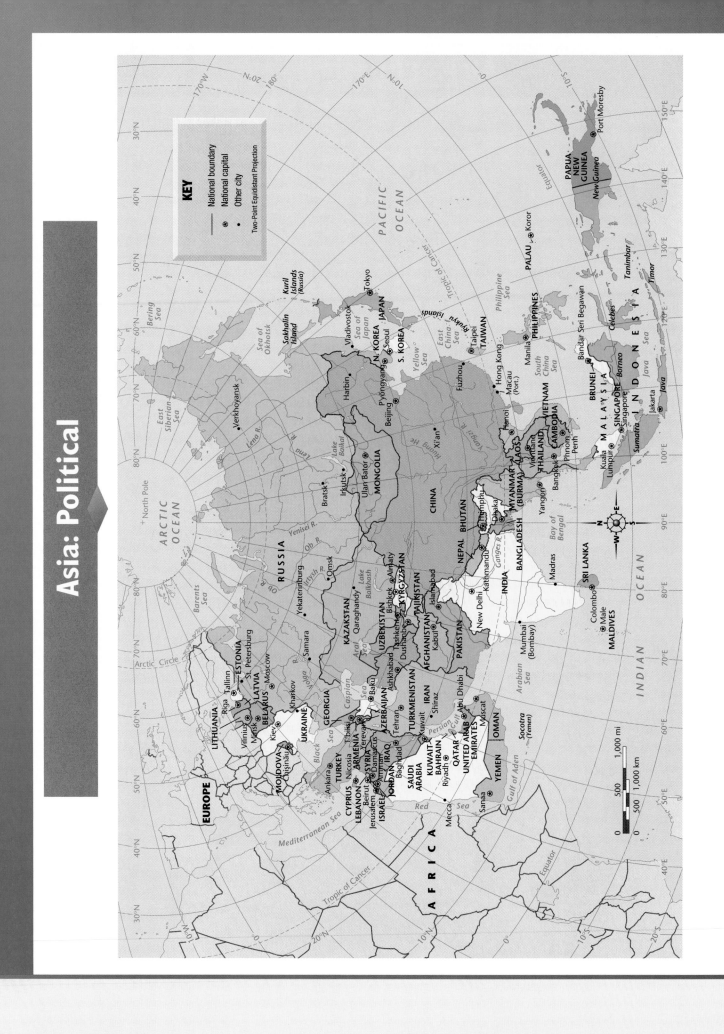

KEY

National boundary
⊛ National capital
• Other city

Two-Point Equidistant Projection

EUROPE

AFRICA

RUSSIA

ARCTIC OCEAN

+ North Pole

PACIFIC OCEAN

INDIAN OCEAN

Bering Sea

East Siberian Sea

Sea of Okhotsk

Sakhalin Island

Kuril Islands (Russia)

Barents Sea

Verkhoyansk

Leno R.

Yenisei R.

Ob R.

Lake Baikal

Bratsk

Irkutsk

Ulan Bator ⊛

MONGOLIA

Vladivostok

Tokyo ⊛

Sea of Japan

JAPAN

N. KOREA

Pyongyang ⊛

Seoul ⊛ S. KOREA

Yellow Sea

Harbin

Beijing ⊛

CHINA

Huang He

Xi'an

Yangtze R.

Fuzhou

East China Sea

Macau (Port.)

Hong Kong

Taipei ⊛

TAIWAN

Ryukyu Islands

Philippine Sea

Manila ⊛

PHILIPPINES

PALAU ⊛ Koror

PAPUA NEW GUINEA

Port Moresby ⊛

New Guinea

Equator

Yekaterinburg

Omsk

Samara

Irtysh R.

Lake Balkhash

Aral Sea

KAZAKSTAN

Qaraghandy

Bishkek ⊛

Almaty

KYRGYZSTAN

Tashkent ⊛

UZBEKISTAN

Dushanbe ⊛

TAJIKISTAN

AFGHANISTAN

Kabul ⊛

Islamabad ⊛

PAKISTAN

Kathmandu ⊛

NEPAL

BHUTAN

Thimphu ⊛

New Delhi ⊛

INDIA

Ganges R.

BANGLADESH

Dhaka ⊛

MYANMAR (BURMA)

Yangon ⊛

Bay of Bengal

Madras

Mumbai (Bombay)

Arabian Sea

Colombo ⊛

SRI LANKA

Male ⊛

MALDIVES

Hanoi ⊛

VIETNAM

LAOS

Vientiane ⊛

THAILAND

Bangkok ⊛

CAMBODIA

Phnom Penh ⊛

Kuala Lumpur ⊛

MALAYSIA

SINGAPORE ⊛

Singapore

Bandar Seri Begawan ⊛

BRUNEI

Borneo

INDONESIA

Sumatra

Java

Jakarta ⊛

Java Sea

Celebes

South China Sea

Tanimbar

Timor

Ashkhabad ⊛

TURKMENISTAN

Caspian Sea

Baku ⊛

AZERBAIJAN

Tehran ⊛

IRAN

Shiraz

Persian Gulf

Kuwait ⊛

KUWAIT

BAHRAIN

QATAR

Abu Dhabi ⊛

UNITED ARAB EMIRATES

Muscat ⊛

OMAN

Socotra (Yemen)

GEORGIA

T'bilisi ⊛

Yerevan ⊛

ARMENIA

TURKEY

Ankara ⊛

Nicosia ⊛

CYPRUS

LEBANON

Beirut ⊛

Damascus ⊛

SYRIA

Amman ⊛

JORDAN

Jerusalem ⊛

ISRAEL

IRAQ

Baghdad ⊛

SAUDI ARABIA

Riyadh ⊛

YEMEN

Sanaa ⊛

Mecca

Red Sea

Gulf of Aden

Gulf of Aden

ESTONIA

Tallinn ⊛

LATVIA

Riga ⊛

LITHUANIA

Vilnius ⊛

BELARUS

Minsk ⊛

St. Petersburg

Moscow ⊛

Kharkov

UKRAINE

Kiev ⊛

MOLDOVA

Chişinău ⊛

Volga R.

Black Sea

Mediterranean Sea

Tropic of Cancer

Tropic of Cancer

Arctic Circle

Equator

1,000 mi

0   500   1,000 km

0   500

90°E   100°E   110°E   120°E   130°E   140°E   150°E

80°E

70°E

60°E

50°E

40°E

30°N   20°N   10°N   0°   10°S   20°S

40°N

50°N

60°N

70°N

80°N

30°N

40°N

50°N

60°N

70°N

80°N

180°   170°W   170°E   160°E   20°N   10°N

N

S

W   E

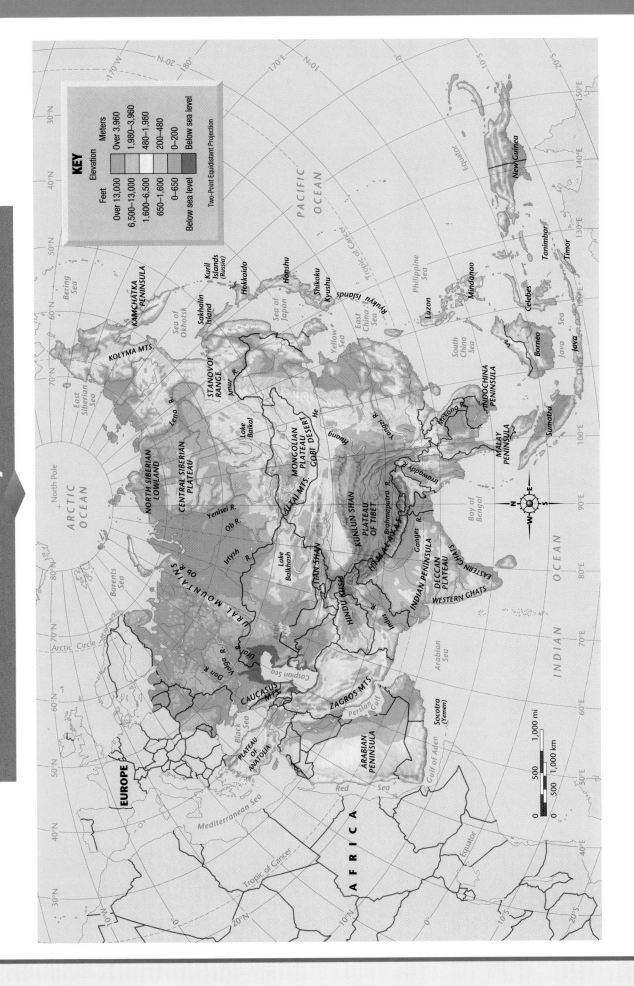

Asia: Physical

KEY

Elevation

Feet	Meters
Over 13,000	Over 3,960
6,500–13,000	1,980–3,960
1,600–6,500	480–1,980
650–1,600	200–480
0–650	0–200
Below sea level	Below sea level

Two-Point Equidistant Projection

ARCTIC OCEAN

North Pole

PACIFIC OCEAN

New Guinea

Equator

Tanimbar

Timor

Tropic of Cancer

Philippine Sea

Mindanao

Celebes

Luzon

Borneo

Java Sea

Java

Sumatra

Ryukyu Islands

South China Sea

Kyushu

Shikoku

Honshu

Hokkaido

Kuril Islands (Russia)

Sakhalin Island

Sea of Japan

Yellow Sea

East China Sea

INDOCHINA PENINSULA

MALAY PENINSULA

Mekong R.

Irrawaddy R.

Bay of Bengal

EASTERN GHATS

WESTERN GHATS

DECCAN PLATEAU

INDIAN PENINSULA

Ganges R.

Brahmaputra R.

HIMALAYAS

PLATEAU OF TIBET

KUNLUN SHAN

Huang

He

Yangtzi R.

GOBI DESERT

MONGOLIAN PLATEAU

ALTAI MTS.

TIAN SHAN

HINDU KUSH

Indus R.

Amur R.

STANOVOI RANGE

Lena R.

Lake Baikal

CENTRAL SIBERIAN PLATEAU

NORTH SIBERIAN LOWLAND

KOLYMA MTS.

KAMCHATKA PENINSULA

Sea of Okhotsk

Bering Sea

East Siberian Sea

Yenisei R.

Ob R.

Irtysh R.

Lake Balkhash

URAL MOUNTAINS

Ob R.

Aral Sea

CAUCASUS MTS.

Caspian Sea

Volga R.

Don R.

Ural R.

ZAGROS MTS.

Persian Gulf

Socotra (Yemen)

Gulf of Aden

ARABIAN PENINSULA

Red Sea

PLATEAU OF ANATOLIA

Black Sea

Mediterranean Sea

Barents Sea

Arctic Circle

EUROPE

AFRICA

Arabian Sea

INDIAN OCEAN

Tropic of Cancer

Equator

1,000 mi

1,000 km

500

500

1,000 km

0

0

N
W E
S

Australia, New Zealand, and the Pacific Islands: Physical–Political

PACIFIC OCEAN

INDIAN OCEAN

Philippine Sea

Arafura Sea

Coral Sea

Tasman Sea

Timor Sea

NORTHERN MARIANA ISLANDS (U.S.)

GUAM (U.S.)

CAROLINE ISLANDS

FEDERATED STATES OF MICRONESIA

⊛ Palikir

MARSHALL ISLANDS

Wake Island (U.S.)

⊛ Tarawa

Gilbert Islands

Midway Islands (U.S.)

Hawaiian Islands (U.S.)

Line Islands

KIRIBATI

NAURU

⊛ Yaren

TUVALU

Funafuti ⊛

WESTERN SAMOA

Apia ⊛

AMERICAN SAMOA (U.S.)

COOK ISLANDS (N.Z.)

Society Islands

FRENCH POLYNESIA (FR.)

Tahiti

PITCAIRN ISLAND (U.K.)

SOLOMON ISLANDS

Honiara ●

VANUATU

New Hebrides

Port-Vila ⊛

NEW CALEDONIA (FR.)

FIJI

Suva ●

TONGA

Nukualofa ⊛

Tropic of Cancer

Equator

Tropic of Capricorn

International Date Line

Auckland ●

North Island

Wellington ⊛

Christchurch ●

Cook Strait

NEW ZEALAND

South Island

Dunedin ●

Stewart Island

AUCKLAND ISLANDS (N.Z.)

Brisbane ⊛

QUEENSLAND

GREAT DIVIDING RANGE

GREAT ARTESIAN BASIN

Darling R.

NEW SOUTH WALES

Sydney ●

Canberra ⊛

Murray R.

VICTORIA

Melbourne ⊛

Bass Strait

TASMANIA

Hobart ⊛

AUSTRALIA

CAPE YORK PENINSULA

ARNHEM LAND

BARKLY TABLELAND

NORTHERN TERRITORY

SIMPSON DESERT

Lake Eyre

SOUTH AUSTRALIA

Adelaide ⊛

Great Australian Bight

NULLARBOR PLAIN

GREAT VICTORIA DESERT

GIBSON DESERT

WESTERN AUSTRALIA

GREAT SANDY DESERT

KIMBERLEY PLATEAU

Darwin ●

Great Barrier Reef

Perth ⊛

DARLING RANGE

KEY

Elevation		
Feet	Meters	
6,500–13,000	1,980–3,960	
1,600–6,500	480–1,980	
650–1,600	200–480	
0–650	0–200	
Below sea level	Below sea level	

⊛ National capital

⊛ State or territorial capital

● Other city

Mercator Projection

0   500   1,000 mi

0   500   1,000 km

The Arctic

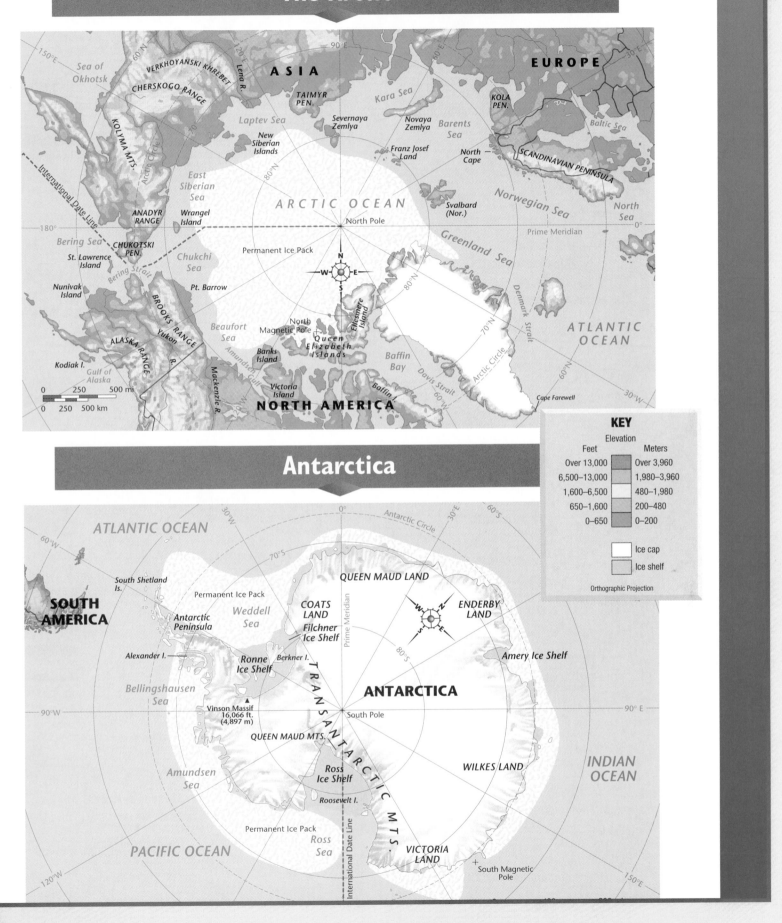

Sea of Okhotsk
VERKHOYANSKI KHREBET
CHERSKOGO RANGE
Lena R.
ASIA
90° E
EUROPE
60° N
150° E
120° E
30° E
TAIMYR PEN.
Kara Sea
KOLA PEN.
KOLYMA MTS.
Laptev Sea
Severnaya Zemlya
Novaya Zemlya
Barents Sea
Baltic Sea
Arctic Circle
80° N
New Siberian Islands
Franz Josef Land
North Cape
SCANDINAVIAN PENINSULA
East Siberian Sea
ARCTIC OCEAN
Svalbard (Nor.)
Norwegian Sea
North Sea
ANADYR RANGE
Wrangel Island
North Pole
0°
Prime Meridian
International Date Line
180°
Bering Sea
CHUKOTSKI PEN.
Chukchi Sea
Permanent Ice Pack
Greenland Sea
80° N
St. Lawrence Island
Denmark Strait
ATLANTIC OCEAN
Bering Strait
Pt. Barrow
Ellesmere Island
Nunivak Island
BROOKS RANGE
Yukon R.
Beaufort Sea
North Magnetic Pole
70° N
Kodiak I.
ALASKA RANGE
Gulf of Alaska
Amundsen Gulf
Banks Island
Queen Elizabeth Islands
Baffin Bay
Arctic Circle
60° N
Victoria Island
Baffin I.
Davis Strait
Cape Farewell
30° W
0   250   500 mi
0   250   500 km
Mackenzie R.
NORTH AMERICA
60° W

Antarctica

ATLANTIC OCEAN
0°
30° W
Antarctic Circle
30° E
60° S
60° W
70° S
QUEEN MAUD LAND
South Shetland Is.
Permanent Ice Pack
COATS LAND
ENDERBY LAND
SOUTH AMERICA
Antarctic Peninsula
Weddell Sea
Filchner Ice Shelf
Prime Meridian
Amery Ice Shelf
Alexander I.
Ronne Ice Shelf
Berkner I.
80° S
Bellingshausen Sea
TRANSANTARCTIC MTS.
ANTARCTICA
90° W
Vinson Massif 16,066 ft. (4,897 m)
South Pole
90° E
QUEEN MAUD MTS.
Amundsen Sea
Ross Ice Shelf
WILKES LAND
INDIAN OCEAN
Roosevelt I.
120° W
Permanent Ice Pack
Ross Sea
International Date Line
VICTORIA LAND
South Magnetic Pole
PACIFIC OCEAN
150° E

KEY

Elevation

Feet		Meters
Over 13,000		Over 3,960
6,500–13,000		1,980–3,960
1,600–6,500		480–1,980
650–1,600		200–480
0–650		0–200

Ice cap

Ice shelf

Orthographic Projection

World View

Afghanistan

CAPITAL: Kabul
POPULATION: 21,251,821
MAJOR LANGUAGES: Pashtu, Afghan Persian, Turkic, and 30 various languages
AREA: 250,010 sq mi; 647,500 sq km
LEADING EXPORTS: fruits and nuts, handwoven carpets, and wool
CONTINENT: Asia

Albania
CAPITAL: Tiranë
POPULATION: 3,413,904
MAJOR LANGUAGES: Albanian, Tosk dialect, and Greek
AREA: 11,101 sq mi; 28,750 sq km
LEADING EXPORTS: asphalt, metals and metallic ores, and electricity
CONTINENT: Europe

Algeria
CAPITAL: Algiers
POPULATION: 28,539,321
MAJOR LANGUAGES: Arabic (official), French, and Berber dialects
AREA: 919,626 sq mi; 2,381,740 sq km
LEADING EXPORTS: petroleum and natural gas
CONTINENT: Africa

Andorra
CAPITAL: Andorra La Vella
POPULATION: 65,780
MAJOR LANGUAGES: Catalan (official), French, and Castilian
AREA: 174 sq mi; 450 sq km
LEADING EXPORTS: electricity, tobacco products, and furniture
CONTINENT: Europe

Angola
CAPITAL: Luanda
POPULATION: 10,069,501
MAJOR LANGUAGES: Portuguese (official), Bantu, and various languages
AREA: 481,370 sq mi; 1,246,700 sq km
LEADING EXPORTS: oil, diamonds, and refined petroleum products
CONTINENT: Africa

Anguilla
CAPITAL: The Valley
POPULATION: 7,099
MAJOR LANGUAGE: English (official)
AREA: 35 sq mi; 91 sq km
LEADING EXPORTS: lobster and salt
LOCATION: Caribbean Sea

Antigua and Barbuda

CAPITAL: Saint John's
POPULATION: 65,176
MAJOR LANGUAGES: English (official) and various dialects
AREA: 170 sq mi; 440 sq km
LEADING EXPORTS: petroleum products and manufactures
LOCATION: Caribbean Sea

Argentina
CAPITAL: Buenos Aires
POPULATION: 34,292,742
MAJOR LANGUAGES: Spanish (official), English, Italian, German, and French
AREA: 1,068,339 sq mi; 2,766,890 sq km
LEADING EXPORTS: meat, wheat, corn, oilseed, and manufactures
CONTINENT: South America

Armenia
CAPITAL: Yerevan
POPULATION: 3,557,284
MAJOR LANGUAGES: Armenian and Russian
AREA: 11,506 sq mi; 29,800 sq km
LEADING EXPORTS: gold and jewelry, and aluminum
CONTINENT: Asia

Australia

CAPITAL: Canberra
POPULATION: 18,322,231
MAJOR LANGUAGES: English and various languages
AREA: 2,968,010 sq mi; 7,686,850 sq km
LEADING EXPORTS: coal, gold, meat, wool, and alumina
CONTINENT: Australia

Austria
CAPITAL: Vienna
POPULATION: 7,986,664
MAJOR LANGUAGE: German
AREA: 32,376 sq mi; 83,850 sq km
LEADING EXPORTS: machinery and equipment, and iron and steel
CONTINENT: Europe

Azerbaijan

CAPITAL: Baku
POPULATION: 7,789,886
MAJOR LANGUAGES: Azeri, Russian, Armenian, and various languages
AREA: 33,438 sq mi; 86,600 sq km
LEADING EXPORTS: oil and gas, chemicals, and oil field equipment
CONTINENT: Europe and Asia

Bahamas

CAPITAL: Nassau
POPULATION: 256,616
MAJOR LANGUAGES: English and Creole
AREA: 5,382 sq mi; 13,940 sq km
LEADING EXPORTS: pharmaceuticals, cement, rum, and crawfish
LOCATION: Caribbean Sea

Bahrain
CAPITAL: Manama
POPULATION: 575,925
MAJOR LANGUAGES: Arabic, English, Farsi, and Urdu
AREA: 239 sq mi; 620 sq km
LEADING EXPORTS: petroleum and petroleum products
CONTINENT: Asia

Bangladesh
CAPITAL: Dhaka
POPULATION: 128,094,948
MAJOR LANGUAGES: Bangla and English
AREA: 55,600 sq mi; 144,000 sq km
LEADING EXPORTS: garments, jute and jute goods, and leather
CONTINENT: Asia

Barbados
CAPITAL: Bridgetown
POPULATION: 256,395
MAJOR LANGUAGE: English
AREA: 166 sq mi; 430 sq km
LEADING EXPORTS: sugar and molasses, and rum
LOCATION: Caribbean Sea

Belarus
CAPITAL: Minsk
POPULATION: 10,437,418
MAJOR LANGUAGES: Byelorussian and Russian
AREA: 79,926 sq mi; 207,600 sq km
LEADING EXPORTS: machinery and transportation equipment
CONTINENT: Europe

Belgium
CAPITAL: Brussels
POPULATION: 10,081,880
MAJOR LANGUAGES: Dutch, French, and German
AREA: 11,780 sq mi; 30,510 sq km
LEADING EXPORTS: iron and steel, and transportation equipment
CONTINENT: Europe

Belize

CAPITAL: Belmopan
POPULATION: 214,061
MAJOR LANGUAGES: English (official), Spanish, Maya, and Garifuna
AREA: 8,865 sq mi; 22,960 sq km
LEADING EXPORTS: sugar, citrus fruits, bananas, and clothing
LOCATION: Caribbean Sea

Benin
CAPITAL: Porto-Novo
POPULATION: 5,522,677
MAJOR LANGUAGES: Fon, Yoruba, and at least 6 various languages
AREA: 43,484 sq mi; 112,620 sq km
LEADING EXPORTS: cotton, crude oil, palm products, and cocoa
CONTINENT: Africa

Bermuda
CAPITAL: Hamilton
POPULATION: 61,629
MAJOR LANGUAGE: English
AREA: 19.3 sq mi; 50 sq km
LEADING EXPORTS: semitropical produce and light manufactures
CONTINENT: North America

Bhutan
CAPITAL: Thimphu
POPULATION: 1,780,638
MAJOR LANGUAGES: Dzongkha (official), Tibetan dialects, and Nepalese dialects
AREA: 18,147 sq mi; 47,000 sq km
LEADING EXPORTS: cardamon, gypsum, timber, and handicrafts
CONTINENT: Asia

Bolivia
CAPITAL: La Paz
POPULATION: 7,896,254
MAJOR LANGUAGES: Spanish, Quechua, and Aymara
AREA: 424,179 sq mi; 1,098,580 sq km
LEADING EXPORTS: metals, natural gas, soybeans, jewelry, and wood
CONTINENT: South America

Bosnia and Herzegovina

CAPITAL: Sarajevo
POPULATION: 3,201,823
MAJOR LANGUAGE: Serbo-Croatian
AREA: 19,782 sq mi; 51,233 sq km
LEADING EXPORTS: none
CONTINENT: Europe

Botswana

CAPITAL: Gaborone
POPULATION: 1,392,414
MAJOR LANGUAGES: English and Setswana
AREA: 231,812 sq mi; 600,370 sq km
LEADING EXPORTS: diamonds, copper and nickel, and meat
CONTINENT: Africa

Brazil
CAPITAL: Brasília
POPULATION: 160,737,489
MAJOR LANGUAGES: Portuguese, Spanish, English, and French
AREA: 3,286,600 sq mi; 8,511,965 sq km
LEADING EXPORTS: iron ore, soybean, bran, and orange juice
CONTINENT: South America

British Virgin Islands

CAPITAL: Road Town
POPULATION: 13,027
MAJOR LANGUAGE: English
AREA: 58 sq mi; 150 sq km
LEADING EXPORTS: rum, fresh fish, gravel, sand, and fruits
LOCATION: Caribbean Sea

Brunei
CAPITAL: Bandar Seri Begawan
POPULATION: 292,266
MAJOR LANGUAGES: Malay, English, and Chinese
AREA: 2,228 sq mi; 5,770 sq km
LEADING EXPORTS: crude oil and liquefied natural gas
CONTINENT: Asia

Bulgaria
CAPITAL: Sofia
POPULATION: 8,775,198
MAJOR LANGUAGE: Bulgarian
AREA: 42,824 sq mi; 110,910 sq km
LEADING EXPORTS: machinery and agricultural products
CONTINENT: Europe

Burkina
CAPITAL: Ouagadougou
POPULATION: 10,422,828
MAJOR LANGUAGES: French (official) and Sudanic languages
AREA: 105,873 sq mi; 274,200 sq km
LEADING EXPORTS: cotton, gold, and animal products
CONTINENT: Africa

Burundi
CAPITAL: Bujumbura
POPULATION: 6,262,429
MAJOR LANGUAGES: Kirundi, French, and Swahili
AREA: 10,746 sq mi; 27,830 sq km
LEADING EXPORTS: coffee, tea, cotton, and hides and skins
CONTINENT: Africa

Cambodia
CAPITAL: Phnom Penh
POPULATION: 10,561,373
MAJOR LANGUAGES: Khmer and French
AREA: 69,902 sq mi; 181,040 sq km
LEADING EXPORTS: timber, rubber, soybeans, and sesame
CONTINENT: Asia

Cameroon

CAPITAL: Yaounde
POPULATION: 13,521,000
MAJOR LANGUAGES: 24 various languages, English, and French
AREA: 183,574 sq mi; 475,440 sq km
LEADING EXPORTS: petroleum products and lumber
CONTINENT: Africa

Canada
CAPITAL: Ottawa
POPULATION: 28,434,545
MAJOR LANGUAGES: English and French
AREA: 3,851,940 sq mi; 9,976,140 sq km
LEADING EXPORTS: newsprint, wood pulp, timber, and crude petroleum
CONTINENT: North America

Cape Verde

CAPITAL: Praia
POPULATION: 435,983
MAJOR LANGUAGES: Portuguese and Crioulo
AREA: 1,556 sq mi; 4,030 sq km
LEADING EXPORTS: fish, bananas, and hides and skins
CONTINENT: Africa

Cayman Islands
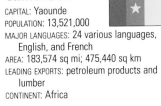
CAPITAL: George Town
POPULATION: 33,192
MAJOR LANGUAGE: English
AREA: 100 sq mi; 260 sq km
LEADING EXPORTS: turtle products and manufactured goods
LOCATION: Caribbean Sea

Central African Republic

CAPITAL: Bangui
POPULATION: 3,209,759
MAJOR LANGUAGES: French, Sangho, Arabic, Hunsa, and Swahili
AREA: 240,542 sq mi; 622,980 sq km
LEADING EXPORTS: diamonds, timber, cotton, coffee, and tobacco
CONTINENT: Africa

Chad
CAPITAL: N'Djamena
POPULATION: 5,586,505
MAJOR LANGUAGES: French, Arabic, Sara, Songo, and over 100 various languages and dialects
AREA: 495,772 sq mi; 1,284,000 sq km
LEADING EXPORTS: cotton, cattle, textiles, and fish
CONTINENT: Africa

Chile

CAPITAL: Santiago
POPULATION: 14,161,216
MAJOR LANGUAGE: Spanish
AREA: 292,269 sq mi; 756,950 sq km
LEADING EXPORTS: copper and other metals and minerals
CONTINENT: South America

China

CAPITAL: Beijing
POPULATION: 1,203,097,268
MAJOR LANGUAGES: Mandarin, Putonghua, Yue, Wu, Minbei, Minnan, Xiang, and Gan and Hakka dialects
AREA: 3,705,533 sq mi; 9,596,960 sq km
LEADING EXPORTS: textiles, garments, footwear, and toys
CONTINENT: Asia

Colombia

CAPITAL: Bogota
POPULATION: 36,200,251
MAJOR LANGUAGE: Spanish
AREA: 439,751 sq mi; 1,138,910 sq km
LEADING EXPORTS: petroleum, coffee, coal, and bananas
CONTINENT: South America

Comoros
CAPITAL: Moroni
POPULATION: 549,338
MAJOR LANGUAGES: Arabic, French, and Comoran
AREA: 838 sq mi; 2,170 sq km
LEADING EXPORTS: vanilla, ylang-ylang, cloves, and perfume oil
LOCATION: Indian Ocean

Congo

CAPITAL: Brazzaville
POPULATION: 2,504,996
MAJOR LANGUAGES: French, Lingala, Kikongo, and other languages
AREA: 132,051 sq mi; 342,000 sq km
LEADING EXPORTS: crude oil, lumber, plywood, sugar, and cocoa
CONTINENT: Africa

Cook Islands

CAPITAL: Avarua
POPULATION: 19,343
MAJOR LANGUAGES: English and Maori
AREA: 95 sq mi; 240 sq km
LEADING EXPORTS: copra, fresh and canned fruit, and clothing
LOCATION: Pacific Ocean

Costa Rica
CAPITAL: San José
POPULATION: 3,419,114
MAJOR LANGUAGES: Spanish and English
AREA: 19,730 sq mi; 51,100 sq km
LEADING EXPORTS: coffee, bananas, textiles, and sugar
CONTINENT: Central America

Côte d'Ivoire
CAPITAL: Yamoussoukro
POPULATION: 14,791,257
MAJOR LANGUAGES: French, Dioula, and 59 other dialects
AREA: 124,507 sq mi; 322,460 sq km
LEADING EXPORTS: cocoa, coffee, tropical woods, and petroleum
CONTINENT: Africa

Croatia
CAPITAL: Zagreb
POPULATION: 4,665,821
MAJOR LANGUAGE: Serbo-Croatian
AREA: 21,830 sq mi; 56,538 sq km
LEADING EXPORTS: machinery and transportation equipment
CONTINENT: Europe

Cuba
CAPITAL: Havana
POPULATION: 10,937,635
MAJOR LANGUAGE: Spanish
AREA: 42,805 sq mi; 110,860 sq km
LEADING EXPORTS: sugar, nickel, shellfish, and tobacco
LOCATION: Caribbean Sea

Cyprus

CAPITAL: Nicosia
POPULATION: 736,636
MAJOR LANGUAGES: Greek, Turkish, and English
AREA: 3,572 sq mi; 9,250 sq km
LEADING EXPORTS: citrus, potatoes, grapes, wines, and cement
LOCATION: Mediterranean Sea

Czech Republic
CAPITAL: Prague
POPULATION: 10,432,774
MAJOR LANGUAGES: Czech and Slovak
AREA: 30,388 sq mi; 78,703 sq km
LEADING EXPORTS: manufactured goods
CONTINENT: Europe

Denmark

CAPITAL: Copenhagen
POPULATION: 5,199,437
MAJOR LANGUAGES: Danish, Faroese, Greenlandic, and German
AREA: 16,630 sq mi; 43,070 sq km
LEADING EXPORTS: meat and meat products, and dairy products
CONTINENT: Europe

Djibouti

CAPITAL: Djibouti
POPULATION: 421,320
MAJOR LANGUAGES: French, Arabic, Somali, and Afar
AREA: 8,495 sq mi; 22,000 sq km
LEADING EXPORTS: hides and skins, and coffee (in transit)
CONTINENT: Africa

Dominica

CAPITAL: Roseau
POPULATION: 82,608
MAJOR LANGUAGES: English and French patois
AREA: 290 sq mi; 750 sq km
LEADING EXPORTS: bananas, soap, bay oil, and vegetables
LOCATION: Caribbean Sea

Dominican Republic

CAPITAL: Santo Domingo
POPULATION: 7,511,263
MAJOR LANGUAGE: Spanish
AREA: 18,815 sq mi; 48,730 sq km
LEADING EXPORTS: ferronickel, sugar, gold, coffee, and cocoa
LOCATION: Caribbean Sea

Ecuador

CAPITAL: Quito
POPULATION: 10,890,950
MAJOR LANGUAGES: Spanish, Quechua, and various languages
AREA: 109,487 sq mi; 283,560 sq km
LEADING EXPORTS: petroleum, bananas, shrimp, and cocoa
CONTINENT: South America

Egypt

CAPITAL: Cairo
POPULATION: 62,359,623
MAJOR LANGUAGES: Arabic, English, and French
AREA: 386,675 sq mi; 1,001,450 sq km
LEADING EXPORTS: crude oil and petroleum products
CONTINENT: Africa

El Salvador

CAPITAL: San Salvador
POPULATION: 5,870,481
MAJOR LANGUAGES: Spanish and Nahua
AREA: 8,124 sq mi; 21,040 sq km
LEADING EXPORTS: coffee, sugar cane, and shrimp
CONTINENT: Central America

Equatorial Guinea

CAPITAL: Malabo
POPULATION: 420,293
MAJOR LANGUAGES: Spanish, Pidgin English, Fang, Bubi, and Ibo
AREA: 10,831 sq mi; 28,050 sq km
LEADING EXPORTS: coffee, timber, and cocoa beans
CONTINENT: Africa

Eritrea

CAPITAL: Asmara
POPULATION: 3,578,709
MAJOR LANGUAGES: Tigre, Kunama, Cushitic dialects, Nora Bana, and Arabic
AREA: 46,844 sq mi; 121,320 sq km
LEADING EXPORTS: salt, hides, cement, and gum arabic
CONTINENT: Africa

Estonia

CAPITAL: Tallinn
POPULATION: 1,625,399
MAJOR LANGUAGES: Estonian, Latvian, Lithuanian, and Russian
AREA: 17,414 sq mi; 45,100 sq km
LEADING EXPORTS: textiles, food products, vehicles, and metals
CONTINENT: Europe

Ethiopia

CAPITAL: Addis Ababa
POPULATION: 55,979,018
MAJOR LANGUAGES: Amharic, Tigrinya, Orominga, Guaraginga, Somali, Arabic, English, and various languages
AREA: 435,201 sq mi; 1,127,127 sq km
LEADING EXPORTS: coffee, leather products, and gold
CONTINENT: Africa

Fiji

CAPITAL: Suva
POPULATION: 772,891
MAJOR LANGUAGES: English, Fijian, and Hindustani
AREA: 7,054 sq mi; 18,270 sq km
LEADING EXPORTS: sugar, clothing, gold, processed fish, and lumber
LOCATION: Pacific Ocean

Finland

CAPITAL: Helsinki
POPULATION: 5,085,206
MAJOR LANGUAGES: Finnish, Swedish, Lapp, and Russian
AREA: 130,132 sq mi; 337,030 sq km
LEADING EXPORTS: paper and pulp, machinery, and chemicals
CONTINENT: Europe

France

CAPITAL: Paris
POPULATION: 58,109,160
MAJOR LANGUAGES: French and regional dialects and languages
AREA: 211,217 sq mi; 547,030 sq km
LEADING EXPORTS: machinery and transportation equipment
CONTINENT: Europe

Gabon

CAPITAL: Libreville
POPULATION: 1,185,749
MAJOR LANGUAGES: French, Fang, Myene, Bateke, Bapounou/Eschira, and Bandjabi
AREA: 103,351 sq mi; 267,670 sq km
LEADING EXPORTS: crude oil, timber, manganese, and uranium
CONTINENT: Africa

The Gambia

CAPITAL: Banjul
POPULATION: 989,273
MAJOR LANGUAGES: English, Mandinka, Wolof, Fula, and various languages
AREA: 4,363 sq mi; 11,300 sq km
LEADING EXPORTS: peanuts and peanut products, and fish
CONTINENT: Africa

Georgia

CAPITAL: T'bilisi
POPULATION: 5,725,972
MAJOR LANGUAGES: Armenian, Azeri, Georgian, Russian, and various languages
AREA: 26,912 sq mi; 69,700 sq km
LEADING EXPORTS: citrus fruits, tea, and wine
CONTINENT: Asia

Germany

CAPITAL: Berlin
POPULATION: 81,337,541
MAJOR LANGUAGE: German
AREA: 137,808 sq mi; 356,910 sq km
LEADING EXPORTS: machines and machine tools, and chemicals
CONTINENT: Europe

Ghana

CAPITAL: Accra
POPULATION: 17,763,138
MAJOR LANGUAGES: English, Akan, Moshi-Dagomba, Ewe, Ga, and various languages
AREA: 92,104 sq mi; 238,540 sq km
LEADING EXPORTS: cocoa, gold, timber, tuna, and bauxite
CONTINENT: Africa

Greece

CAPITAL: Athens
POPULATION: 10,647,511
MAJOR LANGUAGES: Greek, English, and French
AREA: 50,944 sq mi; 131,940 sq km
LEADING EXPORTS: manufactured goods, foodstuffs, and fuels
CONTINENT: Europe

Grenada

CAPITAL: Saint George's
POPULATION: 94,486
MAJOR LANGUAGES: English and French patois
AREA: 131 sq mi; 340 sq km
LEADING EXPORTS: bananas, cocoa, nutmeg, and fruits and vegetables
LOCATION: Caribbean Sea

Guatemala

CAPITAL: Guatemala
POPULATION: 10,998,602
MAJOR LANGUAGES: Spanish, Quiche, Cakchiquel, Kekchi, and various languages and dialects
AREA: 42,044 sq mi; 108,890 sq km
LEADING EXPORTS: coffee, sugar, bananas, cardamom, and beef
CONTINENT: Central America

Guinea

CAPITAL: Conakry
POPULATION: 6,549,336
MAJOR LANGUAGES: French and various languages
AREA: 94,930 sq mi; 245,860 sq km
LEADING EXPORTS: bauxite, alumina, diamonds, gold, and coffee
CONTINENT: Africa

Guinea Bissau

CAPITAL: Bissau
POPULATION: 1,124,537
MAJOR LANGUAGES: Portuguese, Criolo, and various languages
AREA: 13,946 sq mi; 36,210 sq km
LEADING EXPORTS: cashews, fish, peanuts, and palm kernels
CONTINENT: Africa

Guyana

CAPITAL: Georgetown
POPULATION: 723,774
MAJOR LANGUAGES: English and various dialects
AREA: 83,003 sq mi; 214,970 sq km
LEADING EXPORTS: sugar, bauxite/alumina, rice, and shrimp
CONTINENT: South America

Haiti

CAPITAL: Port-au-Prince
POPULATION: 6,539,983
MAJOR LANGUAGES: French and Creole
AREA: 8,784 sq mi; 22,750 sq km
LEADING EXPORTS: light manufactures and coffee
LOCATION: Caribbean Sea

Holy See (Vatican City)

CAPITAL: Vatican City
POPULATION: 830
MAJOR LANGUAGES: Italian, Latin, and various languages
AREA: 17 sq mi; 44 sq km
LEADING EXPORTS: none
CONTINENT: Europe

Honduras

CAPITAL: Tegucigalpa
POPULATION: 5,549,743
MAJOR LANGUAGES: Spanish and various dialects
AREA: 43,280 sq mi; 112,090 sq km
LEADING EXPORTS: bananas, coffee, shrimp, lobsters, and minerals
CONTINENT: Central America

Hungary

CAPITAL: Budapest
POPULATION: 10,318,838
MAJOR LANGUAGES: Hungarian and various languages
AREA: 35,920 sq mi; 93,030 sq km
LEADING EXPORTS: raw materials and semi-finished goods
CONTINENT: Europe

Iceland

CAPITAL: Reykjavik
POPULATION: 265,998
MAJOR LANGUAGE: Icelandic
AREA: 39,770 sq mi; 103,000 sq km
LEADING EXPORTS: fish and fish products, and animal products
CONTINENT: Europe

India

CAPITAL: New Delhi
POPULATION: 936,545,814
MAJOR LANGUAGES: English, Hindi, Bengali, Telugu, Marathi, Tamil, Urdu, Gujarati, Malayam, Kannada, Oriya, Punjabi, Assamese, Kashmiri, Sindhi, Sanskrit, and Hindustani (all official)
AREA: 1,269,389 sq mi; 3,287,590 sq km
LEADING EXPORTS: clothing, and gems and jewelry
CONTINENT: Asia

Indonesia

CAPITAL: Jakarta
POPULATION: 203,583,886
MAJOR LANGUAGES: Bahasa Indonesia, English, Dutch, Javanese, and various dialects
AREA: 741,052 sq mi; 1,919,251 sq km
LEADING EXPORTS: manufactures, fuels, and foodstuffs
CONTINENT: Asia

Iran

CAPITAL: Tehran
POPULATION: 64,625,455
MAJOR LANGUAGES: Farsi (official) and Turkic languages
AREA: 634,562 sq mi; 1,643,452 sq km
LEADING EXPORTS: petroleum, carpets, fruit, nuts, and hides
CONTINENT: Asia

Iraq

CAPITAL: Baghdad
POPULATION: 20,643,769
MAJOR LANGUAGES: Arabic, Kurdish, Assyrian, and Armenian
AREA: 168,760 sq mi; 437,072 sq km
LEADING EXPORTS: crude oil and refined products, and fertilizers
CONTINENT: Asia

Ireland

CAPITAL: Dublin
POPULATION: 3,550,448
MAJOR LANGUAGES: Irish Gaelic and English
AREA: 27,136 sq mi; 70,280 sq km
LEADING EXPORTS: chemicals and data processing equipment
CONTINENT: Europe

Israel

CAPITAL: Jerusalem
POPULATION: 7,566,447
MAJOR LANGUAGES: Hebrew, Arabic, and English
AREA: 10,421 sq mi; 26,990 sq km
LEADING EXPORTS: machinery and equipment, and cut diamonds
CONTINENT: Asia

Italy

CAPITAL: Rome
POPULATION: 58,261,971
MAJOR LANGUAGES: Italian, German, French, and Slovene
AREA: 116,310 sq mi; 301,230 sq km
LEADING EXPORTS: metals, and textiles and clothing
CONTINENT: Europe

Jamaica

CAPITAL: Kingston
POPULATION: 2,574,291
MAJOR LANGUAGES: English and Creole
AREA: 4,243 sq mi; 10,990 sq km
LEADING EXPORTS: alumina, bauxite, sugar, bananas, and rum
LOCATION: Caribbean Sea

Japan

CAPITAL: Tokyo
POPULATION: 125,506,492
MAJOR LANGUAGE: Japanese
AREA: 145,888 sq mi; 377,835 sq km
LEADING EXPORTS: machinery, motor vehicles, and electronics
CONTINENT: Asia

Jordan

CAPITAL: Amman
POPULATION: 4,100,709
MAJOR LANGUAGES: Arabic and English
AREA: 34,447 sq mi; 89,213 sq km
LEADING EXPORTS: phosphates, fertilizers, and potash
CONTINENT: Asia

Kazakhstan

CAPITAL: Almaty
POPULATION: 17,376,615
MAJOR LANGUAGES: Kazakh and Russian
AREA: 1,049,191 sq mi; 2,717,300 sq km
LEADING EXPORTS: oil, and ferrous and nonferrous metals
CONTINENT: Asia

Kenya

CAPITAL: Nairobi
POPULATION: 28,817,227
MAJOR LANGUAGES: English, Swahili, and various languages
AREA: 224,970 sq mi; 582,650 sq km
LEADING EXPORTS: tea, coffee, and petroleum products
CONTINENT: Africa

Kiribati

CAPITAL: Tarawa
POPULATION: 79,386
MAJOR LANGUAGES: English and Gilbertese
AREA: 277 sq mi; 717 sq km
LEADING EXPORTS: copra, seaweed, and fish
LOCATION: Pacific Ocean

Korea, North

CAPITAL: P'yongyang
POPULATION: 23,486,550
MAJOR LANGUAGE: Korean
AREA: 46,542 sq mi; 120,540 sq km
LEADING EXPORTS: minerals and metallurgical products
CONTINENT: Asia

Korea, South

CAPITAL: Seoul
POPULATION: 45,553,882
MAJOR LANGUAGES: Korean and English
AREA: 38,025 sq mi; 98,480 sq km
LEADING EXPORTS: electronic and electrical equipment
CONTINENT: Asia

Kuwait

CAPITAL: Kuwait
POPULATION: 1,817,397
MAJOR LANGUAGES: Arabic and English
AREA: 6,881 sq mi; 17,820 sq km
LEADING EXPORT: oil
CONTINENT: Asia

Kyrgyzstan

CAPITAL: Bishkek
POPULATION: 4,769,877
MAJOR LANGUAGES: Kyrgyz and Russian
AREA: 76,644 sq mi; 198,500 sq km
LEADING EXPORTS: wool, chemicals, cotton, metals, and shoes
CONTINENT: Asia

Laos

CAPITAL: Vientiane
POPULATION: 4,837,237
MAJOR LANGUAGES: Lao, French, English, and various languages
AREA: 91,432 sq mi; 236,800 sq km
LEADING EXPORTS: electricity, wood products, coffee, and tin
CONTINENT: Asia

Latvia

CAPITAL: Riga
POPULATION: 2,762,899
MAJOR LANGUAGES: Lettish, Lithuanian, Russian, and various languages
AREA: 24,750 sq mi; 64,100 sq km
LEADING EXPORTS: oil products, timber, and ferrous metals
CONTINENT: Europe

Lebanon

CAPITAL: Beirut
POPULATION: 3,695,921
MAJOR LANGUAGES: Arabic, French, Armenian, and English
AREA: 4,016 sq mi; 10,400 sq km
LEADING EXPORTS: agricultural products, chemicals, and textiles
CONTINENT: Asia

Lesotho

CAPITAL: Maseru
POPULATION: 1,992,960
MAJOR LANGUAGES: Sesotho, English, Zulu, and Xhosa
AREA: 11,719 sq mi; 30,350 sq km
LEADING EXPORTS: wool, mohair, wheat, cattle, and peas
CONTINENT: Africa

Liberia

CAPITAL: Monrovia
POPULATION: 3,073,245
MAJOR LANGUAGES: English and Niger-Congo
AREA: 43,002 sq mi; 111,370 sq km
LEADING EXPORTS: iron ore, rubber, timber, and coffee
CONTINENT: Africa

Libya
CAPITAL: Tripoli
POPULATION: 5,248,401
MAJOR LANGUAGES: Arabic, Italian, and English
AREA: 679,385 sq mi; 1,759,540 sq km
LEADING EXPORTS: crude oil and refined petroleum products
CONTINENT: Africa

Liechtenstein

CAPITAL: Vaduz
POPULATION: 30,654
MAJOR LANGUAGES: German and Alemannic
AREA: 62 sq mi; 160 sq km
LEADING EXPORTS: small specialty machinery and dental products
CONTINENT: Europe

Lithuania
CAPITAL: Vilnius
POPULATION: 3,876,396
MAJOR LANGUAGES: Lithuanian, Polish, and Russian
AREA: 25,175 sq mi; 65,200 sq km
LEADING EXPORTS: electronics, petroleum products, and food
CONTINENT: Europe

Luxembourg
CAPITAL: Luxembourg
POPULATION: 404,660
MAJOR LANGUAGES: Luxembourgisch, German, French, and English
AREA: 998 sq mi; 2,586 sq km
LEADING EXPORTS: finished steel products and chemicals
CONTINENT: Europe

Macedonia
CAPITAL: Skopje
POPULATION: 2,159,503
MAJOR LANGUAGES: Macedonian, Albanian, Turkish, Serb, Gypsy, and various languages
AREA: 9,781 sq mi; 25,333 sq km
LEADING EXPORTS: manufactured goods and machinery
CONTINENT: Europe

Madagascar
CAPITAL: Antananarivo
POPULATION: 13,862,325
MAJOR LANGUAGES: French and Malagasy
AREA: 226,665 sq mi; 587,040 sq km
LEADING EXPORTS: coffee, vanilla, cloves, shellfish, and sugar
CONTINENT: Africa

Malawi
CAPITAL: Lilongwe
POPULATION: 9,808,384
MAJOR LANGUAGES: English, Chichewa, and various languages
AREA: 45,747 sq mi; 118,480 sq km
LEADING EXPORTS: tobacco, tea, sugar, coffee, and peanuts
CONTINENT: Africa

Malaysia
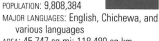
CAPITAL: Kuala Lumpur
POPULATION: 19,723,587
MAJOR LANGUAGES: Malay, English, Mandarin, Tamil, Chinese dialects, and various languages and dialects
AREA: 127,322 sq mi; 329,750 sq km
LEADING EXPORTS: electronic equipment
CONTINENT: Asia

Maldives

CAPITAL: Male
POPULATION: 261,310
MAJOR LANGUAGES: Divehi dialect and English
AREA: 116 sq mi; 300 sq km
LEADING EXPORTS: fish and clothing
CONTINENT: Asia

Mali

CAPITAL: Bamako
POPULATION: 9,375,132
MAJOR LANGUAGES: French, Bambara, and various languages
AREA: 478,783 sq mi; 1,240,000 sq km
LEADING EXPORTS: cotton, livestock, and gold
CONTINENT: Africa

Malta
CAPITAL: Valletta
POPULATION: 369,609
MAJOR LANGUAGES: Maltese and English
AREA: 124 sq mi; 320 sq km
LEADING EXPORTS: machinery and transportation equipment
CONTINENT: Europe

Marshall Islands

CAPITAL: Majuro
POPULATION: 56,157
MAJOR LANGUAGES: English, Marshallese dialects, and Japanese
AREA: 70 sq mi; 181.3 sq km
LEADING EXPORTS: coconut oil, fish, live animals, and trichus shells
LOCATION: Pacific Ocean

Mauritania

CAPITAL: Nouakchott
POPULATION: 2,263,202
MAJOR LANGUAGES: Hasaniya Arabic, Wolof, Pular, and Soninke
AREA: 397,969 sq mi; 1,030,700 sq km
LEADING EXPORTS: iron ore, and fish and fish products
CONTINENT: Africa

Mauritius
CAPITAL: Port Louis
POPULATION: 1,127,068
MAJOR LANGUAGES: English (official), Creole, French, Hindi, Urdu, Hakka, and Bojpoori
AREA: 718 sq mi; 1,860 sq km
LEADING EXPORTS: textiles, sugar, and light manufactures
LOCATION: Indian Ocean

Mayotte
CAPITAL: Mamoutzou
POPULATION: 97,088
MAJOR LANGUAGES: Mahorian and French
AREA: 145 sq mi; 375 sq km
LEADING EXPORTS: ylang-ylang and vanilla
CONTINENT: Africa

Mexico
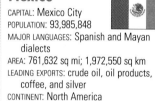
CAPITAL: Mexico City
POPULATION: 93,985,848
MAJOR LANGUAGES: Spanish and Mayan dialects
AREA: 761,632 sq mi; 1,972,550 sq km
LEADING EXPORTS: crude oil, oil products, coffee, and silver
CONTINENT: North America

Micronesia
CAPITAL: Federated states of Kolonia (on the Island of Pohnpei)
*a new capital is being built about 10 km southwest in the Palikir Valley
POPULATION: 122,950
MAJOR LANGUAGES: English, Turkese, Pohnpeian, Yapese, and Kosrean
AREA: 271 sq mi; 702 sq km
LEADING EXPORTS: fish, copra, bananas, and black pepper
LOCATION: Pacific Ocean

Moldova

CAPITAL: Chisinau
POPULATION: 4,489,657
MAJOR LANGUAGES: Moldovan (official), Russian, and Gagauz dialect
AREA: 13,012 sq mi; 33,700 sq km
LEADING EXPORTS: foodstuffs, wine, and tobacco
CONTINENT: Europe

Monaco
CAPITAL: Monaco
POPULATION: 31,515
MAJOR LANGUAGES: French (official), English, Italian, and Monegasque
AREA: .73 sq mi; 1.9 sq km
LEADING EXPORTS: exports through France
CONTINENT: Europe

Mongolia

CAPITAL: Ulaanbaatar
POPULATION: 2,493,615
MAJOR LANGUAGES: Khalkha Mongol, Turkic, Russian, and Chinese
AREA: 604,270 sq mi; 1,565,000 sq km
LEADING EXPORTS: copper, livestock, animal products, and cashmere
CONTINENT: Asia

Morocco
CAPITAL: Rabat
POPULATION: 29,168,848
MAJOR LANGUAGES: Arabic (official), Berber dialects, and French
AREA: 172,420 sq mi; 446,550 sq km
LEADING EXPORTS: food and beverages
CONTINENT: Africa

Mozambique
CAPITAL: Maputo
POPULATION: 18,115,250
MAJOR LANGUAGES: Portuguese and various dialects
AREA: 309,506 sq mi; 801,590 sq km
LEADING EXPORTS: shrimp, cashews, cotton, sugar, copra, and citrus
CONTINENT: Africa

Myanmar (Burma)
CAPITAL: Rangoon
POPULATION: 45,103,809
MAJOR LANGUAGE: Burmese
AREA: 261,979 sq mi; 678,500 sq km
LEADING EXPORTS: pulses and beans, teak, rice, and hardwood
CONTINENT: Asia

Namibia
CAPITAL: Windhoek
POPULATION: 1,651,545
MAJOR LANGUAGES: English (official), Afrikaans, German, Oshivambo, Herero, Nama, and various languages
AREA: 318,707 sq mi; 825,418 sq km
LEADING EXPORTS: diamonds, copper, gold, zinc, and lead
CONTINENT: Africa

Nauru
CAPITAL: Government offices in Yaren District
POPULATION: 10,149
MAJOR LANGUAGES: Nauruan and English
AREA: 8 sq mi; 21 sq km
LEADING EXPORTS: phosphates
LOCATION: Pacific Ocean

Nepal
CAPITAL: Kathmandu
POPULATION: 21,560,869
MAJOR LANGUAGES: Nepali (official) and 20 various languages divided into numerous dialects
AREA: 54,365 sq mi; 140,800 sq km
LEADING EXPORTS: carpets, clothing, and leather goods
CONTINENT: Asia

Netherlands
CAPITAL: Amsterdam
POPULATION: 15,452,903
MAJOR LANGUAGE: Dutch
AREA: 14,414 sq mi; 37,330 sq km
LEADING EXPORTS: metal products and chemicals
CONTINENT: Europe

New Caledonia
CAPITAL: Noumea
POPULATION: 184,552
MAJOR LANGUAGES: French and 28 Melanesian-Polynesian dialects
AREA: 7,359 sq mi; 19,060 sq km
LEADING EXPORTS: nickel metal and nickel ore
LOCATION: Pacific Ocean

New Zealand
CAPITAL: Wellington
POPULATION: 3,407,277
MAJOR LANGUAGES: English and Maori
AREA: 103,741 sq mi; 268,680 sq km
LEADING EXPORTS: wool, lamb, mutton, beef, fish, and cheese
LOCATION: Pacific Ocean

Nicaragua
CAPITAL: Managua
POPULATION: 4,206,353
MAJOR LANGUAGES: Spanish (official), English, and various languages
AREA: 50,000 sq mi; 129,494 sq km
LEADING EXPORTS: meat, coffee, cotton, sugar, seafood, and gold
LOCATION: Caribbean Sea

Niger
CAPITAL: Niamey
POPULATION: 9,280,208
MAJOR LANGUAGES: French (official), Hausa, and Djerma
AREA: 489,208 sq mi; 1,267,000 sq km
LEADING EXPORTS: uranium ore and livestock products
CONTINENT: Africa

Nigeria
CAPITAL: Abuja
POPULATION: 101,232,251
MAJOR LANGUAGES: English (official), Hausa, Yoruba, Ibo, and Fulani
AREA: 356,682 sq mi; 923,770 sq km
LEADING EXPORTS: oil, cocoa, and rubber
CONTINENT: Africa

Niue
CAPITAL: (Free association with New Zealand)
POPULATION: 1,837
MAJOR LANGUAGES: Polynesian and English
AREA: 100 sq mi; 260 sq km
LEADING EXPORTS: canned coconut cream, copra, and honey
LOCATION: Pacific Ocean

Norway
CAPITAL: Oslo
POPULATION: 4,330,951
MAJOR LANGUAGES: Norwegian (official), Lapp, and Finnish
AREA: 125,186 sq mi; 324,220 sq km
LEADING EXPORTS: petroleum and petroleum products
CONTINENT: Europe

Oman
CAPITAL: Muscat
POPULATION: 2,125,089
MAJOR LANGUAGES: Arabic (official), English, Baluchi, Urdu, and Indian dialects
AREA: 82,034 sq mi; 212,460 sq km
LEADING EXPORTS: petroleum, re-exports, and fish
CONTINENT: Asia

Pakistan
CAPITAL: Islamabad
POPULATION: 131,541,920
MAJOR LANGUAGES: Urdu (official), English (official), Punjabi, Sindhi, Pashtu, Urdu, Balochi, and other languages
AREA: 310,414 sq mi; 803,940 sq km
LEADING EXPORTS: cotton, textiles, clothing, rice, and leather
CONTINENT: Asia

Palau
CAPITAL: Koror
POPULATION: 16,661
MAJOR LANGUAGES: English (official), Sonsorolese, Angaur, Japanese, Tobi, and Palauan
AREA: 177 sq mi; 458 sq km
LEADING EXPORTS: trochus, tuna, copra, and handicrafts
LOCATION: Pacific Ocean

Panama
CAPITAL: Panama
POPULATION: 2,680,903
MAJOR LANGUAGES: Spanish (official) and English
AREA: 30,194 sq mi; 78,200 sq km
LEADING EXPORTS: bananas, shrimp, sugar, clothing, and coffee
CONTINENT: Central America

Papua New Guinea
CAPITAL: Port Moresby
POPULATION: 4,294,750
MAJOR LANGUAGES: English, pidgin English, and Motu
AREA: 178,266 sq mi; 461,690 sq km
LEADING EXPORTS: gold, copper ore, oil, logs, and palm oil
LOCATION: Pacific Ocean

Paraguay
CAPITAL: Asuncion
POPULATION: 5,358,198
MAJOR LANGUAGES: Spanish (official) and Guarani
AREA: 157,052 sq mi; 406,750 sq km
LEADING EXPORTS: cotton, soybeans, timber, and vegetable oils
CONTINENT: South America

Peru
CAPITAL: Lima
POPULATION: 24,087,372
MAJOR LANGUAGES: Spanish (official), Quechua (official), and Aymara
AREA: 496,243 sq mi; 1,285,220 sq km
LEADING EXPORTS: copper, zinc, and fish meal
CONTINENT: South America

Philippines
CAPITAL: Manila
POPULATION: 73,265,584
MAJOR LANGUAGES: Pilipino and English (official)
AREA: 115,834 sq mi; 300,000 sq km
LEADING EXPORTS: electronics, textiles, and coconut products
CONTINENT: Asia

Poland
CAPITAL: Warsaw
POPULATION: 38,792,442
MAJOR LANGUAGE: Polish
AREA: 120,731 sq mi; 312,680 sq km
LEADING EXPORTS: intermediate goods
CONTINENT: Europe

Portugal
CAPITAL: Lisbon
POPULATION: 10,562,388
MAJOR LANGUAGE: Portuguese
AREA: 35,553 sq mi; 92,080 sq km
LEADING EXPORTS: clothing and footwear, and machinery
CONTINENT: Europe

Qatar
CAPITAL: Doha
POPULATION: 533,916
MAJOR LANGUAGES: Arabic (official) and English
AREA: 4,247 sq mi; 11,000 sq km
LEADING EXPORTS: petroleum products, steel, and fertilizers
CONTINENT: Asia

Romania
CAPITAL: Bucharest
POPULATION: 23,198,330
MAJOR LANGUAGES: Romanian, Hungarian, and German
AREA: 91,702 sq mi; 237,500 sq km
LEADING EXPORTS: metals and metal products, and mineral products
CONTINENT: Europe

Russia
CAPITAL: Moscow
POPULATION: 149,909,089
MAJOR LANGUAGES: Russian and various languages
AREA: 6,952,996 sq mi; 17,075,200 sq km
LEADING EXPORTS: petroleum and petroleum products
CONTINENT: Europe and Asia

Rwanda
CAPITAL: Kigali
POPULATION: 8,605,307
MAJOR LANGUAGES: Kinyarwanda (official), French (official), and Kiswahili
AREA: 10,170 sq mi; 26,340 sq km
LEADING EXPORTS: coffee, tea, cassiterite, and wolframite
CONTINENT: Africa

Saint Kitts and Nevis
CAPITAL: Basseterre
POPULATION: 40,992
MAJOR LANGUAGE: English
AREA: 104 sq mi; 269 sq km
LEADING EXPORTS: machinery, food, and electronics
LOCATION: Caribbean Sea

Saint Lucia

CAPITAL: Castries
POPULATION: 156,050
MAJOR LANGUAGES: English and French patois
AREA: 239 sq mi; 620 sq km
LEADING EXPORTS: bananas, clothing, cocoa, and vegetables
LOCATION: Caribbean Sea

Saint Vincent and the Grenadines

CAPITAL: Kingstown
POPULATION: 117,344
MAJOR LANGUAGES: English and French patois
AREA: 131 sq mi; 340 sq km
LEADING EXPORTS: bananas, and eddoes and dasheen (taro)
LOCATION: Caribbean Sea

San Marino
CAPITAL: San Marino
POPULATION: 24,313
MAJOR LANGUAGE: Italian
AREA: 23 sq mi; 60 sq km
LEADING EXPORTS: building stone, lime, wood, and chestnuts
CONTINENT: Europe

Sao Tome and Principe

CAPITAL: Sao Tome
POPULATION: 140,423
MAJOR LANGUAGE: Portuguese (official)
AREA: 371 sq mi; 960 sq km
LEADING EXPORTS: cocoa, copra, coffee, and palm oil
CONTINENT: Africa

Saudi Arabia
CAPITAL: Riyadh
POPULATION: 18,729,576
MAJOR LANGUAGE: Arabic
AREA: 757,011 sq mi; 1,960,582 sq km
LEADING EXPORTS: petroleum and petroleum products
CONTINENT: Asia

Senegal
CAPITAL: Dakar
POPULATION: 9,007,080
MAJOR LANGUAGES: French (official), Wolof, Pulaar, Diola, and Mandingo
AREA: 75,752 sq mi; 196,190 sq km
LEADING EXPORTS: fish, ground nuts, and petroleum products
CONTINENT: Africa

Serbia and Montenegro

CAPITAL: Belgrade
POPULATION: 11,101,833
MAJOR LANGUAGES: Serbo-Croatian and Albanian
AREA: 39,436 sq mi; 102,350 sq km
LEADING EXPORTS: none
CONTINENT: Europe

Seychelles
CAPITAL: Victoria
POPULATION: 72,709
MAJOR LANGUAGES: English (official), French (official), and Creole
AREA: 176 sq mi; 455 sq km
LEADING EXPORTS: fish, cinnamon bark, and copra
CONTINENT: Africa

Sierra Leone

CAPITAL: Freetown
POPULATION: 4,753,120
MAJOR LANGUAGES: English (official), Mende, Temne, and Krio
AREA: 27,700 sq mi; 71,740 sq km
LEADING EXPORTS: rutile, bauxite, diamonds, coffee, and cocoa
CONTINENT: Africa

Singapore

CAPITAL: Singapore
POPULATION: 2,890,468
MAJOR LANGUAGES: Chinese, Malay, Tamil, and English
AREA: 244 sq mi; 633 sq km
LEADING EXPORTS: computer equipment
CONTINENT: Asia

Slovakia

CAPITAL: Bratislava
POPULATION: 5,432,383
MAJOR LANGUAGES: Slovak and Hungarian
AREA: 18,860 sq mi; 48,845 sq km
LEADING EXPORTS: machinery and transportation equipment
CONTINENT: Europe

Slovenia

CAPITAL: Ljubljana
POPULATION: 2,051,522
MAJOR LANGUAGES: Slovenian, Serbo-Croatian, and various languages
AREA: 7,837 sq mi; 20,296 sq km
LEADING EXPORTS: machinery and transportation equipment
CONTINENT: Europe

Solomon Islands
CAPITAL: Honiara
POPULATION: 399,206
MAJOR LANGUAGES: Melanesian pidgin and English
AREA: 10,985 sq mi; 28,450 sq km
LEADING EXPORTS: fish, timber, palm oil, cocoa, and copra
LOCATION: Pacific Ocean

Somalia

CAPITAL: Mogadishu
POPULATION: 7,347,554
MAJOR LANGUAGES: Somali (official), Arabic, Italian, and English
AREA: 246,210 sq mi; 637,660 sq km
LEADING EXPORTS: bananas, live animals, fish, and hides
CONTINENT: Africa

South Africa
CAPITAL: Pretoria (administrative), Cape Town (legislative), Bloemfontein (judicial)
POPULATION: 45,095,459
MAJOR LANGUAGES: Afrikaans, English, Ndebele, Pedi, Sotho, Swazi, Tsonga, Tswana, Venda, Xhosa, and Zulu (all official)
AREA: 471,027 sq mi; 1,219,912 sq km
LEADING EXPORTS: gold, other minerals and metals, and food
CONTINENT: Africa

Spain
CAPITAL: Madrid
POPULATION: 39,404,348
MAJOR LANGUAGES: Spanish, Catalan, Galician, and Basque
AREA: 194,892 sq mi; 504,750 sq km
LEADING EXPORTS: cars and trucks, and semifinished goods
CONTINENT: Europe

Sri Lanka

CAPITAL: Colombo
POPULATION: 18,342,660
MAJOR LANGUAGES: Sinhala (official) and Tamil
AREA: 25,333 sq mi; 65,610 sq km
LEADING EXPORTS: garments and textiles, teas, and diamonds
CONTINENT: Asia

Sudan
CAPITAL: Khartoum
POPULATION: 30,120,420
MAJOR LANGUAGES: Arabic (official), Nubian, Ta Bedawie, Nilotic, Nilo-Hamitic, and Sudanic dialects
AREA: 967,532 sq mi; 2,505,810 sq km
LEADING EXPORTS: gum arabic, livestock/meat, and cotton
CONTINENT: Africa

Suriname

CAPITAL: Paramaribo
POPULATION: 429,544
MAJOR LANGUAGES: Dutch (official), English, Sranang, Tongo, Hindustani, and Japanese
AREA: 63,041 sq mi; 163,270 sq km
LEADING EXPORTS: alumina, aluminum, and shrimp and fish
CONTINENT: South America

Swaziland

CAPITAL: Mbabane
POPULATION: 966,977
MAJOR LANGUAGES: English (official) and SiSwati (official)
AREA: 6,641 sq mi; 17,360 sq km
LEADING EXPORTS: sugar, edible concentrates, and wood pulp
CONTINENT: Africa

Sweden

CAPITAL: Stockholm
POPULATION: 8,821,759
MAJOR LANGUAGES: Swedish, Lapp, and Finnish
AREA: 173,738 sq mi; 449,964 sq km
LEADING EXPORTS: machinery, motor vehicles, and paper products
CONTINENT: Europe

Switzerland

CAPITAL: Bern
POPULATION: 7,084,984
MAJOR LANGUAGES: German, French, Italian, Romansch, and various languages
AREA: 15,943 sq mi; 41,290 sq km
LEADING EXPORTS: machinery and equipment
CONTINENT: Europe

Syria

CAPITAL: Damascus
POPULATION: 15,451,917
MAJOR LANGUAGES: Arabic (official), Kurdish, Armenian, Aramaic, Circassian, and French
AREA: 71,501 sq mi; 185,180 sq km
LEADING EXPORTS: petroleum, textiles, cotton, and fruits
CONTINENT: Asia

Taiwan

CAPITAL: Taipei
POPULATION: 21,500,583
MAJOR LANGUAGES: Mandarin Chinese (official), Taiwanese, and Hakka dialects
AREA: 13,892 sq mi; 35,980 sq km
LEADING EXPORTS: electrical machinery and electronics
CONTINENT: Asia

Tajikistan

CAPITAL: Dushanbe
POPULATION: 6,155,474
MAJOR LANGUAGES: Tajik (official) and Russian
AREA: 55,253 sq mi; 143,100 sq km
LEADING EXPORTS: cotton, aluminum, fruits, and vegetable oil
CONTINENT: Asia

Tanzania

CAPITAL: Dar Es Salaam
POPULATION: 28,701,077
MAJOR LANGUAGES: Swahili, English, and various languages
AREA: 364,914 sq mi; 945,090 sq km
LEADING EXPORTS: coffee, cotton, tobacco, tea, and cashew nuts
CONTINENT: Africa

Thailand

CAPITAL: Bangkok
POPULATION: 60,271,300
MAJOR LANGUAGES: Thai and English
AREA: 198,463 sq mi; 511,770 sq km
LEADING EXPORTS: machinery and manufactures
CONTINENT: Asia

Togo

CAPITAL: Lome
POPULATION: 4,410,370
MAJOR LANGUAGES: French, Ewe and Mina, Dagomba, and Kabye
AREA: 21,927 sq mi; 56,790 sq km
LEADING EXPORTS: phosphates, cotton, cocoa, and coffee
CONTINENT: Africa

Tonga

CAPITAL: Nukualofa
POPULATION: 105,600
MAJOR LANGUAGES: Tongan and English
AREA: 289 sq mi; 748 sq km
LEADING EXPORTS: squash, vanilla, fish, root crops, and coconut oil
LOCATION: Pacific Ocean

Trinidad and Tobago

CAPITAL: Port-of-Spain
POPULATION: 1,271,159
MAJOR LANGUAGES: English, Hindu, French, and Spanish
AREA: 1,981 sq mi; 5,130 sq km
LEADING EXPORTS: petroleum and petroleum products
LOCATION: Caribbean Sea

Tunisia

CAPITAL: Tunis
POPULATION: 8,879,845
MAJOR LANGUAGES: Arabic and French
AREA: 63,172 sq mi; 163,610 sq km
LEADING EXPORTS: hydrocarbons and agricultural products
CONTINENT: Africa

Turkey

CAPITAL: Ankara
POPULATION: 63,405,526
MAJOR LANGUAGES: Turkish, Kurdish, and Arabic
AREA: 301,394 sq mi; 780,580 sq km
LEADING EXPORTS: manufactured products, and foodstuffs
CONTINENT: Europe and Asia

Turkmenistan

CAPITAL: Ashgabat
POPULATION: 4,075,316
MAJOR LANGUAGES: Turkmen, Russian, Uzbek, and various languages
AREA: 188,463 sq mi; 488,100 sq km
LEADING EXPORTS: natural gas, cotton, and petroleum products
CONTINENT: Asia

Tuvalu

CAPITAL: Fongafale, on Funafuti atoll
POPULATION: 9,991
MAJOR LANGUAGES: Tuvaluan and English
AREA: 10 sq mi; 26 sq km
LEADING EXPORT: copra
LOCATION: Pacific Ocean

Uganda

CAPITAL: Kampala
POPULATION: 19,573,262
MAJOR LANGUAGES: English, Luganda, Swahili, Bantu languages, and Nilotic languages
AREA: 91,139 sq mi; 236,040 sq km
LEADING EXPORTS: coffee, cotton, and tea
CONTINENT: Africa

Ukraine

CAPITAL: Kiev
POPULATION: 51,867,828
MAJOR LANGUAGES: Ukranian, Russian, Romanian, Polish, and Hungarian
AREA: 233,098 sq mi; 603,700 sq km
LEADING EXPORTS: coal, electric power, and metals
CONTINENT: Europe

United Arab Emirates

CAPITAL: Abu Dhabi
POPULATION: 2,924,594
MAJOR LANGUAGES: Arabic, Persian, English, Hindi, and Urdu
AREA: 29,183 sq mi; 75,581 sq km
LEADING EXPORTS: crude oil, natural gas, re-exports, and dried fish
CONTINENT: Asia

United Kingdom

CAPITAL: London
POPULATION: 58,295,119
MAJOR LANGUAGES: English, Welsh, and Scottish Gaelic
AREA: 94,529 sq mi; 244,820 sq km
LEADING EXPORTS: manufactured goods, machinery, and fuels
CONTINENT: Europe

United States

CAPITAL: Washington, D.C.
POPULATION: 263,814,032
MAJOR LANGUAGES: English and Spanish
AREA: 3,618,908 sq mi; 9,372,610 sq km
LEADING EXPORTS: capital goods and automobiles
CONTINENT: North America

Uruguay

CAPITAL: Montevideo
POPULATION: 3,222,716
MAJOR LANGUAGES: Spanish and Brazilero
AREA: 68,041 sq mi; 176,220 sq km
LEADING EXPORTS: wool and textile manufactures
CONTINENT: South America

Uzbekistan

CAPITAL: Tashkent
POPULATION: 23,089,261
MAJOR LANGUAGES: Uzbek, Russian, Tajik, various languages
AREA: 172,748 sq mi; 447,400 sq km
LEADING EXPORTS: cotton, gold, natural gas, and minerals
CONTINENT: Asia

Vanuatu

CAPITAL: Port-Vila
POPULATION: 173,648
MAJOR LANGUAGES: English, French, pidgin, and Bislama
AREA: 5,699 sq mi; 14,760 sq km
LEADING EXPORTS: copra, beef, cocoa, timber, and coffee
LOCATION: Pacific Ocean

Venezuela

CAPITAL: Caracas
POPULATION: 21,004,773
MAJOR LANGUAGES: Spanish and various languages
AREA: 352,156 sq mi; 912,050 sq km
LEADING EXPORTS: petroleum, bauxite and aluminum, and steel
CONTINENT: South America

Vietnam

CAPITAL: Hanoi
POPULATION: 74,393,324
MAJOR LANGUAGES: Vietnamese, French, Chinese, English, Khmer, and various languages
AREA: 127,248 sq mi; 329,560 sq km
LEADING EXPORTS: petroleum, rice, and agricultural products
CONTINENT: Asia

Western Samoa

CAPITAL: Apia
POPULATION: 209,360
MAJOR LANGUAGES: Samoan and English
AREA: 1,104 sq mi; 2,860 sq km
LEADING EXPORTS: coconut oil and cream, taro, copra, and cocoa
LOCATION: Pacific Ocean

Yemen

CAPITAL: Sanaa
POPULATION: 14,728,474
MAJOR LANGUAGE: Arabic
AREA: 203,857 sq mi; 527,970 sq km
LEADING EXPORTS: crude oil, cotton, coffee, hides, and vegetables
CONTINENT: Asia

Zaire

CAPITAL: Kinshasa
POPULATION: 44,060,636
MAJOR LANGUAGES: French, Lingala, Swahili, Kingwana, Kikongo, and Tshiluba
AREA: 905,599 sq mi; 2,345,410 sq km
LEADING EXPORTS: copper, coffee, diamonds, cobalt, and crude oil
CONTINENT: Africa

Zambia

CAPITAL: Lusaka
POPULATION: 9,445,723
MAJOR LANGUAGES: English (official) and about 70 various languages
AREA: 290,594 sq mi; 752,610 sq km
LEADING EXPORTS: copper, zinc, cobalt, lead, and tobacco
CONTINENT: Africa

Zimbabwe

CAPITAL: Harare
POPULATION: 11,139,961
MAJOR LANGUAGES: English, Shona, and Sindebele
area: 150,809 sq mi; 390,580 sq km
LEADING EXPORTS: agricultural products and manufactures
CONTINENT: Africa

Glossary of Geographic Terms

basin

a depression in the surface of the land; some basins are filled with water

bay

a part of a sea or lake that extends into the land

butte

a small raised area of land with steep sides

▲ butte

canyon

a deep, narrow valley with steep sides; often has a stream flowing through it

cataract

a large waterfall; any strong flood or rush of water

◀ cataract

delta

a triangular-shaped plain at the mouth of a river, formed when sediment is deposited by flowing water

flood plain

a broad plain on either side of a river, formed when sediment settles on the riverbanks

glacier

a huge, slow-moving mass of snow and ice

hill

an area that rises above surrounding land and has a rounded top; lower and usually less steep than a mountain

island

an area of land completely surrounded by water

isthmus

a narrow strip of land that connects two larger areas of land

mesa

a high, flat-topped landform with cliff-like sides; larger than a butte

mountain

an area that rises steeply at least 2,000 feet (300 m) above surrounding land; usually wide at the bottom and rising to a narrow peak or ridge

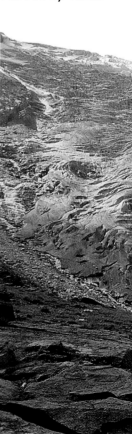

▶ glacier

◄ delta

mountain pass
a gap between mountains

peninsula
an area of land almost completely surrounded by water and connected to the mainland by an isthmus

plain
a large area of flat or gently rolling land

plateau
a large, flat area that rises above the surrounding land; at least one side has a steep slope

river mouth
the point where a river enters a lake or sea

strait
a narrow stretch of water that connects two larger bodies of water

tributary
a river or stream that flows into a larger river

volcano
an opening in the Earth's surface through which molten rock, ashes, and gasses from the Earth's interior escape

► volcano

Gazetteer

A

Africa (10°N, 22°E) world's second-largest continent, surrounded by the Mediterranean Sea, the Atlantic Ocean, and the Red Sea, p. 57

Antarctica (80.15°S, 127°E) the continent lying around the South Pole; almost completely covered by an ice sheet, p. 47

Antarctic Circle (66°30'S) line of latitude around the Earth near the South Pole, p. 29

Arctic region located around the North Pole, p. 59

Arctic Circle (66°30'N) line of latitude around the Earth near the North Pole, p. 29

Asia (50°N, 100°E) the world's largest continent, surrounded by the Arctic Ocean, the Pacific Ocean, the Indian Ocean, and Europe, p. 57

Australia (25°S, 135°E) an island continent in the Southern Hemisphere; a country including the continent and Tasmania, p. 57

C

California Current a southward-flowing oceanic current along the West Coast of North America; flows between 48°N and 23°N, p. 40

Caribbean Sea (14.3°N, 75.3°W) part of the southern Atlantic Ocean, p. 41

China (25.43°N, 99.13°W) a country occupying most of the mainland of East Asia, p. 90

Cuba (22°N, 79°W) the largest island country in the Caribbean, p. 65

E

Egypt (26.58°N, 27.01°E) a country in North Africa, p. 85

Europe

Europe (50°N, 15°E) the world's second-smallest continent, a peninsula of the Eurasian landmass bounded by the Arctic Ocean, the Atlantic Ocean, the Mediterranean Sea, and Asia, p. 57

G

Galapagos Islands (.10°S, 87.45°W) group of islands located in the eastern Pacific Ocean, part of Ecuador, p. 40

Germany (51°N, 10°E) a country in Europe, p. 83

Great Britain (56.3°N, 1.4°W) island located to the west of the European continent, consisting of England, Scotland, and Wales, p. 83

Great Plains (45°N, 104°W) a dry area of short grasses located in North America, stretching from the Rio Grande at the U.S.-Mexico border in the south to the Mackenzie River Delta in the north, and from the Canadian Shield in the east to the Rocky Mountains in the west; also called "The Great American Desert," p. 46

Greenland (74°N, 40°W) a large, self-governing island in the northern Atlantic Ocean, part of Denmark, p.14

Gulf Stream a warm ocean current in the North Atlantic, flowing northeastward off the North American coast, p. 40

I

India (23°N, 77.3°E) a large country occupying most of the Indian subcontinent in South Asia, p. 37

Indian Ocean (10°S, 70°E) the world's third-largest ocean lying between Africa, Asia, and Australia, p. 9

Indonesia (4.38°S, 118.45°E) a country in Southeast Asia consisting of many islands, including Sumatra, Java, Sulawesi (Celebes), Bali, and the western half of New Guinea, p. 68

Israel (32.4°N, 34°E) a country in Southwest Asia, p. 91

Italy (43.58°N, 11.14°E) a boot-shaped country in southern Europe, including the islands of Sicily and Sardinia, p. 89

J

Jakarta (6.17°S, 106.45°E) the capital and largest city of the Republic of Indonesia, p. 68

Japan, (36.3°N, 133.3°E) an island country in the Pacific Ocean off the east coast of Asia, consisting of four main islands—Honshū, Hokkaidō, Kyūshū, and Shikoku, p. 55

M

Mexico (23.45°N, 104°W) a country in North America, p. 41

Milky Way a galaxy consisting of several billions of stars including the sun, p. 27

Mount Everest (28°N, 86.57°E) highest point on the Earth, located on the Great Himalaya Range in Asia, p. 47

Myanmar a country in Southeast Asia, formerly Burma, p. 9

N

Nepal (28.45°N, 83°E) a country in south Asia, p. 47

Nile Valley the fertile land located on both sides of the Nile River in Africa; site of one of the earliest civilizations, p. 58

North America (45°N, 100°W) the world's third-largest continent, consisting of Canada, the United States, Mexico, and many islands, p. 57

North Pole (90°N) northernmost end of the Earth's axis located in the Arctic Ocean, p. 39

P

Pangaea (pan JEE uh) according to scientific theory, a single landmass that broke apart to form today's separate continents; thought to have existed about 180 million years ago, p. 33

Peru Current a cold-water current of the southeast Pacific Ocean; flows between 40°S and 4°S, p. 40

R

Ring of Fire a circle of volcanic mountains that surrounds the Pacific Ocean, including those on the islands of Japan and Indonesia, in the Cascades of North America, and in the Andes of South America, p. 31

S

San Francisco (38°N, 122°W) a seaport city in California, p. 40

South America the world's fourth-largest continent, bounded by the Caribbean Sea, the Atlantic Ocean, and the Pacific Ocean, and linked to North America by the Isthmus of Panama, p. 40

South Pole (90°S) southernmost end of the Earth's axis located in Antarctica, p. 39

St. Louis (38.39°N, 90.15°W) a city in Missouri, p. 40

T

Tropic of Cancer (23 1/2°N) the northern boundary of the tropics, or the band of the Earth that receives the most direct light and heat energy from the sun; this region lies on both sides of the Equator, p. 28

Tropic of Capricorn (23 1/2°S) the southern boundary of the tropics; see above, p. 28

V

Vietnam (18°N, 107°E) a country located in Southeast Asia; officially named the Socialist Republic of Vietnam, p. 66

Glossary

A

acculturation the process of accepting, borrowing, and exchanging ideas and traits among cultures, p. 95

acid rain rain whose high level of chemicals can pollute or damage the environment; usually caused by pollutants from the burning of fossil fuels, p. 118

agriculture farming; includes growing crops and raising livestock, p. 80

atmosphere the multilayered band of gases that surrounds the Earth, p. 35

axis an imaginary line around which a planet turns; the Earth turns around its axis, which runs between its North and South poles, p. 28

B

birthrate the number of live births each year per 1,000 people, p. 61

C

canopy a layer of branches and leaves at the tops of the trees in a forest, p. 44

capitalism an economic system in which people and privately owned companies own both basic and nonbasic businesses and industries, p. 89

cardinal direction one of the four compass points: north, south, east, and west, p. 19

climate the weather patterns that an area typically experiences over a long period of time, p. 38

commercial farming farming that is done by companies; commercial farms are large and use modern technology; also the raising of crops and livestock for sale in outside markets, p. 114

communism an economic system in which the government owns all businesses and industries, p. 90

compass rose a map feature that usually shows the four cardinal directions, p. 19

constitution a set of laws that defines and limits a government's power, p. 91

consumer a person who buys goods and services, p. 88

continental United States the geographical area that includes all states of the United States except Alaska and Hawaii, p. 57

culture the way of life of people who share similar customs and beliefs, p. 78

cultural diffusion the movement of customs and ideas from one culture to another, p. 95

cultural landscape a landscape that has been changed by human beings and that reflects their culture, p. 79

cultural trait a behavioral characteristic of a people, such as a language, skill, or custom, passed from one generation to another, p. 78

D

death rate the number of deaths each year per 1,000 people, p. 61

deforestation the process of clearing land of forests or trees, usually to make room for farms and homes, p. 118

degree a unit of measure used to determine absolute location; on globes and maps, latitude and longitude are measured in degrees, p. 11

demographer a scientist who studies human populations, including their size; growth; density; distribution; and rates of births, marriages, and deaths, p. 55

developed nation a modern industrial society with a well-developed economy, p. 113

developing nation a country with relatively low industrial production, often lacking modern technology, p. 113

dictator a ruler who has complete power over a country, p. 92

direct democracy a system of government in which the people participate directly in decision making, p. 91

distortion a misrepresentation of the original shape; each map projection used by a cartographer produces some distortion, p. 155

E

economy a system for producing, distributing, consuming, and owning goods, services, and wealth, p. 88

ecosystem a community of living things and its environment; the elements of an ecosystem interact with one another, p. 117

Equator an imaginary line that circles the globe at its widest point (halfway between the North and South poles), dividing the Earth into two halves called hemispheres; used as a reference point from which north and south latitudes are measured, p. 11

erosion a process by which water, wind, or ice wears away landforms and carries the material to another place, p. 35

ethics the standards or code of moral behavior that distinguishes between right and wrong for a particular person, religion, group, profession, and so on, p. 85

extended family a family unit that may include parents, children, grandparents, aunts, uncles, cousins, and other relatives, p. 84

F

foreign aid economic and military aid to another country, p. 116

fossil fuel any one of several nonrenewable resources such as coal, oil, or natural gas, created from the remains of plants and animals, p. 108

G

geography the study of the Earth's surface and the processes that shape it, the connections between places, and the relationships between people and their environment, p. 10

global warming a slow increase in the Earth's temperature due to the increasing amount of carbon dioxide in the atmosphere; if there is too much carbon dioxide in the atmosphere, more heat than normal is trapped, and temperatures around the world increase, p. 119

globe a round model of the Earth that shows the continents and oceans in their true shapes, p. 15

goods products that are made to be sold; cars, baskets, computers, and paper are all examples of goods, p. 88

government the system that establishes and enforces the laws and institutions of a society; some governments are controlled by a few people, and others are controlled by many, p. 90

Green Revolution changes in agriculture since the 1950s that have greatly increased the world's food supply; the Green Revolution comes with a price tag, however, since reliance on costly technologies and dangerous pesticides can be both financially and environmentally damaging to nations, p. 61

H

habitat the area in which a plant or animal naturally grows or lives, p. 118

high latitudes the regions between the Arctic Circle and the North Pole and the Antarctic Circle and the South Pole, p. 29

hill a landform that rises above the surrounding land and that has a rounded top; a hill is lower and usually less steep than a mountain, p. 32

I

immigrant a person who moves to a new country in order to settle there, p. 64

K

key the section of a map that explains the symbols for the map features; also called a legend, p. 19

L

landform an area of the Earth's surface with a definite shape; mountains and hills are examples of landforms, p. 32

latitude lines the series of imaginary lines, also called parallels, that circle the Earth parallel to the Equator; used to measure a distance north or south of the Equator in degrees, p. 11

life expectancy the number of years that a person may be expected, on average, to live, p. 61

longitude lines the series of imaginary lines, also called meridians, that run north and south from one pole to the other; used to measure a distance east or west of the Prime Meridian in degrees, p. 11

low latitudes the region between the Tropic of Cancer and the Tropic of Capricorn, p. 29

M

manufacturing the process of turning raw materials into a finished product, p. 112

meridian an imaginary line that circles the globe from north to south and runs through both the North and South poles; the lines of longitude on maps or globes are meridians, p. 11

middle latitudes the regions between the Tropic of Cancer and the Arctic Circle and the Tropic of Capricorn and the Antarctic Circle, p. 30

migration the movement of people from one country or region to another in order to make a new home, p. 64

monarchy a system of authoritarian government headed by a monarch—usually a king or queen—who inherits the throne by birth, p. 91

mountain a landform that usually rises more than 2,000 ft (610 m) above sea level and is wide at the bottom and narrow at the peak, p. 32

N

nonrenewable resource a resource that cannot be replaced once it is used; nonrenewable resources include fossil fuels such as coal and oil, and minerals such as iron, copper, and gold, p. 107

nuclear family a family unit that includes a mother, a father, and their children, p. 83

O

orbit the path followed by one heavenly object as it moves around another, such as that of the Earth as it moves around the sun, p. 28

ozone layer the layer of gas in the upper part of the atmosphere that blocks out most of the sun's harmful ultraviolet rays, p. 119

P

parallel in geography, any of the imaginary lines that circle the Earth parallel to the Equator; a latitude line, p. 11

plain a large area of flat or gently rolling land, often found near a coast, p. 13

plantation a large estate, usually in a warm climate, on which crops are grown by workers living there; plantations usually raise a single crop for export, p. 115

plate in geography, a huge section of the Earth's crust, p. 33

plateau a large, mostly flat area that rises above the surrounding land; at least one side has a steep slope, p. 32

plate tectonics the theory that the Earth's crust is made of huge, slowly moving slabs of rock called plates, p. 33

population the people living in a particular region; especially the total number of people in an area, p. 55

population density the average number of people living in a given area, p. 57

population distribution how a population is spread over an area, p. 55

precipitation all the forms of water, such as rain, sleet, hail, and snow, that fall to the ground from the atmosphere, p. 38

Prime Meridian an imaginary line of longitude, or meridian, that runs from the North Pole to the South Pole through Greenwich, England;

it is designated 0° longitude and is used as a reference point from which east and west lines of longitude are measured, p. 11

producer a person who makes products that are used by other people, p. 88

projection a representation of the Earth's rounded surface on a flat piece of paper, p. 16

"push-pull" theory a theory of migration that says people migrate because certain things in their lives "push" them to leave, and certain things in a new place "pull" them, p. 65

R

raw material a resource or material that is still in its natural state, before being processed or manufactured into a useful product, p. 106

recyclable resource a resource that cycles through natural processes in the environment; water, nitrogen, and carbon are recyclable resources, p. 107

recycle to reuse materials to make new products, p. 121

renewable resource a natural resource that the environment continues to supply or replace as it is used; trees and crops are renewable resources, p. 107

representative democracy a system of government in which the people elect representatives to run the affairs of the country, p. 91

revolution one complete orbit of the Earth around the sun; the Earth completes one revolution every 365 1/4 days, or one year, p. 28

rotation the spinning motion of the Earth, like a top on its axis as it travels through space; the Earth takes about 24 hours to rotate one time, p. 28

rural area an area with low population density, such as a village or the countryside, p. 68

S

scale the size of an area on a map as compared to the area's actual size, p. 15

services work done or duties performed for other people, such as the work of a doctor or of a television repair person, p. 88

socialism an economic system in which the government owns most basic industries, such as transportation, communications, and banking; nonbasic industries are privately owned, p. 89

social structure the ways in which people within a culture are organized into smaller groups; each smaller group has its own particular tasks, p. 82

subsistence farming farming that provides only enough food and animals for the needs of a family or a village, p. 115

T

technology tools and the skills that people need to use them; the practical use of scientific skills, especially in industry, p. 79

temperature the degree of hotness or coldness of something, such as water or air, usually measured with a thermometer, p. 38

tundra a region where temperatures are always cool or cold and where only certain plants, such as low grasses, can grow, p. 46

U

urban area an area with a high population density; a city or town, p. 68

urbanization the growth of city populations caused by the movement of people to cities, p. 68

V

vegetation the plants in an area, p. 43

vertical climate the overall weather patterns of a region as influenced by elevation; the higher the elevation, the colder the climate, p. 47

W

weather the condition of the bottom layer of the Earth's atmosphere in one place over a short period of time, p. 37

weathering the breaking down of rocks by wind, rain, or ice, p. 35

Index

The *italicized* page numbers refer to illustrations. The *m, c, p, t,* or *g* preceding the number refers to maps *(m)*, charts *(c)*, pictures *(p)*, tables *(t)*, or graphs *(g)*.

F

family: cultural importance of, 83, *p 83*; extended, 84; matriarchal, 84; nuclear, 83–84; patriarchal, 84; place of women in, 84

farming: in China, 111; commercial, 114; in developing nations, 113–116; fertilizer used in, 61; importance to cultural development of, 80; Japanese, *p 78*; population distribution and, 56; subsistence, 115; terrace, 78, *p 78*, 79, 81

fast-food stores, 112

fasting: of Muslims during Ramadan, 82

faults, 34

fax, 96

ferns, 44

fertilizer, 61

fiords, *m 56*

fire: discovery of, 80

first-level activities: of resource development, 111, *p 112*

foreign aid, 116

forests: coniferous, *m 44–45*; deciduous, *m 4, m 44–45*, 47; importance of to air quality, 63; in India, 63; in Pakistan, 63; rain, *m 4, 43–44*, 107, *p 107*; preservation of, 94

fossil: plant, 46; fuel, 107

fossil fuel, 107–108, 121

free-market economy, 89, *c 89*

Fujiwara, Megumi, 31

G

galaxy. *See* Milky Way

Galapagos Islands, 40

gasoline shortage (1973), 109

geography: defined, 3, 10; five themes of, 9–13

Germany, 83

glacier, 102

global village, 96

global warming, 120–121; effect on developing nation of, 121

GOES-8, *p 80*

GOES-9, *p 80*

Goizueta, Roberto, 64

gold, *m 106*

goods, 88

government: defined, 90; early forms of, 81. *See also* political systems

Grameen Bank, 88

Grand Bahama Island, *m 18*

grassland, *m 44–45*, 46, 47; in Australia, 57; of the Great Plains, 117

gray whale, *p 118*

Great Britain, 83; constitutional monarchy of, *p 91*

Great Hanshin Earthquake, 31

Great Plains (U.S.), 46, 117

Greek alphabet: origin of, 85

Green Belt Movement, 117

greenhouse effect, *p 119*

Greenland, 16, *p 16*

Green Revolution, 61

grid, *m 18*, 19

groundwater, 36

Gulf of Mexico, *m 13*

Gulf Stream, 40

H

habitat, 118

hacker. *See* computer hacker

Haiti, 65

Hawaiian islands, 34

health care: advances in, 61

hemlock, 74

herders, *m 114*, 115

hill: defined, 32

Hinduism, *m 86*

Hiroshima, Japan, *m 57*

homework: importance of, to Japanese students, 77

Huang He, 111

humidity, 45

hurricane: Andrew, 40, 51; defined, 41; wind speeds of, 41

hydroponics, 61

I

ice caps. *See* polar ice caps

ice pack, *m 44–45*

Iftar, 82

immigrants, 64, *p 95*; Irish, 66; Vietnamese, 66

immigration: of convicts, 67; Irish, 66; Vietnamese, 66

India, 4, *m 4*, 37; cultural landscape of, 79

Indiana Dunes National Park, 121

Indian Ocean, *m 4*, 9, *m 32*

indigo, 93

Indo-European language group, *m 84*

industrial nation, 112

Industrial Revolution, 113

Internet, 79, 95, 96

Inuits, 14, 85

Iran: petroleum production of, *g 109*

irrigation, 12, 36, 81

Islam, 82, 85, 86, *m 86*

isolines, 57

Israel: representative democracy of, 91

Italy: socialist economy of, 89

Ithaca Hours, *p 88*

J

Jakarta, Indonesia, 68

Jamaica, 65

Japan, 113; capitalism and, 89; contour map of, *m 57*; farming in, *p 78*; Hiroshima, *m 57*; Kobe, 31; language group of, *m 84*; limited petroleum resources of, 109; population of, 55; Tokyo, 55, *p 55*

Japanese and Korean language group, *m 84*

Judaism, 86, *m 86*

judo, 77

K

Kalahari Desert, 115

KAP. *See* Kids Against Pollution (KAP)

karate, 77

Kazakstan, 118

Keaton, Julius, 40–41

Kennedy, John F., *p 66*

Kenya, Africa, *p 12*

Kenyatta National Hospital, *p 61*

key: map, *m 18*, 19

Khatun, Sufiya, 87

Kids Against Pollution (KAP), 122, 123

Kobe, Japan, 31

L

Lake Naivasha, *p 12*

Lancaster, Pennsylvania, *p 58*

landform, 57; defined, 32, effect of, on climate, 38–39

language: groups, *m 84*; cultural importance of, 78, 85

language groups, *m 84*

latitude, 11, 19; effect of, on climate, 38–39; high, 29; low, 29; middle, 30;

lead, *m 106*

lichens, 46, 47

life expectancy, 61; in selected countries, *g 62*

Lighthawk, 45

literature, 74–75, 102–103

Lixing, Li, 111

longitude, 11, 19

M

Maathai, Wangari, 117

magma, 34

Malayo-Polynesian language group, *m 84*

Malaysia, *p 83*

Maldive Islands, 9

manufacturing, 112–114, *m 114*; automobile, 113, *p 113*

mapmakers, 15, 16

maps and globes, 10, *m 10*, 14–15; distortion in, 15; distribution maps, 70–71; latitude and longitude in, 10, *m 10*, 11, *m 11*, 29; Mercator projection and, 16, *m 16*; parts of a map, 18; Peters projection and, *m 17*; physical map, 2–3, 13; Robinson projection and, *m 17*; scale in, 15

maps: of continental movement, 33; of continents, oceans, and seas, 32; contour, of Japan, 57; of Cuba and the U.S. Gulf Coast, 65; of major language groups, 84; of major religions, 86; of ocean currents, 41; physical, of North America, 13; physical, of Norway, 56; of plate boundaries, 34; of population distribution of Mexico, 71; of South America, 3; of South Asian climate regions, 5; of South Asian population density, 5; of South Asian vegetation regions, 4; of world climate regions, 38–39; of world economic activity, 114; of world natural resources, 106; of world natural vegetation, 44–45; of world ocean currents, 41; of world population density, 6; of world wind patterns, 35; of zones of latitudes, 29

Marshall Islands, *p 14*

Martha's Vineyard, Massachusetts, 105

matriarchal family, 84

measles, 61

Mediterranean Sea, 85

Mediterranean vegetation, *m 44–45*

mental map, 7

Mercator projection, 16, *m 16*

meridians, 11, 19

meteorologists, *p 80*

Mexico, 65, 70–71; petroleum production of, *g 109*; population distribution of, *m 71*

middle latitude, 45

Midnight Sun, 29

migration, 64. *See also* immigration

Milky Way, 27

Minnesota, 65

mixed economy, *c 89*

Morocco, 67

Acknowledgments

Program Development, Design, Illustration, and Production

Proof Positive/Farrowlyne Associates, Inc.

Cover Design

Olena Serbyn and Bruce Bond

Cover Photo

Jon Chomitz

Maps

GeoSystems Global Corp.

Text

9, Excerpt from *Carrying the Fire* by Michael Collins. Copyright © 1974 by Michael Collins. Reprinted by permission from Farrar, Straus & Giroux, Inc. 27, Excerpt from *North American Indian Mythology* by Cottie Burland, rev. by Marion Wood. Copyright © 1965 by Cottie Burland, Copyright © renewed 1985 by the Estate of Cottie Burland. Reproduced by permission of Reed Books. 31, Excerpt from "The Kobe Earthquake: A Chance to Serve," by Megumi Fujiwara, *JAMA,* January 3, 1996, volume 275, p. 79. Copyright © 1996, American Medical Association. Reprinted with permission of the American Medical Association. 74, From *My Side of the Mountain* by Jean Craighead George. Copyright © 1959 by Jean Craighead George, renewed 1987 by Jean Craighead George. Used by permission of Dutton Children's Books, a division of Penguin Books USA Inc. 102, "Rough Country" copyright © 1991 by Dana Gioia. Reprinted from *The Gods of Winter* with the permission of Graywolf Press, Saint Paul, Minnesota.

Photos

1 T, © Karen Kasmauski/Woodfin Camp & Associates, 1 BL, © SuperStock International, 1 BR, © Paul Chesley/Tony Stone Images, 2 T, © Ken Graham/Tony Stone Images, 2 B, Peter Carmichael/Tony Stone Images, 3 T, © Alan Abromowitz/Tony Stone Images, 3 B, Robert Frerck/Odyssey Productions, 4, © Mark Thayer, Boston, 8, © Baron Wolman/Tony Stone Images, 9, © Kevin Kelley/Tony Stone Images, 12, The Rift Valley—Lake Naivasha, by Edwin Rioba, age 16, Kenya. Courtesy of the International Children's Art Museum, 14, © British Museum, 15 T, M, BL, BR, © Custom Medical Stock Photo, 20, 21, © David Young-Wolff/PhotoEdit, 24 L, © Mike McQueen/Tony Stone Images, 24 R, © Stephen Studd/Tony Stone Images, 26, © ESA/TSADD/Tom Stack & Associates, 27, © Photri, 37, © David Falconer/Tony Stone Images, 43, © Rod Planck/Tom Stack & Associates, 46 TR, © John Beatty/Tony Stone Images, 46 BL, © Jonathan Nourok/PhotoEdit, 49, © Grant Taylor/Tony Stone Images, 53, © David Young-Wolff/PhotoEdit, 54, © Robert Fox/Impact Visuals, 55, © Paul Chesley/Tony Stone Images, 56, © Tony Stone Images, 58 TL, © Connie Coleman/Tony Stone Images, 58 TR, © Bill Pogue/Tony Stone Images, 58 B, SuperStock International, 61, © Jason Laure'/Laure' Communications, 64, © Chris Brown/SABA Press Photos, 66, © Ted Streshinsky/Corbis, 67, © Mariella Furrer/SABA Press Photos, 69, © Donna DeCesare/Impact Visuals, 70, © Earth Imaging/Tony Stone Images, 74, © Carr Clifton/Carr Clifton Photography, 76, © Lawrence Migdale/Tony Stone Images, 77, © Paul Conklin/PhotoEdit, 78, © Don Smetzer/Tony Stone Images, 79, © David Young-Wolff/PhotoEdit, 82, © Donna DeCesare/Impact Visuals, 83 TL, © David Young-Wolff/PhotoEdit, 83 TR, © Inga Spence/Tom Stack & Associates, 83 B, © Andrew Errington/Tony Stone Images, 87, © Julia Vindasius/Vindasius, 88 T, B, © Ithaca Money, 89, © AP/World Wide Photos, 90, Untitled, by Olga Loceva, age 14, Russia. Courtesy of the International Children's Art Museum, 91, © Adam Woolfitt/Corbis, 92, © Hulton Deutsch Collection/Corbis, 93, © Robert Frerck/Tony Stone Images, 94, © Felicia Martinez/PhotoEdit, 95, © The Granger Collection, 97, © Jose Carrillo/PhotoEdit, 98, © Billy E. Barnes/PhotoEdit, 103 L, © Philip & Karen Smith/Tony Stone Images, 103 M, © Bruce Hands/Tony Stone Images, 103 R, Peter Pearson/Tony Stone Images, © 104, © Manfred Gottschalk/Tom Stack & Associates, 105, © SuperStock International, 107, © Larry Tackett/Tom Stack & Associates, 110, © Dennis MacDonald/PhotoEdit, 112 T, © Paul Conklin/PhotoEdit, 113, © Andy Sacks/Tony Stone Images, 115, © Radhika Chalasani/Gamma Liaison International, 116, © Jean-Marc Giboux/Gamma Liaison International, 117, © Mike Bacon/Tom Stack & Associates, 118, © Rich Frishman/Tony Stone Images, 121, © David M. Dennis/Tom Stack & Associates, 122, © Jonathan Nourok/PhotoEdit, 123, © Michael Newman/PhotoEdit, 126, © Mark Thayer, Boston, 127, © Roger Chester/Trip Photographic, 154 T, © A & L Sinibaldi/Tony Stone Images, 154 B, © John Beatty/Tony Stone Images, 155 T, © Hans Strand/Tony Stone Images, 155 BL, © Spencer Swanger/Tom Stack & Associates, 155 BR, © Paul Chesley/Tony Stone Images.